THESE UNITED STATES

THESE UNITED STATES

A SYMPOSIUM

Edited by
ERNEST GRUENING

FIRST SERIES

BONI AND LIVERIGHT
PUBLISHERS :: NEW YORK

PRINTED IN THE UNITED STATES OF AMERICA

PREFACE

That America is changing has been a truism throughout the century and a half of our national existence. Expansion and development have been concomitants of every decade, but hitherto our progress has steered its charted course. The transformation that is now taking place is in many ways of a different character. Fundamental doctrines are being abandoned, or basically reinterpreted.

Most obvious among the physical changes is the cessation of the westward march. For the first time in our history the center of population has remained stationary for a decade. With the restriction of immigration the current which has flowed persistently throughout American history has been checked at the source—and the implications of this change alone are far-reaching. Closely related is the disappearance of free land. The country is filled up. The period of flux is over, that of crystallization has begun.

Among the factors influencing the present transmutation was the great war. It lifted the United States into dominance as a world power. It altered our international relations. It shattered time-honored concepts. It brought with it a burden of taxation hitherto unborne, prohibition and numerous spiritual changes. It revealed altered attitudes toward varying forms of dissent, toward the problems ushered in with the industrial era a generation ago, but which had never been fully faced. Owing largely to America's relative freedom from caste and because of our abundant raw material, the industrial revolution wrought proportionately profounder changes here than in other countries. And although it accentuated regional differences, it also stimulated a new national unity by providing rapid communication, the cultural ties of nationally distributed magazines, plays and motion pictures, and quantitatively produced commodities of everyday use. The frontier has gone and much of the old individualism is passing.

Whatever the personal attitude of the American toward the great variety of issues, political, economic, social, that confront us, whether he views their manifestations with alarm or with satisfaction, he will not deny that it is a changing America of which he is a part. Thus the time seems especially appropriate for a revaluation of our national heritage.

The essays on the States that compose our Republic, collected in this volume, first appeared in the *Nation,* several of them in a somewhat abbreviated form. The announcement preceding the publication expressed the hope that the series would furnish an enlightening perspective of America today in the somewhat arbitrary terms of politico-geographic boundaries, and that it would be a valuable contribution to the new literature of national self-analysis. No attempt was made to secure uniformity either of approach or of treatment. The writers of the twenty-seven articles in the first volume, as well as those in the remainder of the series, to be published subsequently, differ considerably in political and economic convictions, in their professions and in their mode of life. Each one was free to choose his material and his method of presentation, and each expressed his individual reaction to his State. In consequence, the articles are pitched in varying keys; are, in fact, a miscellaneous collection of adventures in description, analysis, exposition, criticism, and comment. No effort has been made to prove any thesis. Whatever editorial suggestion has gone to the writers has been to emphasize the essential characteristic of each commonwealth, not for the purpose of developing local and sectional differences, but that the collective effort should convey a composite of the great abundance and variety of the United States, of the problems that are inevitably raised by our historical, physiographic, racial, and economic heterogeneity and of the part which these various factors play in our twentieth-century civilization. Some of the writers selected a special phase of life within the State for discussion; others saw fit to picture problems of more than State-wide significance against the local background. No claim for exclusive authority is made on behalf of these presentations. If the editor has deemed the writers thoroughly qualified to present their point of view for their respective States, he may and does differ with certain of their interpretations. Obviously, also, another equally qualified group of contributors might, with the assignments, have presented many different aspects and reached widely different conclusions.

The suggestion made above that no leitmotif threads its way through the series is subject to one basic exception. This is found not merely in the subject nor in the writers' community of interest and affection for those things in America which they hold dear. It lies in the one fundamental thing that all Americans have in common—the faith in the American ideal. However considerable and tragic and repeated may be the lapse therefrom, however completely our human frailty may nullify it here and there, it, alone, persists and will persist, a standard to which all Americans may repair for all time.

ERNEST GRUENING.

CONTENTS

THESE UNITED STATES

THESE UNITED STATES

KANSAS

A PURITAN SURVIVAL

By WILLIAM ALLEN WHITE

It is curious how State lines mark differences in Americans. There are no climatic differences between Kansas and Missouri, and small climatic differences between Kansas and Nebraska; yet the three States hold populations in which are marked differences—differences at least which Americans may distinguish. Doubtless to Chinamen all Americans look alike! But Americans know the differences between Americans North, East, South and West, and dwellers in a section know minor differences between persons living in neighboring States in the same section of the United States. The larger sectional differences in Americans may be somewhat the result of climatic influences. But the distinguishing points between a Kansan and a Missourian, between a New Yorker and a citizen of Vermont, between a Georgian and a Virginian or a Louisianian, or between an Oregonian and a Southern Californian arise from the changes in men made by social and political institutions.

Kansans are marked by Puritanism. "Kansas," said our greatest statesman, John J. Ingalls, nearly forty years ago, "is the child of Plymouth Rock." In the beginning of the settlement of Kansas, the State was invaded by immigrants from New England or sons and daughters of New Englanders, who came to Kansas to make this a Free State. Congress left the question of slavery to the voters of the new State. A fair fight in an open field ensued; the abolitionists crowded out the proslavery people, outvoted them, and captured Kansas. The first Kansans, therefore, were crusaders, intellectual and social pioneers, covenanters of various sorts; which, if you like to live comfortably upon your soft yesterdays, means that Kansas was full of cranks. Slavery being abolished your Kansan had to begin abolishing something else. Abolitionism was more than a conviction; it was a temperamental habit. It is a good or a bad habit according as you feel that you are your brother's keeper or that the devil should take the hindermost. Soldiers from the great war for the Union flooded into Kansas attracted by the free homesteads. But only Union soldiers could get free land, so Kansas was settled in the seventies and eighties almost exclusively by Northerners—partisans, bitterly controversial and biologically marked by a blue stripe under the waistcoat; Yankees and children of Yankees. Something had to happen to Kansas with such a population. It happened. It was prohibition, adopted forty years ago. Curiously enough the Republican Party in Kansas always indorsed prohibition in its State platforms and through its candidates, while the Democratic Party, representing the feeble protest of the easy-going citizenship that had come into Kansas in the fifties and sixties bringing slaves, opposed prohibition. But the Democratic minority was negligible and the prohibitionists took away the liquor of their less scrupulous neighbors as their slaves had been taken. For two decades the prohibition problem engaged Kansas. It was a hard fight, but it never wavered. The Puritan won. The Law and Order League in every town and county worked day and night, and to make the victory surer, five years after prohibition came in, the State allowed women to vote in municipal matters, and women having the ballot in the towns where liquor was sold never stopped until prohibition succeeded. It required laws which permitted search and seizure, which prohibited doctors from prescribing liquor, and druggists from keeping it in stock, laws which permitted the confiscation of liquor-running automobiles, and which made the second offense of the liquor seller a felony, sending him to the penitentiary for it—but in the end, prohibition won. Your Puritan is no slouch; he is thorough at all costs; thorough and fairly consistent.

For then came Populism. Populism had its genesis in the South probably; and it ran a mild course in the Dakotas and Colorado and Nebraska, States all more or less like Kansas in climate, in economic status, and in blood and breed. But because of the blood and breed, because of the Puritan inheritance of Kansas, the dour deadly desire to fight what was deemed wrong for the sheer sake of obliterating wrong, Kansas took Populism much more seriously than her sister States. Kansas produced most of the leadership of Populism. And long after Populism was defeated and forgotten Kansas clung to it, adopted its creed, and forced a dilution of Populism upon an unwilling nation. The insurgence of insurgency, the progressiveness of the Bull Moose, was the restless spirit of Kansas trying to realize the dream of Populism. Murdock, Bristow, Stubbs, Allen, and Capper in the uprising of the first two decades of the century gave to the national movement a certain blind crusader's enthusiasm. It was with a ghoulish grin that Victor Murdock met a fellow Kansan the morning when Roosevelt threw his hat into the ring in 1912.

"Well—he's finally in," said the Kansan.

"And it's a fine joke on him," says Victor.

"Why?" says the Kansan.

"Because he thinks it's '60 and it's only '48," chuckled the Puritan, delighted that a great man was to aid a good cause and go to defeat in it, even if the great man did not dream what was ahead of him.

That was the Kansas of it. Murdock had no remote thought of hesitating because he saw the inevitable defeat. Defeat was his meat and drink. But he had his sneaking doubts about the Puritan zeal of Roosevelt, who was practical Dutch, doughty, and gorgeously militant; but with a sly sweet tooth for victory and its fruits. Your Puritan regards any sweet tooth as a weakness bordering upon sin! So Kansas has delighted in causes rather than conquests.

After prohibition succeeded and Populism passed, the pioneer spirit of Kansas engaged itself in several social and political experiments, most revolutionary then; but now they have become sane and commonplace attitudes in the ordinary way of life. The theory, for instance, that the State has a right to interfere in the individual's habits on behalf of the better health of the people of the State. Under the State Board of Health, which had unusual police powers, Kansas abolished the common drinking cup and the roller towel from public places, took over the distribution of various toxins against contagious diseases, inspected hotels and food stores, and closed them up when they were unsanitary. The State also guaranteed bank deposits and restricted the sale of stocks and bonds to projects that had State approval; established a State hospital where crippled children may be cured at State expense; printed its own school textbooks and distributed the books at cost; tightened its grip on public utilities operating in the State; passed a law which virtually socializes all Kansas industry except agriculture, and passed the long line of legislation, once referred to as socialistic and now merely sneered at as laws of Meddlesome Mattie, but accepted by most of the progressive States of the Union and loudly bewailed by those who believe in the laissez-faire theory of morals and economics.

Kansas delighted in being among the first to pass all of these and actually the first to enact many of them. Again it was the Puritan spirit cropping out. Prohibition had kept out of Kansas hundreds of thousands of Germans and Scandinavians and Bohemians who flooded Nebraska and the Dakotas in the eighties and nineties, and the New England strains of blood continued to dominate the life of the State. Nearly 77 per cent of our population is of American-born parents. The Puritan blood even now is the strongest current —almost the only current directing our thought in Kansas. We censor the movies and prohibit them on Sundays. We forbid race-track gambling—indeed, gambling of all kinds is illegal; stop the sale of cigarettes—or try to. We permit Sunday baseball, but only because it is amateur sport and is not commercialized. We prohibited the thing called white slavery before the passage of the Mann act, and commercialized prostitution has been stopped in Kansas, as entirely as commercialized horse-stealing or commercialized arson or commercialized larceny of any kind. All these inhibitions against the natural tendency of depraved man cut loose from the apron-strings we are pleased to call moral restrictions. We make the questions moral issues arising before and after the passage of our restrictive laws. We go to the churches and schools for our political majorities. The politician who tries to assemble a majority without the churches and schools, without the women, and without what is known as the best influences in the community always finds himself leading a minority. He rails at the long-haired men and short-haired women; he rages at the Pecksniffian attitude of life. But it is deeply ingrained in the Kansas character. It seems so infernally pious; so hypercritical to those who oppose these causes. Yet at base these questions—abolition, prohibition, health, stability of savings, cigarettes, prostitution, gambling, and social and industrial justice—are not moral but economic in their value to society. Slavery would not work in a modern world; neither does the saloon; cigarettes and common drinking cups and prostitutes and roller towels and impure foods and long working hours cut down the producing power of men, cripple their economic efficiency; so puritanism, which is always keen about the main chance, makes a cause out of abolishing them, sings hymns—as, for instance, "Onward, Christian Soldiers," or "Where Is My Wandering Boy Tonight?" or "The Slave's Lament"—and quotes texts and holds prayer meetings to gild the main chance with the golden glow of piety. But after all it is the main chance the Puritan is after. He is an idealist planning a great democratic civilization; but one wherein a dollar will travel further, work harder, and bring in more of the fruits of civilization than any other dollar in the world. The waste of slavery, the social expense of the saloon, the venereal disease, the crooked stock seller, the purveyor of expensive schoolbooks or impure food, or the dishonest banker—each immediately becomes a check to the Puritan scheme of things and automatically is invested with evil! Meddlesome Mattie is the machinist operator who is forever listening into the works to hear a knock or a bur-r-r; and hearing it, jabs her monkey wrench into a lot of fun for some one, not because it is fun, but because it costs too much to maintain the bad adjustment.

So much for the institutions of Kansas—for her society and politics. Now for the life of Kansas, for which she has instituted her laws and social standards and upon which they rest. What manner of people are these Puritans who sing hymns and quote texts and glorify moral issues to cover the main chance, who glorify God to grease their busy dollars? As a pragmatic proposition does their civilization work? Is it worth while? Are people freer, happier, more prosperous, more comfortable and wise under this order of things than they are under the scheme of things which shrugs its Latin shoulders and says it does not care; says to waste is human, to enjoy is divine? First let us look at the material side. As to wealth, for instance. Ten years ago the figures indicated that the county in the United States with the largest assessed valuation was Marion County, Kansas, a county in central Kansas, not materially different from any other county; Marion County happened to have a larger per capita of bank deposits than any other American county. Its average of per capita wealth and per capita bank deposits was not much higher than the Kansas average. Yet no man in Marion County was then rated as a millionaire, but the jails and poorhouses were practically empty. The great per capita of wealth was actually distributed among the people who earned it. They were sober, so they saved; they were healthy, so they worked. They were well schooled, so they worked to purpose and with direction and made money. They were clear-brained, well-bred, cold-blooded Yankees, who knew exactly what they wanted, how to get it, and where to put it. That is your Kansan. Typically he lives either upon an eighty-acre farm or in a detached house within a fifty-foot lot, near a schoolhouse, with an automobile in the garage, whether farmer or town dweller; if a farmer he lives upon a rural free-delivery route along which the postman brings to him at least one daily paper, one weekly paper, and one monthly; if a town dweller he lives upon a paved street, a sewer line, a telephone wire, an electric light and power conduit and a gas main. In the county wherein these lines are written, an ordinary Kansas county, the number of telephones exceeds the number of families, the daily newspaper prints as many copies as there are heads of families, and in the towns the number of electric light connections is more than the number of residences. Water and gas are common, and the bank deposits for the town and county are $6,260,000 and the number of depositors 21,500 in a county with a total population of 26,496 people. Ninety per cent of the families are within five miles of a high school in this county, and 25 per cent of the children of high-school age attend the high school. The county contains two colleges, and the attendance from the county in the colleges is 623! A farm agent who receives $2,200 a year advises the farmers about crops, helps them to overcome bugs and pests, and organizes them for marketing. The county is spending a quarter of a million upon its own hospital and no citizen of the county is in jail. Twenty-five miles of hard-surfaced roads are under construction and as much more ordered in. It cost less than $2,000 last year to try all the criminals that infested the courts, and a preacher is police judge of the county-seat town. He commits less than a dozen men a year to jail—and this in a town of 12,000 surrounded by a county of 26,496.

This is a Kansas average, and there is your ideal Puritan civilization: a prosperous people, neither burdened by an idle and luxurious class who are rich, nor taxed to support a sodden and footless class verging upon pauperism. A sober people practically without a criminal class, an intelligent people in so far as intelligence covers a knowledge of getting an honest living, saving an occasional penny, and living in a rather high degree of common comfort; a moral people in so far as morals consist in obedience to the legally expressed will of the majority with no very great patience for the vagaries of protesting minorities. A just and righteous people in so far as justice concerns the equitable distribution of material things, and righteousness requires men to live at peace among men of good-will. A free people in so far as freedom allows men and women to have and hold all that they earn, and makes them earn all that they get. But a people neighbor-minded in the Golden Rule, a people neighbor-bound by ties of duty, by a sense of obligation, by a belief in the social compact, in the value of the herd, in the destiny of the race. All these social totems are concentrated in the idea of God in the Kansas heart. We are a deeply religious people. Time was when they used to say in Kansas that the Republican Party and the Methodist church were the spiritual forces that controlled the State. "Ad astra per aspera," to the stars by hard ways, is the State motto, and kindly note the "hard ways." Ours is no easy approach to grace, no royal road to happiness, no backstairs to beneficence. There is no earthly trail paralleling the primrose path in which one can avoid the wrath of God and the lady next door. Life and liberty are indeed highly esteemed in Kansas; but the pursuit of happiness only upon conditions set forth in the Ten Commandments, the Golden Rule, and their interpretation by the Kansas statutes.

Still we are not a joyless people. We laugh easily, and for the most part kindly. But we often approve the things we laugh at; we laugh one way and vote another. Our sense of humor saves us, but not entirely whole; we have never laughed ourselves out of our essential Puritanism. Laughter as a solvent has been tried—the anti-prohibitionists tried it, the opponents of Populism tried it, the defenders of Cannon and Aldrich and conservatism tried it. But they all failed as flatly as the Missourians and the gay Southerners failed who tried to laugh at the abolition rifles by dubbing them "Beecher's Bibles." Deep in our hearts is the obsessed fanaticism of John Brown. Joy is an incident, not the business of life.

Justice as it works out under a Christian civilization is the chief end of man in Kansas.

But alas, this is begging the question. For who can say that the establishment of justice is the chief end of a State? Indeed, who can say even what justice is? Is it just that every man should earn what he gets and get what he earns? Or is it just that those who see and feel and aspire to do great things—to make life beautiful for themselves and others—should be pared down to the norm in their relations with mankind? Is it justice to establish a State where the weak may thrive easily and the strong shall be fettered irrevocably in their most earnest endeavors? Should a State brag of the fact that it distributes its wealth equitably—almost evenly—when it has produced no great poet, no great painter, no great musician, no great writer or philosopher? Surely the dead level of economic and political democracy is futile if out of it something worthy—something eternally worthy—does not come. The tree shall be known by its fruit. What is the fruit of Kansas? Is happiness for the many worth striving for? What is the chief end of a civilization? What is the highest justice?

What we lack most keenly is a sense of beauty and the love of it. Nothing is more gorgeous in color and form than a Kansas sunset; yet it is hidden from us. The Kansas prairies are as mysterious and moody as the sea in their loveliness, yet we graze them and plow them and mark them with roads and do not see them. The wind in the cottonwoods lisps songs as full of meaning as those the tides sing, and we are deaf. The meadow lark, the redbird, the quail live with us and pipe to us all through the year, but our musicians have not returned the song. The wide skies at night present the age-old mystery of life, in splendor and baffling magnificence, yet only one Kansas poet, Eugene Ware, has ever worn Arcturus as a bosom pin. The human spirit—whatever it is in God's creation—here under these winds and droughts and wintry blasts, here under these drear and gloomy circumstances of life, has battled with ruthless fate as bravely and as tragically as Laocoön; yet the story is untold, and life no richer for the nobility that has passed untitled in marble or in bronze or in prose. Surely the righteousness which exalts a nation does not also blind its eyes and cramp its hands and make it dumb that beauty may slip past unscathed. Surely all joy, all happiness, all permanent delight that restores the soul of man, does not come from the wine, women, and song, which Kansas frowns upon.

Yet why—why is the golden bowl broken, the pitcher at the fountain broken, and in our art the wheel at the cistern still? This question is not peculiarly a Kansas question. It is tremendously American.

MARYLAND

APEX OF NORMALCY

By H. L. MENCKEN

In all tables of statistics Maryland seems to gravitate toward a safe middle place, neither alarming nor depressing. The colony was settled after Massachusetts and Virginia, but before Pennsylvania and the Carolinas; the State lies today about halfway down the list of American commonwealths, in population, in the value of its manufactures, and in its production of natural wealth. I thumb all sorts of strange volumes of figures and find this median quality holding out. The percentage of native-born whites of native parentage in the country as a whole is somewhere between 55 and 60; in Maryland it is also between 55 and 60; below lie the very low percentages of such States as New York, and above lie the very high percentages of such States as Arkansas. In the whole United States the percentage of illiteracy is 7.7; in Maryland it is 7.2. In the whole country the blind number 62.3 in every 100,000 of population; in Maryland they number 61.9. Ranging the States in the order of the average salary paid to a high-school principal, Maryland is twenty-third among the 48; ranging them in the order of automobile licenses issued, it is twenty-ninth; ranging them in the order of the ratio of Roman Catholics to all Christian communicants it is twenty-second.

The chief city of Maryland, Baltimore, lies halfway down the list of great American cities; the State's average temperature, winter and summer, is halfway between the American maximum and minimum. It is in the middle of the road in its annual average of murders, suicides, and divorces, in the average date of its first killing frost, in the number of its moving-picture parlors per 100,000 of population, in the circulation of its newspapers, in the ratio between its street-railway mileage and its population, in the number of its people converted annually at religious revivals, and in the percentage of its lawyers sent to prison yearly for felony.

Popular opinion holds the Mason and Dixon line to be the division between the North and the South; this is untrue geographically, culturally, and historically. The real frontier leaps out of the West Virginia wilderness somewhere near Harper's Ferry, runs down the Potomac to Washington, and then proceeds irregularly eastward, cutting off three counties of the Maryland Western Shore and four of the Eastern Shore. Washington is as much a Northern town as Buffalo, despite the summer temperature and the swarms of Negroes; Alexandria, Va., across the river, is as thoroughly Southern as Macon, Ga. In Maryland the division is just as noticeable. The vegetation changes, the mode of life changes, the very people change. A Marylander from St. Mary's County or from the lower reaches of the Eastern Shore is as much a stranger to a Marylander from along the Pennsylvania boundary, or even from Baltimore, as he would be to a man from Maine or Wisconsin. He thinks differently; he has different prejudices, superstitions, and enthusiasms; he actually looks different. During the Civil War the State was even more sharply divided than Kentucky or Missouri, and that division still persists. It results in constant compromises—an almost Swiss need to reconcile divergent traditions and instincts. Virginia to the southward is always Democratic and Pennsylvania to the northward is always Republican, but Maryland is sometimes one and sometimes the other, and when Baltimore is one the counties are commonly the other. The influence of this single big city, housing nearly half the population of the State, is thrown toward maintaining the balance. It has *nearly* half the population, but not *quite* half; thus the rural Marylanders must always pay heed to it, but need never submit to it slavishly. The result is a curious moderation in politics. Maryland is liberal and swiftly punishes political corruption, but it is suspicious of all the new sure-cures that come out of the South and Middle West—the recall of judges, the city manager system, prohibition, the initiative, government ownership, and so on. That moderation extends to all the social and economic relationships. Though there are large minorities of Negroes in every political division, there is seldom any trouble between the races, and even in the darkest counties every well-behaved Negro is now allowed to vote. Though Baltimore, in some parts, is alive with foreigners, they are not harassed and persecuted by the usual 100 per cent poltroons, and even during the war and at the height of the ensuing alarm about radicals they were reasonably protected in their rights. And though the typical Marylander, once a farmer, is now a hand in a factory, industrial disputes of any seriousness are relatively rare, and even the Maryland miner, though his brothers to both sides, in Pennsylvania and West Virginia, are constantly in difficulties, is but seldom butchered by the State militia.

In brief, Maryland bulges with normalcy. Freed, by the providence of God, from the droughts and dervishes, the cyclones and circular insanities of the Middle West, and from the moldering doctrinairism and appalling bugaboos of the South, and from the biological decay of New England, and from the incurable corruption and menacing unrest of the other industrial States, it represents, in a sense, the ideal toward which the rest of the Republic is striving. It is safe, fat, and unconcerned. It can feed itself, and have plenty to spare. It drives a good trade, foreign and domestic; makes a good profit; banks a fair share of it. It seldom freezes in winter, and it stops short of actual roasting in summer. It is bathed in a singular and various beauty, from the stately estuaries of the Chesapeake to the peaks of the Blue Ridge. It is unthreatened by floods, Tulsa riots, Nonpartisan Leagues, Bolshevism, or Ku Klux Klans. It is bare of Len Smalls, Mayor Thompsons, Lusks, Hylans, A. Mitchell Palmers, Bryans, Vardamans, Volsteads, Upton Sinclairs, Parkhursts, Margaret Sangers, Mrs. Carrie Chapman Catts, Monk Eastmans, Debses, Hearsts, Mrs. Kate O'Hares, Prof. Scott Nearings, John D. Rockefellers, Stillmans, Harry Thaws, Jack Johnsons, La Follettes, Affinity Earles, Judge Cohalans, W. E. Burghardt Du Boises, Percy Stickney Grants, Dreisers, Cabells, Amy Lowells, Mrs. Eddys,

Ornsteins, General Woods, William Z. Fosters, Theodore Roosevelt, Jrs., Cal Coolidges. Its Federal judge believes in and upholds the Constitution. Its Governor is the handsomest man in public life west of Cherbourg. The Mayor of its chief city is a former Grand Supreme Dictator of the Loyal Order of Moose. It has its own national hymn, and a flag older than the Stars and Stripes. It is the home of the oyster, of the deviled crab, of hog and hominy, of fried chicken *à la* Maryland. It has never gone dry.

I depict, you may say, Utopia, Elysium, the New Jerusalem. My own words, in fact, make me reel with State pride; another *Lis'l* of that capital moonshine *Löwenbräu,* and I'll mount the keg and begin bawling "Maryland, My Maryland." Here, it appears, is the dream paradise of every true Americano, the heaven imagined by the Rotary Club, the Knights of Pythias, and the American Legion. Here is the goal whither all the rest of the Republic is striving and pining to drift. Here, as I have said, is normalcy made real and visible. Well, what is life like in arcadian Maryland? How does it feel to live amid scenes so idyllic, among a people so virtuous and so happy, on the hooks of statistics so magnificently meridional? I answer frankly and firstly: it is dull. I answer secondly: it is depressing. I answer thirdly: it steadily grows worse. Everywhere in the United States, indeed, there is that encroaching shadow of gloom. Regimentation in morals, in political theory, in every department of thought has brought with it a stiffening, almost a deadening in manners, so that the old goatishness of the free democrat—how all the English authors of American travel-books denounced it two or three generations ago!—has got itself exchanged for a timorous reserve, a curious psychical flabbiness, an almost complete incapacity for innocent joy. To be happy takes on the character of the illicit: it is jazz, spooning on the back seat, the Follies, dancing without corsets, wood alcohol. It tends to be an adventure reserved for special castes of antinomians, or, at all events, for special occasions. On all ordinary days, for all ordinary Americans, the standard carnality has come to be going into a silent and stuffy hall, and there, in the dark, gaping stupidly at idiotic pictures in monochrome. No light, no color, no sound!

So everywhere in the Republic, from Oregon's icy mountains to Florida's coral strand. But in Maryland there is a special darkening, due to an historical contrast. Save only Louisiana, and, for very brief spaces, Kentucky and California, Maryland is the only American State that ever had a name for gaiety. Even in the earliest days it knew nothing of the religious bigotry that racked New England, nor of the Indian wars that ravaged Georgia and New York, nor of the class conflicts that menaced Virginia. Established on the shores of its incomparably rich waters, its early planters led a life of peace, tolerance, and ease, and out of their happy estate there grew a civilization that, in its best days, must have been even more charming than that of Virginia. That civilization was aristocratic in character, and under it the bonds of all classes were loose. Even the slaves had easy work, and plenty of time for jamborees when work was done, and perhaps a good deal more to eat than was good for them. The upper classes founded their life upon that of the English country gentry, but they had more money, and, I incline to think, showed a better average of intelligence. They developed their lands to a superb productiveness, they opened mines and built wharves, they lined the Chesapeake with stately mansions—and in the hours of their leisure they chased the fox, fished the rivers, visited their neighbors, danced, flirted, ate, and drank. It was then that the foundation of Maryland's fame as a gastronomical paradise was laid; it was those ancients who penetrated to the last secrets of the oyster, the crab, and the barnyard fowl. Nor were they mere guzzlers and tipplers. Annapolis, down to Washington's presidency, was perhaps the most civilized town in America. It had the best theater, it had the best inns, and it also had the best society. To this day a faint trace of its old charm survives; it is sleepy, but it is lovely.

What overturned the squirearchy, of course, and with it Maryland civilization, was the rise of the industrial system. It shifted the center of gravity from the great estates to the rushing, pushing, dirty, and, after a while, turbulent and hoggish town of Baltimore, and so, bit by bit, the old social organization fell to pieces, and the very landscape itself began to lose its old beauty. Wherever there was a manor house along the Bay in the eighteenth century there is now a squalid town, and wherever there is a town there is a stinking cannery, or an even more odoriferous factory for making fish guano. For years there was a more or less fair and equal struggle between town and country. Baltimore grew and grew, but the old landed gentry hung on to their immemorial leadership, in politics if not in trade. Even so recently as a generation ago, half of the counties were still dominated by their old land-owning families; out of them came the supply of judges, State senators, governors, congressmen. Even into our own day they retain tenaciously a disproportionate share of seats in the State Assembly. But it was a losing fight, and as year followed year the advantages of the new industrial magnates grew more visible. As in so many other States, it was a railroad—the Baltimore & Ohio—that gave mere money the final victory over race. The Baltimore & Ohio, for more than fifty years, steadily debauched the State. Then it was overthrown, and the political system that it had created went with it, but by that time it was too late to revive the aristocratic system of a more spacious day. Today the State is run by the men who pay the wages of its people. They do it, it must be said for them, with reasonable decency, but they do it absolutely without imagination, and all links with the past are broken forever. Maryland was once a state of mind; now it is a machine.

The tightening of the screws goes on unbrokenly; the end, I suppose, as everywhere else in These States, will be a complete obliteration of distinction, a wiping out of all the old traditions, a massive triumph of regimentation. It is curious to note some of the current symptoms of the process. There is, for example, the Fordization of the Johns Hopkins University. The Johns Hopkins was founded upon a plan that was quite novel in the United States: it was to be, not a mere college for the propagation of the humanities among the upper classes, but a genuine university in the Continental sense, devoted almost wholly to research. To that end it set up shop in a few plain buildings in a back street—and within twenty years its fame was world-wide, and its influence upon all other American universities of the first rank was marked. It had no campus, no dormitories, no clubs of college snobs, no college yells, but if you go through the roster of its students during its first two or three decades you will go through a roster of the principal American scholars and men of science of today. The death of Daniel Coit Gilman was a calamity to the university, and following it came demoralization. Today the Johns Hopkins is reorganized, but upon a new plan. It has a large and beautiful campus; its buildings begin to rise in huge groups; it challenges Harvard and Princeton. Interiorly it turns to the new efficiency, the multitudinous manufacture of sharp, competent, $10,000-a-year men. There is a summer-school for country schoolmarms eager for six weeks of applied psychology, official history, and folk-singing. There is instruction for young men eager to be managers of street railways, automobile engineers, and city editors of newspapers. There is patriotic drilling on the campus. There is a growing college spirit. Gifts and endowments increase. Everything is booming. But the old Johns Hopkins is dead.

Turn now to Baltimore society. In the old days it was extraordinarily exclusive—not in the sense of stupid snobbishness, but in the sense of prudent reserve. The aristocracy of the State was a sound one, for it was firmly rooted in the land, and it looked with proper misgivings upon all newcomers who lacked that foundation. It had friendly relations with the aristocracy of Virginia, but with the industrial magnates of the North and their wives and daughters it was inclined to be a bit stand-offish. When it gave a party in Baltimore or in one of the county towns, the display of clothes was perhaps not startling, but there was at least a show of very pretty girls, and their pa's and ma's were indubitably gentlemen and ladies. I am still almost too young, as the saying is, to know my own mind, but I well remember the scandal that arose when the first millionaire bounders tried to horn in by *force majeure*. Even the proletariat was against them, as it would have been against a corporation lawyer who presumed to climb upon the bench with the judge. But today—God save the mark! The old landed aristocracy, put beside the new magnates and their women, seems shabby and unimportant; it has lost its old social leadership, and it has even begun to lose its land, its traditions, and its *amour propre*. The munitions millionaires of the war years entered to the tune of loud wind music; a fashionable ball today is an amazing collection of gilded nobodies; all eyes are turned, not toward the South, but toward New York. There are leaders of fashion in Baltimore today whose mothers were far from unfamiliar with the washtub; there are others whose grandmothers could not speak English. The whole show descends to a fatuous and tedious burlesque. It has the brilliance of a circus parade, and the cultural significance of an annual convention of the Elks.

The decay of the Johns Hopkins is accompanied by a general eclipse of intellectualism. Music becomes a mere fashionable diversion; it is good medicine for pushers to go to opera and symphony concert and suffer there for an hour or two. As for intellectual society, it simply doesn't exist. If some archaic bluestocking were to set up a *salon,* it would be mistaken for a saloon, and raided by some snouting cleric. In Baltimore lives Lizette Woodworth Reese, perhaps the finest poet of her generation yet alive in America. Some time ago a waggish newspaper man there had the thought to find out how Baltimore itself regarded her. Accordingly, he called up all of the town magnificoes, from the president of the Johns Hopkins down to the presidents of the principal women's clubs. He found that more than half of the persons he thus disturbed had never so much as heard of Miss Reese, and that all save two or three of the remainder had never read a line of her poetry! Edgar Allan Poe is buried in the town, in the yard of a decrepit Presbyterian church, on the edge of the old red-light district. It took sixteen years to raise enough money to pay for a modest tombstone to his memory; it took seventy-two years to provide even an inadequate monument. During that time Baltimore has erected elaborate memorials to two founders of tin-pot fraternal orders, to a former Mayor whose long service left the city in the physical state of a hog-pen, and to the president of an obscure and bankrupt railroad. These memorials are on main streets. That to Poe is hidden in a park that half the people of Baltimore have never so much as visited. And on the pedestal there is a thumping misquotation from his poetry!

Such is Maryland in this hundred-and-forty-sixth

year of the Republic—a great, a rich, and a puissant State, but somehow flabby underneath, somehow dead-looking in the eyes. It has all the great boons and usufructs of current American civilization: steel-works along the bay, movies in every town, schools to teach the young how to read and write, high schools to ground them in a safe and sane Americanism, colleges for their final training, jails to keep them in order, a State police, a judiciary not wholly imbecile, great newspapers, good roads. It has vice crusaders, charity operators, drive managers, chambers of commerce, policewomen, Y. M. C. A.'s, women's clubs, Chautauquas, Carnegie libraries, laws against barking dogs, the budget system, an active clergy, uplifters of all models and gauges. It is orderly, industrious, virtuous, normal, free from Bolshevism and atheism. . . . Still, there is something wrong. At the moment, thousands seem to be out of work. Wages fall. Men are ironed out. Ideas are suspect. No one appears to be happy. Life is dull.

MISSISSIPPI

HEART OF DIXIE

By BEULAH AMIDON RATLIFF

IT is hard, perhaps impossible for a Northerner to understand Mississippi: that is, to realize its past, to accept its social and economic present, to feel at home living according to its standards, to face its future with hope and assurance. Though Mississippi has grown neurotic over its "war-time anguish," there is no doubt that the State suffered cruelly during the war and reconstruction. Except Virginia, no other State was the scene of so much actual fighting.

At the end of the war, the State debt, according to Attorney General Harris, was over $16,300,000. Prices rivaled the staggering quotations from Vienna and Moscow today: men's boots sold at $200 a pair at Natchez; a coat was priced at $350; flour, $50 a barrel; salt, $4 a pound; soap, 75 cents a cake. The State finances were hopelessly involved after several issues of railroad scrip, treasury notes and State bonds. The repudiation of the huge debt incurred "in aid of the rebellion" complicated instead of simplifying the financial tangle. The fields had not been tilled for four years. The stock had died or been driven off to feed the armies. Buildings and fences had fallen into decay. Railroads and such highways as once existed had deteriorated till they were almost useless. Levees had been cut by both Union and Confederate armies and thousand of acres were flooded. According to the United States census of 1860 and the State census of 1866, the population had decreased 66,585; the decrease of the white population being 10,499 and of the black population 56,146. (Famine and disease took such toll among the Negroes during the war and reconstruction that Governor Sharkey stated in 1866 that half the Negroes of the State had perished, and the race seemed doomed to early extinction.) Such schools as the State had possessed were utterly destroyed and the printing presses had not fared much better. The economic system, in use since Colonial days, was scrapped, and the laborers wandered about the country, refusing to work under the belief that "Marse Linkum gwine gib ebry niggah fo'ty acres an' a mule ob his own." The State leaders who had survived the war were humiliated and uncertain.

History fails to record an instance of a victorious people dealing mercifully and patiently with their late enemies. The Federal Government made harsh and stupid blunders in meeting the problems of reconstruction. Both the presidential and congressional reconstruction policies were hastily formed and tactlessly administered. Beaten, impoverished, weary, confused, the State was in no temper to accept calmly and judge on their merits the startling innovations of the victorious Northerners. To people reared in a society based on human slavery, and accepting that institution as the just and necessary foundation of economic life, it was sufficiently revolutionary to have their late property suddenly snatched away, without compensation, by an arbitrary law in the making of which they had no voice. But in addition to this, they were expected to accept their former slaves as voters, office-holders, and court witnesses—in short, to have their cattle transformed overnight into citizens.

Carpet-baggers, sufficiently clever and unscrupulous to exploit to the limit the disorganized conditions of the State and the childish ignorance and egotism of the Negroes, made their disgraceful contribution to the misery of the situation. From the paralysis of utter panic, Mississippians passed to a state of resentment which culminated in the well-organized "Revolt of 1875." The carpet-baggers were driven out. Negro office-holders were unseated. White franchise was established. Mississippi had made a successful beginning in blotting out the odious Thirteenth, Fourteenth and Fifteenth amendments from the life of the State.

The Mississippi of today bases its activity and its ideals on the rosy tradition of "befo' de wah." The "Revolt of '75" destroyed, as far as Mississippi was concerned, the fruits of the war: emancipation and Negro citizenship. Since then, the effort has been to go on as though there had been no war. Slavery, of course, could not exist in name, but as far as possible the institution has been preserved in fact. Naturally, this effort has been more successful in remote country places than in the towns. Today there is a marked difference between "field niggers" and "town niggers."

Practically all plantations are divided into small farms of from five to twenty-five acres, which are "let" to a Negro farmer for a "season" on the "tenant-farmer" plan. That is, the Negro and his family work the land, using the stock and tools of the landowner, pick the cotton and sell it, either to a cotton buyer, to a gin, or to the planter himself. The planter furnishes food and kerosene to his hands on credit, and advances small sums of money till the crop is sold. Then there is a "settlement," when the accumulated debt of the tenant is set off against the value of his crop, minus the rent of the land, and the cash balance due him is paid the tenant. Often the end of the season finds the Negro possessed of a debt instead of a balance. Then he must remain another season to "work off his debt," or the planter may "sell" him to another planter, who pays the amount of the debt, in which case the Negro is bound to his new "boss" for the amount of the "purchase price."

The planter has numerous opportunities to profit under the "tenant-farmer" system:

1. The planter divides up the land to suit himself. The farm he "lets" as 20 acres may contain 20 acres, or it may contain 15 or 16 acres. Most planters "let" at least a fifth more land than they own.

2. Supplies are furnished the Negroes from the commissary, the plantation store. The planter fixes his own prices, does his own bookkeeping, and adds a percentage, usually 20 per cent, to all accounts "for carrying."

3. The tenant must accept the planter's figures for the settlement. There is no tribunal to which he can appeal if he considers the settlement unjust. I heard a planter tell, with roars of laughter, that "Jeff done

sued me fo' seven hundred dollahs aftah the settlement," elaborating on the tenant's "fine bookkeeping" and "the smart Aleck lawyer" he got to file the suit. I inquired when the case would be tried. I was met with a stare of blank amazement, and then the indignant question, "Do you think theah's a co't in Mississippi gwine entertain a nigger's suit against a white man? That there suit was throwed out o' co't mos' afore it got in."

4. Classing cotton takes a high degree of skill and intelligence. It is easy for the planter to buy the tenant's cotton at many grades below its real worth, selling it at its true value, and realizing a big profit on every bale.

Contracts for the coming season are made the first of each January. After a Negro has made his "contract" he is bound to his "boss" as completely as in slavery days. He must purchase his supplies at the commissary. He must not change employers nor leave the plantation. If a Negro "runs away" the planter may pursue him, bring him back by force, punish him with a whipping and stand over him with a gun to prevent another runaway. Various Southern writers have vehemently denied that planters of the present day whip their negroes. I can only testify to what I have seen and heard. A Negro woman was once whipped in my hearing for quarreling with another Negress. "As crazy as a nigger woman gettin' a lickin'" was the simile used by a leading Greenville lawyer in my hearing. A neighbor asked a planter, in my presence, what had become of a certain Negro. The reply was: "He run away. I never did figger out how. Lit out one night. I went after him and come up with him at R——'s. Owed me close to $400. I brought him back and whipped him till he couldn't stand up. Thought that would hold him awhile. But next morning he was gone. Never got a trace of him. I'd sure like to know how he got off. He couldn't stand up when I got through with him."

A friend once telephoned me: "We can't get in to play cards tonight. S—— had to give a nigger a whippin' today and it always makes him so nervous he can't do anything but go to bed."

The jovial, singing, courteous Negro of Southern plantations has passed away from Mississippi, if he ever existed outside fiction. Field-hands of the present are unbelievably slow and stupid. "Jes' sense enough to hold a plow and yell at a mule," a planter once described them to me, and the characterization is apt.

Their speech is so thick and mumbled it scarcely seems like human articulation. They are dull and surly, apparently without ambition or human affection. Nine field Negroes out of ten cannot tell you how old they are, where they were born, whether their parents are living, how often they have been married, or how many children they have. Their sex life is utterly bestial.

Ask a piccaninny whose child he is and he will reply, "Norah's boy" or "Kate's boy." Neither the child nor his mother could state his paternity

In many country districts there are no schools for colored children. In the more progressive counties, like Warren, there is a term of five months for colored children, and in many of the schools, thanks to the Jeanes fund, some form of industrial training has been introduced. Other counties have terms varying from ninety days to seven months for colored children. In all counties, the country schools for blacks are wretchedly equipped. I quote from the last "Survey of Negro Education" revised to 1919, published by the Department of the Interior, vol. II, p. 15: "The Negro schoolhouses (rural) are miserable beyond description. They are usually without comfort, equipment, proper lighting, or sanitation. Most of the teachers are absolutely untrained, and have been given certificates by the county board not because they have passed the examination, but because it is necessary to have some kind of a Negro teacher. Among the Negro schools I have visited, I have found only one in which the highest class knew the multiplication table."[1]

From the age of five or six, the children go into the fields, "chopping" cotton with a hoe or picking cotton. Cornbread, biscuits, molasses, rice and salt pork form the diet of plantation Negroes of all ages. Few families have the energy to raise vegetables or chickens to vary the coarse, ill-balanced fare, though around every cabin there is plenty of space for a "garden patch."

The life of the Mississippi plantation Negro is toil, ignorance, hopelessness, animal stupidity and bestiality. He is a filthy, stolid, unloved and unlovely creature, as far from the "merry, singing hoe-hand" of fiction as is the dirty, diseased reservation Indian from Cooper's "noble red man."

[1] For a detailed description of a typical rural Negro school, see "Paradise Negro School," by Howard Snyder. *Yale Review*, Oct., 1921.

The patience with which a Mississippi planter deals with his dull, irresponsible labor is almost unbelievable to a Northerner. If he is harsh in punishing a "runaway," too shrewd in his contracts, quick to take advantage of all his opportunities to exploit, the planter is also the long-suffering guardian of these difficult children. If a hand falls sick, the planter's physician is called. The planter purchases the necessary medicines, and he or his wife watches through the night beside the sick person, for no plantation Negro can be depended upon to administer medicine regularly or in the prescribed doses. Family or community quarrels are patiently heard and decided. Many planters give an annual barbecue, when all the hands are invited to a feast and merrymaking. A Negro cheated by another Negro or by a white man can count on his "boss" to safeguard his rights. The planter protects his Negroes from the countless "agents" who are always trying to sell the hands some trifle at an exorbitant price. The average planter looks on his hands as responsibilities to be fed, clothed, guarded, and cared for in sickness or disaster. At the same time, he is unalterably opposed to anything that would help these "children" grow up. As a civic duty, he would assist in tarring and feathering any "interfering Yankee" who urged the Negroes to obtain an education, buy a farm, learn a trade, leave the land, or, most heinous crime of all, organize.[1] As far as he can achieve it, the Mississippi planter will keep the Negroes slaves, overworked, mal-

[1] There are 161,027 Negro farmers in Mississippi, of whom 23,179 are landowners, 137,848, tenant-farmers (1920 Census, "Agriculture," p. 12, line 81). That is, 14 per cent of the Negro farmers own land, 86 per cent are landless.

nourished, terrorized into submission by corporal punishment, lacking initiative or ambition, dull, landless.

The "town Negroes" are markedly different. In Vicksburg Negroes act successfully as teachers, physicians and dentists to their own race, and to both races as trained nurses, cooks, nursemaids, plumbers, carpenters, plasterers, dressmakers, store clerks, mail carriers, chauffeurs, mechanics, painters and paperhangers, brick masons and truck drivers. "Town Negroes" are, of course, in closer touch with the white race and with the white man's way of living than the field hands. They try, and with startling success, to arrange their houses, prepare their food and dress "like white folks."

One of my cooks was an interesting example of the difference between "field Negroes" and "town Negroes." Effie had been born on a plantation, but at the age of six she was taken to Vicksburg by the daughter of the planter for whom her mother worked and brought up as the playmate of a little white girl. This meant that she was kept seasonably and neatly dressed, shared the meals of her little charge, played with the same toys, learned to read and write at the same time, had attention paid to her speech and manners, and for ten years was exposed to the influences of a refined and pleasant home. I sometimes saw Effie's mother and sisters when they trudged in from the country, typical dull, awkward, ugly field Negroes. But Effie was immaculate in her person and clothing, dainty and attractive in appearance and carriage, intelligent, courteous, able to read simple books and to write and spell fully as well as the average ten-year-old public-school child, an advanced degree of erudition for a Mississippi Negro. The difference in environment and training made Effie seem of a different race from her "cornfield relations."

The Negro school buildings and equipment in Vicksburg (and in other large towns, I was told) compare favorably with the white schools. The teachers are graduates of colored high schools and colleges in many cases. There are pictures, playgrounds, and even a few victrolas, "visiting days" with very creditable programs, and a little industrial training. But there is neither incentive nor opportunity for progress beyond the grades, and most colored children drop out of school as soon as possible.[1]

There are a number of Negro educational institutions in Mississippi, bearing the name of "colleges." The largest, the Alcorn Agricultural and Mechanical College (colored), is maintained by the State. The others are largely supported by the Home Mission boards of various churches in the North and by private donations. These attempts to provide educational opportunities for Mississippi Negroes are much to be commended, but when a Mississippian states that "there are nearly twenty colored colleges in our State," it must be realized that the word "college" is not to be understood in the sense in which it is used in the North. From the "Survey of Negro Education" [2] and

[1] The total high-school enrolment of Mississippi (white and colored) is 6,319. There are three high schools for Negroes in the entire State with the following enrolment: 9th grade, 139; 10th grade, 103; 11th grade, 75; 12th grade, 0. Total, 317. (Biennial Survey of Education, Bureau of Education, in 4 vols., vol. IV, p. 212.)

[2] U. S. Department of the Interior, in 2 vols., revised in 1919, vol. II, p. 344 ff.

the "Reference List of Southern Colored Schools"[1] I give the descriptions and enrolments of the largest and most important Negro "colleges" in Mississippi:

Alcorn Agricultural and Mechanical College (colored): "A school of secondary grade with two-thirds of its pupils in the elementary department. . . . The second year of the preparatory department and the four years of the so-called college constitute a fairly good high-school course." Enrolment: Total, 485; between 7th grade and college, 372; college, 45.

Tougaloo College: "A school of secondary grade with a few pupils in collegiate classes and a large elementary attendance." Enrolment: Total, 351; 7th grade-college, 181; college, 12.

Campbell College: "A large school of elementary and secondary grade giving some instruction in commercial and theological subjects." Enrolment, 235; 7th grade-college, 129; college, 0.

Rust College: Enrolment, 589; secondary, 267; college, 14.

Jackson College: "A secondary school for both boys and girls with a large elementary enrolment. A teachers' course is listed but there are no pupils." Enrolment, 285; secondary, 244; college, 6.

The "color line" in Mississippi is a devious thing for Northerners to trace. There are, of course, "Jim Crow" cars on the trains, "Jim Crow" waiting-rooms, theater galleries and street-car sections. The school systems are entirely separate, as are the churches. But Negroes patronize "white stores" and are at liberty to try on any hat, garment or pair of shoes they fancy I have often seen Negresses "trying on" ex-

[1] John F. Slater Fund, Occasional Papers, No. 20, 2nd ed. 1921.

pensive dresses, which were hung back on the racks and later tried on and purchased by white customers. "Town Negroes" use the banks and stand in line beside white people, though they could not do so in a street-car aisle. Doctors and dentists minister to white and colored alike. There are separate wards in the hospitals, with colored nurses for the colored wards, working under the direction of white nurses. White children of the well-to-do class are left almost entirely to the care of colored nurses. Incidentally, "the charming Southern accent" and "the delightful Southern drawl" are to be traced to this fact, a number of Southerners have informed me. The little children, in learning to talk from their nurses, pick up also the slovenly Negro articulation and the Negro's whining intonation, and later training, while it corrects in a measure, the Negro grammar and diction of early childhood, leaves the "accent" and "drawl."

There are numerous colored prostitutes and "kept women" are as apt to be colored as white. There are two remarkable statements I have heard again and again from Mississippians, in the same breath in which they protested, "By God, there'll never be social equality or mingling of the races in this State": "There isn't a full-blooded nigger in the State of Mississippi" and "There's not a virgin Negress over fourteen years old in this State."

"Town Negroes" take and leave employment as they choose. They appear in court as witnesses, and I recall a case in Warren County where a white man was hanged on the testimony of a Negro. I never heard of a suit brought by a Negro against a white man in Vicksburg, but I feel sure that such a suit would not be summarily "thrown out of court" there or in any of the other large towns. Communications from colored people on matters of general interest are printed in the Vicksburg papers, and such matters as colored school programs, the death of respected colored citizens, colored Red Cross activities and charities are fully reported.

But even in Vicksburg, where the relations between the two races are particularly good, the Negroes are "kept in their place." They are not citizens. They neither vote nor hold office, though they pay taxes. A crime against a Negro is not punished as severely as a crime against a white person. For example, during the war Mississippians held that everyone able to work must work. Various patriots appointed themselves to enforce this rule. Four such patriots (white) in Vicksburg went to the home of a Negro woman who was not working, seized her by force, whipped her, and tarred and feathered her. She was pregnant and lost her child, almost losing her own life, as the result of the experience. Nearly two years later, the four patriots were tried on a minor charge ("assault," I believe) and sentenced to six months in jail, but the sentence was not served. Though I asked many people about it, I never heard of a Negro voting or attempting to vote in Mississippi. A prominent man from the north of the State told me: "They don't come to the polls in our county. None of our niggers are crazy to commit suicide."

Mob rule and "lynch law" are sometimes resorted to in punishing Negro criminals, or those suspected of crime. While I was living in Mississippi I knew of Negroes being killed for the following causes: attacking a white woman, 1; trying to enter a movie theater on the "white side," 1; trying to enter a "white restaurant," 1; house-breaking, 1; helping a Negro murderer to escape, 1; killing a white man, 1; shooting a white man, 4; drawing a gun on a white man, 1. In the case of the Negro helping the murderer to escape, the victim was tortured in a fruitless attempt to secure a confession, before he was hanged. The Negro killed for attacking a white woman was burned alive, after horrible tortures. The victim of the attack, who was uninjured, failed to identify him as her assailant and once stated that he was not the man. The Negro who tried to enter the theater with "white folks" and the one who wanted to eat in the "white restaurant" were both ex-service men in uniform, recently returned from France. This does not pretend to be a complete list of the lynchings that occurred during the two and a half years I lived in the State. It is, merely, a list of those of which I heard the facts from reliable sources. I also know of two cases in which a Negro who killed a white man was legally tried and executed.

Mississippi is a State that appears at the bottom of the list in most tables of statistics. It has fewer hospitals than any other State in the Union. Its educational appropriation is $7.49 per "educable child," the lowest in the country, a seventh of the amount appropriated in Middle Western States. Because of the inadequate schools, and, till very recently, of no compulsory education law, illiteracy among whites as well as blacks is not uncommon.[1] Mississippi's first compulsory education law was passed in 1920. It provides that all children, regardless of race, between the ages of 6 and 14, must attend school at least 80 days each year; parents and guardians are held responsible for violations of the law. The law went into effect August 1, 1920. The State Superintendent of Public Instruction states that the first year after the passage of the law, the enrolment in the public schools was increased by 30,000, indicating both the need for the law and the fact that it is being enforced.[2]

The child-labor laws of Mississippi are entirely inadequate, as they are in most Southern States. Boys under 12 and girls under 14 are not to be employed in factories, canneries, cotton or knitting mills. Provision is made for a semi-annual inspection of all establishments "where child labor is employed." Violation of the law is made a misdemeanor, punishable by a small fine or a few days in jail.[3] The lax enforce-

[1] Bureau of Education, No. 90, "Biennial Survey of Education," in 4 vols., vol. III, p. 198. Other educational statistics for Mississippi (same ref.) are:

Percentage of total tax levy devoted to education, U. S. av. 28.67; Miss., 12.46, second lowest in the country.

Value of school property, per child enrolled: U. S. average, $95.12. Miss., $8.97, the lowest in the list. Second lowest, N. C., $22.55.

Salaries of teachers (p. 164), U. S. average, $635. Miss., $291, second lowest.

Average per capita cost of schools: U. S., $7.26 (p. 198), Miss., $2.13, the lowest in the country.

[2] The percentage of illiterates in the United States is 7.7. Illiteracy among the native whites is 3.7, among Negroes 30.4. The figures for Miss. are, all classes 22.4; native whites, 5.3; Negroes, 35.6. ("Bien. Surv. of Ed." vol. III, p. 145.) Louisiana has the greatest percentage of illiteracy among native whites and also among Negroes; Alabama is second; Mississippi is third.

[3] Mississippi Code: C 1906 s 5061; 1908 C 99 s 1-8 as amend.; 1912 C 165; 1914 C 164 s 1-8.

ment of the inadequate regulations, including the age limit, and the terrible conditions under which children toil in the oyster and shrimp canneries of the Gulf Coast are described in detail in Bureau Publication No. 98 (1922) of the Children's Bureau, U. S. Department of Labor.

Mississippians admit, many of them regretfully, the backwardness of their State. They speak with pathetic apology of "the horrors of war"; the "reconstruction debts" which still oppress several of the leading towns; "the flower of the State dead in battle only one generation ago"; the financial burden of the Confederate pensions; "the poverty following the war"; "more than half our population ignorant blacks"—all of which are, doubtless, contributing factors. But I believe that Mississippi's backwardness has its cause in something more fundamental than the aftermath of war or the color of the population.

Human slavery is an outworn and discarded institution. That, at least, humanity has left behind. A society based upon an institution tested, found basically wrong and cast aside cannot itself be sound and capable of normal growth. Mississippi has made every effort to keep her Negro population slaves in fact if not in name. To oppress an inferior race is not so degrading to the oppressed as to the oppressors. In attempting to retard the normal development of the Negroes, the whites have retarded and perverted their own development.

Mississippi does not want "damyankee notions upsetting the niggers," so Mississippi has shut itself off from the North as completely as possible. Northern ideas of business, education, agriculture, road-building, finance and public health have been stubbornly resisted. The hostile attitude of the State toward the attempted pellagra investigation in the fall of 1921 is typical. "The good old days" have been the ideal, and Mississippi has scorned the community efforts that have developed in other sections, clinging to the intense individualism of sixty years ago. The bad schools and the isolation from the rest of the country have inevitably resulted in a smug, impenetrable provincialism that is appalling. "We do it so in Mississippi," or "We don't do it so in Mississippi," permits or forbids anything.

And yet Mississippi and Mississippians have such splendid possibilities! There are a few Mississippi women whose charm and humor and loveliness of spirit and person I have not seen excelled in this country. They are, of course, of the "quality," widely traveled and fairly well read. If they had had the education and the horizon of Northern college women they would be among the leaders of American womanhood.

The climate of Mississippi, with malaria controlled and good roads and decent hotels built, would make it a tourist paradise. It has the softness of Florida and the invigorating air of the West blended into what is, seven months of the year, the "perfect atmosphere." In addition, Mississippi has the lavish, open-handed beauty of a mild climate blessed with plenty of rain. Anything will grow and blossom with half a chance—roses and fruit trees and children and flowers. The land is rich and, if scientifically farmed, it would yield enormous wealth. Experiments like the truck gardens around Crystal Springs have shown what production the State is capable of, when dragged away from "co'n an' cotton" to twentieth-century crop rotation and fertilization.

Criticism of anything Mississippian is hotly resented, particularly criticism of the existing order. Anyone, but especially a Northerner, comments on the "Negro problem" at his peril. Even a calm and impartial description of actual conditions is resented. "It's our business"; "It's something no Yankee can understand"; "We don't want our affairs written up in no damyankee paper."

When this article first appeared in the *Nation* it was bitterly assailed by adverse criticisms from citizens of Mississippi. About twenty Mississippians wrote letters, long, violent, oratorical, vituperative, even profane and obscene, seldom bothering to quote facts, and in only two instances quoting facts correctly, but confirming with unimpeachable evidence one of the most regrettable weaknesses of Mississippi. That weakness is the refusal to face facts; the resentment of criticism however well founded and kindly meant; the firm belief that life in Mississippi now is all that life should be (only two critics admitted that perhaps the State is a little backward in some things!), the desire for eulogy, whether deserved or not; the certainty that Mississippi is apart from the rest of the country, with "peculiar problems" and "peculiar conditions" that only Mississippians can understand; and, finally, the conviction that the race problem is a local, not a national concern, and one that only Southerners should study, observe, discuss, or even meditate upon.

This attitude is characteristic of Mississippians of all classes. It is part of that narrowness of outlook and utter complacency that we call "provincialism." It is partly the fault of the State's history. Mostly, it is due to the low standards of education, the few and meager libraries, the small, intensely local newspapers, the unwillingness to travel, and the resentment of ideas from other parts of the world.

Most of those who have criticized this article so violently could (and would) have written an article about Mississippi that would have been highly approved throughout the State—a eulogistic, rosy article, savored with the atmosphere of Southern novels and romances: wistaria and live oaks, and soft voices and faithful old "mammies" and courteous squires and benign old colonels and mint juleps and charming belles and white-columned plantation houses. If such a description were not quite true to fact, it would at least be true to tradition. And in the "Heart of Dixie" tradition is infinitely more precious than truth.

VERMONT

OUR RICH LITTLE POOR STATE

By DOROTHY CANFIELD FISHER

EVERYBODY knows that New York State is a glowing, queenly creature, with a gold crown on her head and a flowing purple velvet cloak. The face of Louisiana is as familiar—dark-eyed, fascinating, temperamental. Virginia is a white-haired, dignified *grande dame* with ancient, well-mended fine lace and thin old silver spoons. Massachusetts is a man, a serious, middle-aged man, with a hard conscientious intelligent face, and hair thinned by intellectual application. And if I am not mistaken, Pennsylvania is a man too, a well-dressed business man, with plenty of money in his pockets and the consciousness of his prosperity written large on his smooth indoor face and in his kindly calculating eyes.

These State countenances are familiar to all of us, and many more; but back of this throng of affluent, thriving personalities, quite conscious of their own importance in the world, stands one, known to fewer Americans, lean, rather gaunt compared to the well-fed curves of the others, anything but fine, aristocratic, or picturesque. Yet the little group of mountaineers who know the physiognomy of Vermont from having grown up with it have the most crabbed, obstinate affection and respect for their State, which they see as a tall, powerful man, with thick gray hair, rough outdoor clothes, a sinewy axman's hand and arm, a humorous, candid, shrewd mouth and a weather-beaten face from which look out the most quietly fearless eyes ever set in any man's head. They know there is little money in the pockets of that woodman's coat, but there is strength in the long, corded arm, an unhurried sense of fun lies behind the ironic glint in the eyes, and the life animating all the quaint, strong, unspoiled personality is tinctured to its last fiber by an unenvious satisfaction with plain ways which is quite literally worth a million dollars to any possessor. Not to envy other people is an inheritance rich enough; but Vermont adds to that treasure the greater one of not being afraid. It seems incredible, in our modern world, so tormented with fears about its safety, that a whole Stateful of people have no ground for apprehension; but it is true. The Vermonter is so used to the moral freedom of not dreading anything that he is hardly conscious of it. It is the breath he draws, this lack of fear, it is the marrow of his bones. Why should he be afraid of anybody or anything?

What are some of the things that other people fear? Well, most of them are afraid of being poor. This fear, rather more than love, is what makes the modern world go round. The Vermonter is not afraid of being poor because he is poor already and has been for a hundred and fifty years, and it hasn't hurt him a bit. To trade for money this lack of fear of poverty would seem to him the most idiotic of bargains, and if there is one thing on which he prides himself it is on not making poor bargains. This quality makes him by no means a favorite with people who try to organize the world along what they call "strictly business lines of industrial efficiency." Most of their operations are based on their certainty that people are afraid to be poor. We Vermonters often notice a considerable heat of exasperation in such devotees of industrialism when they encounter the natives of our State. We make no comment on this at the time, taking them in with the silent attentive observation which they furiously dub "bucolic stolidity"; but after they have gone back to the city we laugh to ourselves, and some old fellow among us hits on just the droll, ironic phrase to describe the encounter. For years afterwards, we quote this to the mystification of the outsider.

Another well-known and much-described fear is that of not keeping up with the social procession, of being obliged to step down a rung on the social ladder. This is another fear which stops short before it gets into Vermont. That small section of the country has never kept up with other people's processions and has found it no hardship to walk along at its own gait. And as for social ladders, any glimpse of a social ladder or of purely social distinctions moves a Vermonter to the unaffected, pitying, perhaps rather coarsely hearty mirth which white people feel at the sight of the complicated taboo of savage tribes. Of course, the Vermonter pays for his high-handed scoffing at sacred social distinctions by a rough plainness, not to say abruptness, of speech and manner which people from outside do not relish and which they describe in far from complimentary terms. This is a pity. But I dare say you can't have something for nothing morally, any more than materially, and perhaps it is not too high a price to pay for the total absence in our world of any sort of servility or overbearing arrogance or any sort of pretentiousness. Every man to his taste. We like it better the way we have it.

Another fear, perhaps the most corroding one in our world of possessors of material wealth, is the panic alarm at any glimpse of possible changes in the social fabric which may make things uncomfortable for possessors. The Latin poet who many years ago described the light-hearted stride of a poor man across a dark plain infested with robbers described the care-free gait at which Vermont moves through the uncertain and troubled modern world. Vermont, like some of the remote valleys in the Pyrenees, has always been too far out of the furiously swirling current of modern industrial life to be much affected by it or to dread its vagaries. For generations now, when times get hard and manufactures are flat and deflated and the mills in the industrial States around us are shut down, and the newspapers are talking about bankruptcies and bread-lines, the Vermont family, exactly as rich and exactly as poor as it ever was, remarks with a kindliness tinged with pride: "Well, we'd better ask Lem's folks up to stay a spell, till times get better. I guess it's pretty hard sledding for them." And when times get better and Lem's family leave the poor little frame farm-house which has been their refuge, and drive off down the steep stony road which is the first stage of their journey back to wages and movies, the Vermont family stand looking after them, still with friendliness.

They realize shrewdly that already they seem countrified to their mill-town, factory-hand guests, but this does not worry them: rather it makes an ironic quirk come into the corner of their mouths, as at the transparent absurdity of a child. They continue to stand and wave their hands with undiminished kindliness, this time tinged by an amused humor which would be distinctly unpalatable to the others if they could understand it. I am afraid there is an element of sinful pride in the granite-like comfort they take in the security given them by their plain tastes and ability to deal with life at first hand. No dependence on employers for them!

Another problem of which we read occasionally as bothering serious-minded folks in other parts is what to do with accumulated wealth. It bothers us as little as how to fight cobras. For the most part, society in Vermont is organized along the most obviously solid and natural lines, primitive and elemental. Everybody is working. Yes, working, you jeering step-lively outsiders, although Vermonters may not hit up the hectic pace of factory hands and although some leisure for talking things over and reading the papers and cracking jokes about life, and going hunting and nutting is a necessity for Vermonters even if they are obliged to pay for it by the forgoing of sacred dollars. Almost everybody is working, and at the plainest, most visible, most understandable jobs, to raise food, or grind corn, or make shoes, or put houses together, or repair Fords, or teach children. It is very rare when anybody in Vermont fails to secure a fair amount of shelter and clothing and food and education; and it is equally rare when anybody secures very much more than that. There are, so to speak, no accumulated possessions at all.

But perhaps what Vermont is least afraid of, and what other people fear and hate most, is politics. You know as well as I do that most Americans are low in their minds about politics. They feel that politics is really beyond them, that they never will be able to get what they want through their political action. The "fatalism of the multitude" weighs like lead upon their hearts. When there are so many, what can one man do? Well, you see in Vermont there aren't so many. There isn't any multitude. Self-government may not be perfection there, any more than anywhere else, but it bears the closest, realest relationship to the citizens, and is not at all given over to professional politicians who are always below the level of the best voters. Vermonters see nothing in self-government (especially local self-government) inherently more complicated than keeping your bank-book balanced. Perhaps this is because Vermont puts up as little as possible with that lazy substitute for self-government known as the "representative system," under which you tell somebody else to do the governing for you and not to bother you about it lest your money-making be disturbed. There is so little money to make in Vermont that few people are absorbed in making it. Nearly everybody has sufficient strength and time left over, and more than sufficient interest, to give to self-government. The Town Meeting is self-government, direct, articulate, personal. It is the annual assemblage not of the representatives of the governed, but of every one of the governed themselves. Anybody—you who are governed by a non-existing entity called "the county" cannot understand this, but it is true—anybody at all who does not like the way things are going in his town can stand up and say so, and propose a cure, as pungently as his command of his native tongue will allow. And Czar Public Opinion not only lets him do this, but rather admires a man who has something to say for his own point of view.

Every question concerning the welfare of the town, to the last forgotten valley in the mountains, is brought up at this open meeting and decided after loud and open discussion. When it is over and the teams and Fords and lean wiry men stream away from the Town Hall over the rutted roads in the sharp March air, they are all tingling with that wonderfully stimulating experience, having spoken their minds out freely on what concerns them. They step heavily in their great shoes through the mud, which on March-meeting Day is awful beyond belief, but they hold up their heads. They have settled their own affairs. The physical atmosphere of town-meeting is rather strong with tobacco and sawdust and close air, but the moral atmosphere is like that on a mountain-peak compared to any political life I ever saw elsewhere, either in France or in other American States. There is none of that stultifying, bored, cynical, disillusioned conviction that the rogues will beat the honest men again this time, as always. Not on your life! The honest men are on the job, with remarkably big and knotty fists, their dander ready to rise if somebody tries to put something over on them. And although they might not be able to cope with specially adroit political rogues, there is blessedly so little money involved in most Vermont operations that it is hardly worth the while of specially adroit rogues to frequent town-meetings. The Vermonter has for a century and a half found self-government not so very daunting, and often the highest form of entertainment.

This tradition of looking the world in the eye and asking no odds of it, probably seems to the rest of you a rather curious tradition for a small, poor, rustic State with hardly a millionaire to its name, no political pull of any sort, and nothing to distinguish it in the eyes of the outside world. But all Vermonters know where it comes from, straight down from our forefathers who did look the world in the eye and made the world back down. With nothing on their side but their fearlessness and a sense of human rights as against property rights, they held out stoutly and successfully against oppression and injustice, though dressed up in all the fine names of "legality" and "loyalty to the organization of society."

Not many people outside Vermont know the dramatic story of the State's early life, but everybody inside the State does. There are fewer people in the whole State of Vermont than in the city of Buffalo, which is not at all huge as cities go now. But even at that, there are a good many men, women, and children in the State, over three hundred thousand. There is hardly one of this number who does not know about the history of the New Hampshire Grants, and how our great-grandfathers stood up against all the then existing British state for their naked human rights; and won the fight.

I know you are vague on this point, though you probably had it as a lesson one day in high school; so

I will give you a sketch of it, compressed to a brevity which ought not to bore you too much. After the end of the French and Indian War, Vermont was safe ground for American settlers and the bolder spirits began to come in from New Hampshire and Connecticut. They settled, went through the terribly wearing toil of pioneers, felled trees, reclaimed land, drained swamps, built houses and mills, braved isolation, poverty, danger, health-breaking labor, and made Vermont a region of homes. They had learned to love it as we love it now, silently, undramatically, steadfastly, detesting any florid, high-flown talk about it, burying our love in our hearts and pretending to outsiders that it is not there. Vermonters are not sentimental, articulate Celts, but hermetically sealed Yankees. But they live on this love for their homes and they have shown themselves quite ready to die for it.

Back there in the eighteenth century, just when the settlers had definitely proved that they could make homes out of the wilderness, they were informed that by a legal technicality the grants by which they held their land were not valid; and that the King of England authorized New York lawyers to send officers of the law to take the Vermont land away from the men who had reclaimed it. It was then to be given to soft-handed, well-to-do men, with political influence who had no more rightful connection with that land than did the inhabitants of Peking. The Vermont settlers did not pretend to understand the law of that day. They only knew in their hearts that the land they had so painfully reclaimed, worked over, brought up their children on, was theirs, if anything ever belonged to anybody. A shout went up from Vermont to the New York officers of the law: "Just come and take it away, if you dare!" And they got down their long rifles, ran some bullets, and dried their powder.

The hated "York State men" tried to do this, ventured into the Vermont settlements, were roughly treated, and sent home. They were afraid to try it again and retreated to the Albany courts of law, which summoned the Vermonters to submit the matter to trial. With nothing but their inherent human rights back of them, the Vermonters went down to Albany (no true Vermonter can abide the name of Albany since then!) and there went through the solemn twaddle of a law-trial, where the standards were not those of human rightness and fair-dealing, but were drawn from yellow parchments. Of course the parchments won. That is their habit in law-courts.

Ethan Allen was in Albany through this trial, to help the Vermonters. After the decision was rendered, he walked out of the law-court, on his way home, surrounded by a mocking crowd of York State men. The whole history is so familiar to us Vermonters that any one of us would know just what is coming next in this episode. When, in speaking to a Vermont audience, you begin this story, you can see people lay down their umbrellas and handbags to have their hands free to applaud, and you can see every backbone straighten as you go on in the phrases consecrated by time. "They shouted jeeringly at Allen: 'Now, do you know you're beaten? Now will you lie down and give up?' Ethan Allen drew himself to the full height of his magnificent manhood" (we never use any less fine a phrase than this) "and cried out in a ringing voice, 'The gods of the mountains are not the gods of the plains,' and strode away leaving them silenced." (Here is where the speaker always has to wait for people to get through clapping.) He strode back to Vermont and organized a resistance. Was there ever a more absurd, pitiable, pretentious attempt? A handful of rough ignorant mountaineers, without a legal leg to stand on, to try and defend themselves against the British law! And their only pretext, the preposterous one that they had earned what they held!

Well, to make a long and complicated story short, the rough handful of ignorant men did continue to hold the land they had earned, and we, their descendants, are living on it now. They did more. For fourteen years after that, those men, our great-grandfathers, ruled Vermont, free of any sovereignty, an independent republic on the continent of North America. You never heard that quaint and colorful fact about our little State, did you? Yes, for fourteen years they stood straight and strong on their own feet, owing allegiance to nothing in creation but their own consciences. They stood steady in a whirling, shifting world, and proved to their own satisfaction that to stand steady is not an impossible task.

Down to this day, down to the last corner of our green, wooded, mountain-bedecked State, we all stand steadier because of that memory back of us. Every foot of the land on which we live was held for us by the courage, almost absurd in its simple-heartedness, of our tall, lean, ironic grandfathers, and by their candid faith in the inherent strength of a just cause.

They risked their fortunes and their lives on their faith in this principle: that those who work and create have certain sacred rights, no matter what laws may be, more than those who do nothing. With that principle as our main inheritance, we Vermonters can cock our feet up on the railing of the porch and with a tranquil heart read the news of the modern world and the frightened guessing of other folks at what is coming next!

NEW JERSEY

THE SLAVE OF TWO CITIES

By EDMUND WILSON, JR.

FROM the first fringe of houses that one leaves on emerging from the Pennsylvania Tunnel and that litters the slope of the hill like the scum of a receding sea, from the yellowed and foundering marshes and the rusty back-yards of factories, from the tangled grooves of railroad tracks and the greasy black of Newark Bay, one finds oneself immersed in an atmosphere of tarnishment and mess. The cities are indifferent and dingy; the people are seedy and dull; a kind of sloppiness and mediocrity seems to have fallen on the fields themselves, as if Nature herself had turned slattern and could no longer keep herself dressed. The chances are that you merely pass through, on your way to Pennsylvania or the South, and that New Jersey seems to you essentially a region that one traverses to go somewhere else, a kind of suburb and No Man's Land between New York and Philadelphia. It has the look of a dreary dumping-ground for odds and ends not wanted in the cities, a scrap-heap of ignoble manufactures and uninteresting amusements, that manages to cheapen even the silence of its southern pines. And in this first unflattering impression you would not be far wrong. It is precisely its suburban function which gives New Jersey such character as it has. It is precisely a place where people do not live to develop a society of their own but where they merely pass or sojourn on their way to do something else. Its distinction among Eastern States is that it has attained no independent life, that it is the door-mat, the servant, and the picnic-ground of the social organisms which drain it.

Almost every characteristic phase of New Jersey takes its function from the nearness of the cities. This is largely what prevents its minor cities from rising above their flatness and drabness. They are content to leave to New York and Philadelphia ambition, liveliness, and brilliance. Where a small Western city, however barren and crude, may command attention through the violence of its energy and the freshness of its enthusiasm, a similar place in New Jersey is likely to lapse into a leaden sleep scarcely distinguishable from death. For the Western town, isolated, thrown in on its own resources, and without a base already laid in the past to support the activities of the present, is obliged to be a success or it is nothing at all; it depends on the efforts of the present generation to make it a going concern; whereas the New Jersey town exists very largely either as a sleeping-place for commuters, who have their business, their amusements, and their associates in New York, or as a mere blackened stump of a town, from which all the more enterprising people have departed, leaving only the feebler to nest in the trunk which their ancestors have planted. The commuters, in their less fashionable phases, are the pure type of American suburbans—lawn-mowing, baseball-watching, Sunday-paper-reading merchants or business men: they live in new concrete houses and own Buicks and Red Seal Victrola records. But the remnants left behind of the original local society decay drearily in great box-like houses which they seem gradually to have ceased to paint, dwelling languidly amid family photographs and shabby Victorian furniture, asking nothing of the commerce of the town but what the grocer and the drug-store can supply, breathing the stale tepid air of an atmosphere where even gossip has lost some of its virulence. They keep not even the charm of social ideals which are admirable even in decay—such as one finds in the South or New England; such taste and manners as there have been have long since emigrated or worn off; nor is there enough energy left behind to launch the town on a vulgar career of booming. Only Newark, so far as I remember, has ever tried anything of this kind and that was more of a special centenary than a prolonged campaign of boost. The best they could do for a slogan was "Newark Knows How" and their mean and dingy imaginations rose no higher than mean and dingy boasts. "History shows us that when poets appear," ran the legend on one of the gala arches, "civilization has begun to decay. Newark has produced no poets."

But the smarter communities come even further from fostering an independent local life. It is either a question of well-to-do commuters who are fundamentally New Yorkers and who never really identify themselves with New Jersey as citizens of that State or of people with country houses who merely come down to New Jersey for a few months in the summer. And they do not even carry smartness to a particularly brilliant point. Rich brokers and powder manufacturers build houses like huge hotels, where their families go about the familiar business of motor and country club. There are the regular tennis, golf, and polo, and, occasionally, a half-hearted fox-hunt. Scattered fragments of a local squirearchy live in the country all the year 'round, accustomed to the society of their horses and dogs and not greatly missing any other. The children of both these elements, rather unusually stupid flappers and youths, pursue a monotonous round of recreation of which they never seem to tire. They are neither very sprightly nor very wild and between the beach club, the tennis club, and the country club attain a sun-baked, untroubled comeliness of healthy solid young animals. They have not even much of a heritage of snobbery to give them the distinction of a point of view.

As for the vulgar resorts that strew the coast culminating in Atlantic City, they have even less charm than the fashionable ones. Here on sticky summer evenings the inland horde swarms like flies. They plunge shrieking on roller-coasters, explore the amorous tunnels of the Old Mill, and listen to phonograph records of Al Jolson on musical slot-machines; they have their pictures taken on buttons, consult negroid gypsy fortune-tellers, bid for bogus *objets d'art* at elegantly conducted auctions, eat pop-corn and salt-water taffy, win fans at Japanese ball-rolling games, shout with laughter at the Magic Mirrors, look on at sand-sculptors modeling President Harding, and squeal with glee as they grab each other's legs in the squirming eel-pot of the surf.

No, New Jersey can boast no Cannes nor even any Provincetown. Here the ancient loud-murmuring sea that breaks so grandly on the coast of New England, that laps the soft smooth sands of Long Island with its little crystal waves—affronted by nightmare villas, pricked by endless piers and casinos, befouled with the droppings of picnics, garbage-pailfuls of egg-shells and orange-skins, balked abruptly of its long sweep of shore by the encroachments of bulkheads and beach clubs—chafes dully against its curb, bleaching out the flimsy summer cottages and in the winter gnawing sullen chunks from the bathing pavilions and boardwalks. Only at such comparatively remote and unpopular refuges as Mantoloking does one find the open yellow sands free for men and children to play on, where, unencumbered by boardwalks and beach clubs, you may sprawl as naked as you please, turning orange at the pressure of the sun among the dark green garlands of the seaweed, while the sea softly worries the shore like a friendly and playful dog. For the rest, the turbid surf made stale with a million hired bathing-suits, the bleak private beaches where cottages lodge like the sea-dried mummies of fish.

Even the countryside of New Jersey has largely lost its local flavor. Where fifty years ago a tranquil race not unlike that of New England went about the work of farm and village in faithful allegiance to the church, which formed the center of a genuine community with a civilized society of its own, there is nothing today but great truck-gardens to feed the straining populations of the city and towns which have been gored by the motor roads and are losing their identity as gasoline stations. I take as symbol an amiable old lady inhabiting a low white house, built close against the road but screened off with yellow rambler and clematis; in the dining-room are smooth mahogany and some fine thin old silver; in the bookcase are Shakespeare, Milton, Dickens, and Frank Stockton. The road, now become a State highway, buries the rambler and the clematis in dust; the old lady dies of lacerated nerves from the shrieking of joy-rides to the shore; the mahogany is bought up at auction by the wife of a gasket manufacturer.

Only three kinds of life in New Jersey are really free of subservience to the cities and these do not contribute much that is vivid to the stagnant society of the State. There are, first, the industrial centers, like Paterson, Newark, and Trenton, which do their share to blacken the landscape and spread desolation on man. They are as grimy and as dismal as possible, but it is characteristic of New Jersey that not even the horrible here attains really heroic proportions. In the plumbing and rubber goods of Trenton, the sewing-machines of Elizabeth, the silk mills of Paterson, and the petroleum of Bayonne, and in the jungle of diversified industries which gives Newark a sort of grim richness: the Agatine Shoe Hooks, the Metal Buttons and Novelties, the Jigs, Fixtures, and Dies, the Grey Iron Castings, the Washers and Steam Discs, the Milling Cutters and Reamers, the Celluloid, Varnish, and Corsets, the Artificial Leather Products, and the Electric Hoisting Machinery—you get the blank brick walls, the leaden streets, and the cramped smudgy life of industry without the epic sky-blasting monsters that one finds in the steel-mills of Pittsburgh. But here life reaches what is almost the only intensity it ever attains in New Jersey: the grinding and bitter conflicts which make an industrial ulcer of Paterson.

Another element of New Jersey society which exists independently of the cities is the settlement of poor white trash or "pine rats" which infests the southern pines. Below Lakewood one enters an arid tropics of pine-needles and sand. The air is like molten flannel; the streams dry up to green streaks. To whole tracts of this desolate wilderness there has never come anyone but the surveyor, and the very landmarks have been branded with such sinister names as Mount Misery. But scattered about the edges of this desert are found rudimentary communities of men who manage to live in a perpetual state of indolence and destitution. Without lawyer, doctor, or clergy, in the crudest of timber shacks, devoured daily by fleas, mosquitoes, sand-ticks, and gigantic flies, they ask nothing of the world but to be allowed to deteriorate in peace. They have practically nothing except gin that civilization can supply. They are interrupted only by sociologists who find them a useful laboratory of degeneracy. I remember that the last thing I saw as I was leaving one of these settlements one summer was a huge snake being assaulted by two half-naked little girls who savagely did it to death with large tree-branches for bludgeons. These are perhaps the only autochthonous and autonomous Jerseymen.

But it cannot be altogether the suburbs which give New Jersey its tarnished quality. There is something in the very climate which seems to blur life out of clearness. The sticky winds from the sea, the miasmal vapors from the marshes, the muggy suffocating summers, and the long dissolution of the fall spread a haze and a kind of blowziness upon the human life of the State. Does the flatness of the country itself tend to flatten the lives of the inhabitants? Is it for this reason that when I think of New Jersey it tends to appear to me as a set of phenomena so uniformly blighted with a lack of stature or distinction? I see the dusty and smelly ailanthus trees of the dog-eared public park in Newark, the crazy husks of summer hotels deserted and collapsing on the shore, sparse groves slowly turning to junk-heaps with accretions of cans and old shoes, wooden houses turned abjectly into billboards for long extinct brands of Liver Pills, a man in a furry green hat wrangling rancidly with his wife in a country club, a puncture in a soft red road at the edge of a settlement of Negroes, an imitation of the Villa d'Este (with overtones of the Hanging Gardens of Babylon) by a Jewish theatrical manager, "Souvenir of Atlantic City," root-beer booths beside the road, three actors catching sallygrowlers on an hilarious outing in a rowboat, women reading the *Ladies' Home Journal* by blue and green glass soda-fountain reading-lamps, a State Senator bribed in a lavatory, a Sunday-school excursion to Ocean Grove, the public library of a large town which never gets the works of H. G. Wells, oyster-openers at Keyport striking because the Board of Health had perforated their buckets and thus, allowing the juice to escape, had made it necessary for them to open more oysters, girls in the Passaic handkerchief factories trying to bring down the price of the thread which, though an essential material of their work, they are forced to buy from their masters.

Yet, on the other hand, one should not blame too harshly the landscape and the climate. After all, our unhappy State must once have had its charm like another. When Colonial standards still prevailed, New Jersey must have been nearly as attractive as the South or New England. It is true that this earlier civilization seems to have been more completely obliterated than elsewhere: the old towns, like Perth Amboy or Elizabeth, with beautiful or distinguished names, have become now the most hideous of all. Perth Amboy is a scrofulous common glared upon by ghastly corpse-like houses; Elizabeth's ancient church is wedged tight between dry-goods stores and banks; at New Brunswick the fine sweep of the Raritan is begrudged by a huddle of factories. But here and there, none the less, one finds a relic of the old quality. At Princeton, most of all, is it possible to guess what life must once have been. Here, at last, whatever tone New Jersey has may be seen at its best; for Yale and Harvard are not more of New England than is Princeton of New Jersey. Here where clear windows and polished knockers are still bright on Colonial houses, where Nassau Hall, in dry grace of proportion, still wears the dignity of the eighteenth century, the eternal lowland haze becomes charming, the languor a kind of freedom. Here, as elsewhere in New Jersey, it is as if life were on the point of stopping, turning no face to the future, not caring if the future ever comes; so careless, so untroubled by the tides of life are the gestures and voices of its men that our visitors from New England universities have been known to rail at Princeton for idleness, for drifting gaily through delightful days in a backwater of the world, as the other inhabitants of New Jersey may be supposed to drift dully through shoddy ones. One seems at last to have reached a place where no one cares what is happening in New York. . . . An old Negro in a rickety hack rattles listlessly along Nassau Street . . . men in white hats and white flannels lounge gently toward the tennis-courts . . . cries flung from the playing-fields are lost in the wide flat silence of the countryside . . . on the canal a lock-keeper and his wife live forever in a small white lock-house and the white ducks bob and float on the green surface of the canal . . . crows hawk in the low wet woods where the lady-slipper lifts her pink . . . the tame locomotive that runs lazily between the town and the junction pants and shuffles vaguely in the distance like a comfortable pet. . . . And at night from the campus rise fragments of song, friendly names tossed at open windows, spray of music splashed lightly from casements to dissolve in the quiet air—half-meant, half-heard, half-finished, thrown careless to the careless night. . . . But by as much as Princeton is moribund from the point of view of the cities by so much does she suit herself better to be a place of reflection and play. The flowers of poetry and of learning scarcely open in our crowded air. There are too many interruptions and too little patience to tend them. But at Princeton it is possible, at least, for men to find their forebears again and to practice the arts which they cherished in an atmosphere not different from their own. If the tempo of life is indolent, why, indolence nourishes poetry; if the outlines of things are blurred, why, one is so much less beset by the real. Here at least New Jersey the slattern may lift nobly the head of a Muse. . . .

Yes: one must not fall into the error of making Nature a scapegoat for everything: she might be dignified and charming enough even in the mild fields of New Jersey if the beings who insist upon infesting her did not murder those qualities with their own.

UTAH

APOCALYPSE OF THE DESERT

By MURRAY E. KING

More than three-fourths of the people of Utah are Mormons. Stretching away from Salt Lake City, Ogden, from the smelter towns and mining camps, which are half Gentile and indistinguishable from similar centers in other parts of the West, is a rural hinterland almost wholly Mormon. Here one sees the Utahan in his native setting. Here life is uniquely organized, and here is rooted the power that dominates the State religiously, socially, and politically.

A sight of the Mormon conference crowd in Salt Lake City every April and October should dispel impressions of the Mormons that have grown out of stories of polygamous escapades, Danites, and Avenging Angels. It is Mormon Utah assembled. From a tenth to an eighth of the State's half-million inhabitants gather semi-annually at the call of the church for a general spiritual refilling. The multitude on the Tabernacle grounds looks much like any predominantly rural crowd anywhere between Duluth and Dallas. It differs neither in dress nor in physiognomy. It is not less good-natured and sturdy. Certain backwoods, puritanical, and patriarchal touches impart a picturesque effect, but its only striking peculiarity is that the older generation is an unusual patchwork of nationalities. Many blond, sunburned, rawboned, and stolid Norsemen, largely peasant types, from all parts of the State and from counties almost solidly Scandinavian contrast with groups of dark, stocky Welshmen and women talking excitedly with hands and tongues. These are largely from exclusively Welsh rural settlements and coal-mining camps. English folk are much in evidence—under-sized factory workers, Cockneys, stolid Yorkshire farmers—Icelanders from Spanish Fork, Hawaiians from bleak Skull Valley, and a sprinkling of Germans, Dutch, Scotch. Notwithstanding physical divergencies, this crowd is noticeably homogeneous. A common spirit imparts a clearly collective character. One senses a self-conscious, optimistic, literal, and provincial mind brimming over with local pride and conceit. It is Mormonism manifesting itself through varying types. This religion and its outworkings distinguishes the people of Utah.

The Mormon religion is so simple and literal; it appeals so strongly to the love of the spectacular, dramatic, and miraculous; it promises such large and quick results; it is so directly and solidly authoritarian that it has a peculiar hold on primitive minds. The whole spiritual universe is explained in materialistic terms and analogies. God is a perfected human being with "body, parts, and passions." He is a good Mormon with many wives and is literally the father, his wives the mothers, of our spirits. He placed us on earth to test us and to educate us in a school of experience. After the resurrection we will have immortalized bodies and will eat, drink, and enjoy physical existence and beget children forever. Believers will attain different degrees of glory according to their merits. The highest glory, the celestial, can be attained only through the practice of plural marriage. The polygamist Mormon will become a god and will beget children and construct solar systems for his descendants "out in space" forever, while his monogamic or bachelor brother will continue to exist as a mere angel.

Mormonism keeps its adherents in a perpetual state of spiritual enthusiasm by promising everything to the present generation. It is a "last days" preparation for a "winding-up scene" always a decade or two away. Hence the Mormon is a Latter-Day Saint who expects to live to see dreadful, spectacular, and glorious events that are to accompany the gathering of Israel to the region of Utah, the destruction of all the wicked who refuse to accept the Gospel, the return of the Lost Tribes of Israel from the region of the North Pole, the founding of the city of Zion at Independence, Jackson County, Missouri, the second coming of Christ, the first [1] resurrection, the translation into immortal beings of all good Saints then living, the beginning of the millennium. Before 1891, that date was set by thousands of Latter-Day Saints as the year of the second coming of Christ. The belief was based upon a passage in the Doctrine and Covenants, the Mormon book of revelations, in which God informs Joseph Smith, the founder of the church, that if he lives until he is eighty-five

[1] When the Mormons speak of the first resurrection they ignore the accepted resurrection of Christ nineteen centuries ago and refer to a supposed general resurrection of the righteous, which they say will take place at a comparatively early date. Long after this will come the second resurrection, which will consist of the resurrection of the wicked after they have been purged sufficiently of their sins.

years old he will "see the face of the coming of the Son of Man." Mormons now explain that Joseph Smith did not live until he was eighty-five. These abnormal expectations have culminated from time to time in periods of religious excitement and miracles when whole communities have been rebaptized and have started life anew. Such occurrences have become less and less frequent, but today there are thousands of aged persons in Utah who are happy in the belief that they will see the "winding-up scene" and will become immortal beings without having to die.

The main Mormon arguments for polygamy are: the exemplary and approved personages in the Bible practiced it; it supplies human bodies more rapidly than monogamy for the hosts of waiting spirits who must be "born under the covenant" before the end of the world; it is necessary for the purification of women by earthly trial. In practice it broke or crushed women or drove them into ungovernable rebellion. Children of polygamist parents turned upon their fathers and demanded the abolition of the practice. Caught between a young Mormon element and the Government, the authorities promulgated a revelation in 1891 suspending the practice. At that time, it is said, 7 per cent of Utah families were polygamic. Secret plural marriages developed later and the church authorities were compelled by public opinion to excommunicate the offenders. Cases of this kind have not come to light for about ten years, but relics of the institution still survive. Old men quietly cling to their former wives and support them. But despite the passing of polygamy, Mormons continue to live that part of their religion which requires the rearing of large families. A Provo, Utah, school teacher recently asked her geography class, "What are the principal means of transportation in Utah?" A small boy promptly answered, "Baby carriages."

Celestial marriages have taken the place of plural marriages. A celestial marriage is a secret Temple rite wherein men have dead women "sealed" to them as their wives for eternity, and unattached women are sealed to dead husbands. There is no evidence that the ghost has any choice in the matter. These harmless ceremonies open the gates to the celestial glory temporarily closed by the revelation of 1891. An unsuccessful bachelor may collect the names of decedent old maids or wives of other men not married "under the covenant." At the Temple after the "sealing ordinance" he is given a record of the heavenly names of these celestial wives. Only by repeating these names at the gates of heaven can he get them inside. This explains what a grief-stricken Mormon bachelor in Salt Lake City several years ago meant when he sobbed, "I have lost my wives: the mice have eaten them up!"

A Latter-Day Saint will tell you that the distinguishing principle of his religion is "continued revelation." He means that his church is ruled and guided from heaven through the constituted authorities here. All good saints may receive "testimonies," see visions, or perform miracles for themselves in accordance with church authority, but only one man, the president, prophet, seer, and revelator of the church, may receive revelations from God for the guidance of the church or any part of it. Many devout Mormons accept this doctrine without qualification. It confers upon the Mormon hierarchy a potential political power that may well be a challenge to democratic institutions. Many Mormons, however, accept it with reservations, or ignore it. This, combined with the caution and cunning of the leaders, prevents it from being pushed to extreme lengths. The practice of promulgating revelations has declined to such an extent that no authorized revelations have appeared in Utah for years. On the other hand, the authorities have been greatly embarrassed by the competition of self-constituted prophets. Not many years ago an aspiring John the Baptist in southern Utah paved the way for the advent of a certain son in a certain family who would be "the chosen one" to lead the saints back to Jackson County, Missouri. As the natal day approached the excitement grew among the followers of the unborn Messiah. Suddenly the whole movement miraculously collapsed and the church was saved. The expected boy turned out to be a girl.

The average Mormon is a composite product of this religion, the desert, the mountain land with which he blends, and a modern American world which pushes in upon him and changes him in spite of himself. Stop at his home and one of the first questions he asks is, "Do you belong to the church?" If you do, he will reveal himself as an enthusiast very much enamored with the visions of miraculous things about to transpire. If you do not, he will discover to you a practical, common-sense, shrewd, fairly human and neighborly individual interested in a great many worldly, materialistic, and modern things. Despite his belief in polygamy he has a rigid code of sex morality. There is not an unusual amount of immorality or illegitimacy in Mormon communities. Notwithstanding his belief in "continued revelation," his head is full of canny and stubborn reservations which save him from being the priest-ridden creature one might expect to find. Assertions of independence often come with quaint effect from stern old believers, as in the case of a Welsh brother who, having been pressed a little too hard for church contributions, shouted in church: "I tell 'oo the church do look after itself furst. I hereby serve notice that henceforth I will look out for David Evans furst, and the church after." An old Danish peasant in Ferron compromised between his spirit of independence and religious fears by declaring to the congregation: "Ay tank yet dis is de church of God, but Ay tank no longah you ah de Lord's people."

To hear whole Mormon congregations in village meeting houses on Sundays shouting their hymns to the mountains is to realize the love of this people for the country they dwell in.

> O ye mountains high, where the clear blue sky
> Arches over the vales of the sea,

they shout. Or they sing,

> O Babylon, O Babylon, we bid thee farewell;
> We are going to the mountains of Ephraim to dwell,

or thunder,

> For the strength of the hills we bless Thee,
> Our God, our fathers' God.

The preachers lovingly refer to Utah as "the Valleys of the Mountains," or "Deseret." The natural ties that unite the people and country are augmented by religious and historical bonds. The Mormons came from Missouri and Illinois, a hunted people, and found valleys that were places of refuge and mountains that were walls of defense. The deserts, valley rivers, and salt lakes realized the visions of the wilderness, of the Jordan and Dead Sea of ancient Palestine, and stamped the country as the new Land of Promise. Here the somber and apocalyptic imagination of a modern Israel finds its home.

Picture a wild tumble of forest-splashed mountain ranges flung in a great semicircle from the middle of the northern boundary of the State to the southwest corner. To the west and north of this a vast, gray desert—wide, flat valleys, far, lone hills, low, sunburned ranges, salt-rimmed lakes, glistening alkaline flats, blinding-white salt deserts—all spreading with increasing desolation to Nevada and beyond. To the east and south an immense red sandstone desert beats in tumultuous rock waves from the edge of the State to the base of the mountains—a mesa land, abysmally gorged, savagely painted, weirdly weathered and sculptured, and touched with a thorny, subtropical vegetation. This is Utah in outline. Its inhabitants cling tenaciously to the central crescent of mountains. They huddle along the edges of the red and the gray deserts. But only rarely and timidly do they follow the river valleys out into these wastes.

If this is a forbidding picture, you have not learned the lure and deception of Utah. Through the heart of the mountains for three hundred miles north and south runs a single connected chain of watered valleys, green in the north among the jumbled, snow-capped peaks of the Wasatches, gray among the naked, forest-fringed mountains of the south, except where the little settlements have spread their rugs of green—Cache Valley, Ogden Valley, Salt Lake Valley, Provo Valley, Indianola Valley, San Pete Valley, Sevier Valley, Circle Valley, Panguitch Valley, Grass Valley. Here along torrents emerging from canyons, or on the banks of valley rivers, in cozy towns and villages girdled by green fields and smothered in orchards and shade trees, dwell more than half the rural folk of Utah.

Not less picturesquely placed are the towns on the edge of the gray desert at the mouths of the canyons of the Pavant and Tushar mountains. From each of these green deltas, which look down upon the wide desert fading to purple and azure in the distance, rises a green lane beside torrential waters through ragged gorges to a cool upland of lakes, woods, and meadows. But strangest of all are the settlements on the edge of the red desert in Utah's Dixie. The gorges of the painted desert head in little, funnel-shaped canyons at the base of the mountains. Canyon torrents drop sheer to these through zones of fir, white pine, long-leaf pine, cottonwood, squaw bush, chaparral, cactus and Joshua trees, and are diverted by the settlers to the hot, sandy soil. The canyon floors and the mesas above become bowers of subtropical foliage, flower, and fruit in the midst of gaunt desolation.

The farming communities in this setting embody what is basic in Utah. The location of more than three-fourths of them at the mouths of canyons is most propitious for delightful contrasts of climate and scenery and communal self-sufficiency. The canyon is a boulevard and a summer resort; the canyon stream an exclusive community possession for turning the industries and conquering the desert and transforming it into a fruitful Eden; the mountains a great, free timber reserve and summer pasture; the valley an empire of land in process of conquest; the desert a winter range. These communities are compact and self-sufficient, and are separated by respectable distances of field or desert space from neighboring towns. Around them are zones of green or russet fields gradually advancing upon the desert as methods of irrigation improve. This zone is quite without houses and outbuildings. The owners of its fenced plots live in the town and fare forth daily during the busy season to cultivate the land and haul in the crops. The church, the desert, and the canyon stream have conspired to produce this village concentration. The church has created so many religious activities and so monopolizes social activities that it cannot carry out its program except in organized communities. There is little isolated rural living in Utah. The man who cultivates the soil is the main pillar of a highly structured town life, a life that is indeed tinged with communism. Many towns have coöperative stores, creameries, cheese factories, and canneries. The irrigation system is owned and administered coöperatively. Milch cows and work horses graze placidly on a common pasture. The church has a communal provision against indigence. Part of the "tithing," Relief Society, and fast-day "offerings" is used to provide for those who are unable to provide for themselves. The result of all these conditions is an unusual diffusion of comfort and absence of extreme poverty. The 1920 census shows that only 10.9 per cent of Utah farmers are tenants, as against 38.1 per cent of the farmers of the remainder of the United States.

The town is a regular arrangement of substantial brick homes. Each house stands in an orchard and garden plot of about an acre, with barn and corrals in the opposite corner of the lot. The square, fenced blocks are like wicker baskets bursting with fruits and flowers. The sidewalks are bordered by running water and smothered under shade trees. The meeting-house, tithing office, and other church buildings are great bulks of red brick. Schoolhouses are plentiful. Utah ranks fourth among the States in secular education; but the church administers an immediate antidote in the shape of the most complete system of religious education in the United States.

Quaint and various are the religious manifestations. A venerable patriarch, with flowing beard, solemnly blesses awed young boys and girls, reveals the tribes of Israel from which they have descended, and foretells their futures. Elders cast out devils, lay hands on the sick, anoint them with olive oil, and pray for their recovery. Dances are opened and closed by prayer, and religious instructors teach proper "round dancing." Everybody fasts once a month and turns the equivalent of the meals saved to the church for the poor. Young and old assemble at the meeting-house fast day for "testimony meetings." These are Pentecostal affairs where all who feel "moved by the spirit" arise, confess their faults, ask forgiveness, and bear their testimonies. These consist of the narration of miraculous incidents in the course of which the emotions of the assemblage are often loosed and some of the speakers become incoherent. Young ward teachers visit all the families each month and question the members about their religious and moral conduct and condition of faith and report back to the bishop, who is the "temporal" head of the community. The women of the Relief Society have sewing bees for the benefit of the poor and a granary stored with wheat against the predicted famines of the "last days." Life is one continual round of meetings—Sunday schools and religion classes for the children, the Young Men's and Young Women's M. I. A., deacons' and teachers' meetings for youth, Relief Society meetings for women, priesthood meetings of all orders of the priesthood for men, general meetings of all kinds for everybody.

The church utilizes every resource of organization, education, and spiritual hope to erect its formidable power and counteract Gentile and modern influences. Every male member over ten or twelve is required to join the priesthood. The ascending orders of the priesthood are: deacons, teachers, priests, elders, high priests, seventies, the Twelve Apostles, the first presidency, consisting of the president and his two councilors. In addition to its enormous educational activities in each community the church has a system of academies and colleges. Its Temple work of "sealing," "ordinances," "endowments," vicarious baptisms grips the Mormon imagination powerfully. Its missionary work requires every young man to leave Utah and proselyte among the Gentiles several years. Of all methods calculated to produce an ingrained Mormonism, this is the most effective.

Out of all this has developed a political power potentially incalculable. Devout Mormons deny this, notwithstanding the bitter political fight between Gentiles and independent Mormons on one side and the church and its devoted followers on the other, which has torn the State asunder for a generation. The political purpose of the church has been to keep Utah as much as possible in the camp of the dominant political party in order to obtain for Mormonism an advantageous and influential position in the nation. In the course of the long fight the church has swung around from the position of a power that fought the United States army under Johnston to one that teaches patriotism and proclaims the Constitution a divinely inspired instrument. The visible method used to swing the State politically is to drop gentle hints at public meetings as to what "would be best for Zion at this time." There have always been enough church members who literally accept the divine authority of the dignitaries and put the interests of the church above everything else to constitute a comfortable balance of power in the hands of the authorities. But the independent Mormon element has been growing steadily and the practice of such methods has developed scandals within the church resulting in "trials" of overzealous members. They end usually in the overzealous brother receiving solemn censure from an Apostle who mayhap also winked the other eye. The church has gradually become more cautious in its methods and the conflict less direct and bitter, until today external peace prevails in the State.

Perhaps the most sinister development of the church is its gigantic material power. It bases its strength increasingly on the acquisition of property. This control has been secured with funds created out of a system of taxes and levies probably without parallel. Every member is required to pay annually one-tenth of his or her gross income as "tithing." In addition there are fast offerings, Relief Society offerings, missionary contributions, and donations of all sorts for building and other purposes. For many years the church has been investing part of these funds in various financial and industrial enterprises. It now owns or controls several shoe and overall factories, several publications and printing and publishing houses, great funds for the aid of reservoir and irrigation projects, the Deseret National Bank, Zion's Savings and Trust Company, Zion's Coöperative Mercantile Institution, Hotel Utah, the Utah-Idaho Sugar Company, with nineteen plants in Utah, large ranches upon which it has colonized members, much real estate, and sugar plantations in Hawaii. It employs church members and deducts its tithing from their pay checks. Unions are not tolerated by this gigantic employer. There is mutual and bitter hostility between the labor unions and the Mormon church. Encouraged by public statements of church authorities in the Tabernacle, sons of Mormon farmers "scab" on union strikers in the mining camps. The late Mormon President, Joseph F. Smith, once offered as principal justification for opposing labor unions that they were secret societies! It is said in Salt Lake City business circles that the church authorities are enriching themselves from these investments; but of vastly greater consequence is the capital and the investment fund that remain the property of the church. Fed from the pockets of hundreds of thousands of members, these expand abnormally, threatening the whole State with a form of dominance intolerable to contemplate.

Yet in spite of this highly mobilized religion and church, the Mormons—and Utah—are responding rapidly to Gentile and modern influences. Originally the church was so determined to develop a separate and peculiar people that the Utah settlements were made as self-sustaining, interdependent, and coöperative as circumstances would allow. These efforts culminated in the establishment at Kingston, Orderville, and other places in the early eighties of communistic colonies. These efforts developed a spirit that made it possible to keep the Mormons out of the gold rush to California, and later when the surrounding States were filled with prospectors all that was necessary to keep the saints for several decades out of the great mining movement was a warning from the church that the opening up of mineral riches in Utah would cause Zion to be submerged by inrushing hordes of Gentiles. In those days the Mormon religion was a terrific reality. Life in Utah was a continuous riot of miracles and visions. The steady trickle into the Great Basin of Gentile cattlemen, prospectors, and merchants was bitterly resented. Church authorities thundered constantly in the meetings against association or intermarriage with these intruders. The feelings aroused resulted in acts of persecution and violence against Gentiles culminating in the Mountain Meadow massacre.

Remembering these former intensities, the grip of Mormonism and the organized power of the church, one may well be amazed over present conditions in Utah. The Mormon, with some exceptions, is a greatly changed and modernized person. The Gentile is everywhere. Scarcely a town or village is free from his presence. He finds his way into Mormon circles and homes. He is still treated with a lingering aloofness and clannishness, but with increasing courtesy. There are intermarriages. Where a considerable number of Mormons and Gentiles dwell in the same community, and the Gentile church looks superciliously across the street upon the Mormon meeting-house, society tends toward two exclusive social divisions, but the feeling of aloofness and superiority is as much on one side as on the other.

Two things have struck Mormon isolation and exclusiveness staggering blows. America has closed in on the Mormon with an infiltrating intellectual environment of current ideas, opinions, phrases, news, literature, which in the long run affect him more than his Book of Mormon or Doctrine and Covenants, which he hardly ever reads any more, or his *Deseret Evening News,* and church magazines, which he does read. Utah Gentilery has released ponderous industrial and commercial forces that are changing his incentives, habits, and social organization. It is boasted locally that Salt Lake City is the greatest smelter center in the world. Utah is already one of the leading mining

States. In the feverish industrial foci of the State the struggle for trade advantage makes the major claim on life. Here Gentile and Mormon business men mingle closely and approximate despite themselves the mentality and standards of life that belong to this environment. Here Mormon and Gentile workers rub elbows and the Mormons, drawn into labor organizations in spite of the church, develop interests, motives, and views that blend them with the great mass of American toilers. Here the Mormon church becomes a competing sect among sects and must conform to certain standards of religious competition. Here the Mormon comes gradually to ignore those religious doctrines that fail to square with this material and intellectual environment. Often he remains a Mormon only in name, or according to his own interpretations of Mormonism, because he does not wish to disconnect himself from a people he still regards his own.

SOUTH CAROLINA

A LINGERING FRAGRANCE

By LUDWIG LEWISOHN

A TINY tongue of land extending from Broad Street in Charleston to the beautiful bay formed by the confluence of the Ashley and the Cooper rivers is all of South Carolina that has counted in the past; the memories that cling to the little peninsula are all that count today. More than thirty years have passed since Ben Tillman led the revolt of the agrarians, the "poor white trash," the "wool-hats" of the "upper country" against the old Charlestonian aristocracy. He won. The time-spirit was with him. The new men control the State; they control the State University; they will not send their sons to the College of Charleston; they have industrialized the "upper country" and made it hum with spindles and prosperity and their particular brand of righteousness. Spartanburg is both a more progressive and a more moral city than Charleston. It even indulges in cultural gestures and is visited by a symphony orchestra once a year. It is the headquarters of the cotton-mill men and of the Methodists; it is the seat of Wofford College, where they cultivate Christian prosperity and the tradition of the sainted Bishop Duncan: "In my time I used to read Shakespeare and Scott and all those writers. But nowadays I read nothing but the Bible because I know it is the word of my God. . . ."

The new men brought neither freedom nor enlightenment. They oppress and bedevil the Negro without the old gentry's vivid and human, even if strictly feudal, sympathy with his character and needs; they sentimentalize in political speeches and commencement orations about the Old South. Of its genuine qualities, as these were represented in old Charleston, they know nothing. It was, indeed, in mute deference to them that the president of the College of Charleston ceased, long before the days of prohibition, to serve wine at his receptions and permitted engineering courses to be added to the undergraduate curriculum. In this atmosphere the sons of the Charleston gentry who, until a few years ago, studied Greek as a matter of course, have sunk into that appalling and intolerant ignorance and meanness of spirit that mark the cultural vacuum known as the New South. They no longer study in Europe or found periodicals or issue shy volumes of verse or cultivate a perfectly genuine though somewhat pseudo-Roman and oratorical spirit of service to the State and nation. They are letting their civilization perish without resistance.

They are, of course, vastly outnumbered and energy died out of the stock long before they were born. They are mere descendants and cling to the husks. In the early years of the present century one of the last of the Pinckneys wrote a "Life of Calhoun" in which he defended the doctrine of nullification as fundamentally necessary to the structure of American government. Then he went mad. At the reunions of Confederate Veterans the contemporaries of this gentleman spoke with tears of the glories of the Old South. They did not mean the spirit of true civilization which, somehow, old Charleston had possessed; they meant the "peculiar institution of slavery" and the oligarchical rule of the planters of the seaboard counties. Yet at that very time faint remnants of the old Charleston spirit could be observed. The Master in Equity, a *novus homo,* but long accepted through association and marriage into, let us say, the South Carolina Society and the St. Cecilia Society, desired to publish in a volume the poems he had written in the course of a lifetime beautifully though rather ineffectually dedicated to literature and learning. A group of his friends—colleagues of the Charleston bar—made up a purse for him and the book was duly brought out by a New York firm noted for its sharp business practice and its long association with American literature. That was a last flicker of the life of old Charleston. . . .

I seem to be detailing gossip. But these anecdotes are significant and they are, at least, authentic. They should be corrected in the impression they convey by others. The old Charleston group had its darker side. William Gilmore Sims was treated shabbily, though I am willing to believe that he was a man of rude manners and unprintable speech; Henry Timrod, the best of their poets, was treated abominably. He was, in the first place, the son of a German tradesman and poor and a tutor in planters' families. More sinister in its meaning is the bit of gossip which floated down the years that he or the young woman to whom he was betrothed had "a touch of the tar-brush." This thing—interesting and picturesque if true of the poet himself—was whispered to me in a kind of murderous secrecy as a sufficient excuse for whatever need, misery, humiliation poor Timrod was permitted to endure. The old Charlestonians, in brief, loved letters and learning and romance. They were often capable of a fine and gallant and even intellectual gesture; they bore themselves not without distinction. Under that cultivation and distinction, as under the cultivation and distinction of the eighteenth-century type everywhere, lurked cruelty, violent intolerances, stealthy and relentless lusts. . . .

It is hard to realize that today. Quiet has stolen into the old houses of the lower city; scarcely a breath seems to ruffle the wistaria vines in spring! In such a spring Mr. Owen Wister visited shady drawing-rooms —and talked to exquisite old ladies and wrote "Lady Baltimore." Henry James communed with such frail figures during his last stay in this country. He saw a long disused harp, a lovely colonial cabinet, autograph letters of Hayne, and was told that Mr. Thackeray, when he lectured here, took tea in this very room. And it caressed his ear when old ladies with delicate shadows amid their porcelain-like wrinkles sounded the vowels of English as he knew, from the rhymes, Pope must have sounded them, but as he never expected to hear them upon mortal lips. These "values" pleased him amid the violent and raw distractions of the American scene. They are soothing. I, too, have lingered among them and savored them. But they do not tell the complete story of the civilization from which they derived.

That tight and peculiar Charleston culture was created by settlers partly of English, partly of French descent. Names, put down almost at random, will help to convey its quality and atmosphere. Among the English names are Wragg, Middleton, Pinckney, Gadsden, Drayton, Hayne, Trescott, Bull; among the French are Manigault, Gaillard, Huger, Simon, Legaré, Porcher, de Saussure, Jervey (Gervais). The Ravanels were probably Marranos; the French settlers were Huguenots and though many of them, under the political and cultural domination of Britain, went to augment the Anglican parishes of St. Michael and St. Philip, enough clung to their ancestral faith to make the only Huguenot church in America a quaint and agreeable Charleston landmark to this day. There were dissenters from other countries, like the Dutch Mazycks; there was, from a very early period on, a small colony of Sephardic Jews—Lopez, De Leon, Moise, Ottolengui. All the names I have mentioned exist in Charleston today. Of the immediate youngsters I cannot speak. The bearers of these names who are now approaching middle age all, or nearly all, preserved within them something of the spirit of their ancestral civilization.

They were not Puritans in the fierce, vulgar, persecuting and self-persecuting sense. Their theological and moralistic assents were social gestures; they had, themselves, large mental reservations and though in their own persons they considered it rather bad form to parade those reservations, they were not intolerant of the type of conscience that held silence to be hypocritical. They were snobs to the marrow, but a few of them, at least, were capable of contemplating that fact consciously and a little sorrowfully. A Charleston gentleman, almost of the ancient régime, was heard to say to a friend of his: "I don't blame you at all for leaving a city where your social standing will never be quite what you deserve. It is a pity; Charleston needs you. But I should do the same in your place. . . ." Yes, they were snobs and facile assenters who made the free life more difficult. But they had a real respect for the arts, for the things of the mind, for the critical spirit they could never quite share. They were and are, when every deduction has been made, among the most civilized of Americans. They had, in addition, grace, ease, personal charm. When I think of the people who are pressing them hard—the horse-dealer from central Georgia, some hustler from the Middle West—I am inclined to lend them an almost legendary worth. I must, at all events, set down this fact: the present descendants of most of the old Charleston families are poor. The men are still members of the learned professions, as their fathers were. They still consider them learned professions—even the law. The handsome new houses in Charleston are the houses of new people. Many a beautiful and time-mellowed mansion on Legaré Street is in a state of gradual decay.

The history of the old Charleston group is, of course, like the history of other such urban and patrician groups in other parts of the world. It can be matched in Mantua and in Lübeck. The pathos of its downfall lies in the fact that it has gone down not before the authentic spirit of the modern world, but before the mean barbarism of sharp business men and Ku Klux Klanners. Its enemies and conquerors would consider the personalities it produced at its best moments—

Hugh Swinton Legaré, Paul Hamilton Hayne, William Henry Trescott—very much as a Tulsa or Winesburg hundred percenter would consider, if he could consider them at all, Nietzsche or Verlaine or Bertrand Russell. For what Legaré and Trescott had was the critical and distinguishing mind, the culture of the intellect. Legaré, a diplomat, a scholar, a brilliant and romantic personality, a writer like the Edinburgh reviewers of the early days, hastened home from Brussels to protest against secession; Trescott, a statesman who cultivated quietly a gift for extraordinarily limpid and expressive prose, wrote, soon after the Civil War, reflections that blended human warmth with philosophical detachment.

These men and Robert Hayne and Calhoun were, however, less intimately characteristic of the Charleston culture that projects feebly into the present than the minors—the shy spiritual and literary adventurers found in almost every family. In the very early days they were bolder, like Washington Allston, the poet and painter and friend of Coleridge. Later their efforts were more tentative and hushed, like the verses of the Simon brothers, or the really admirable poems of the almost legendary James Mathew Legaré, or the Crashaw-like outpourings of Caroline Poyas. Often they sought anonymity and printed verse and prose in the Charleston periodicals which succeeded each other from before the Revolution to the founding of the *Nineteenth Century* in 1870. And when one considers that the contents of these magazines were all written in Charleston and that Charleston, which has fewer than seventy thousand inhabitants today, was a very small town indeed, one gains a high notion of the pervasiveness of the literary culture and spiritual aliveness that existed in the city between the Revolution and the Civil War. Much of this writing was, of course, feeble and jejune. There is scarcely an original note. The Byronic lyric succeeds the couplet and the didacticism of the late eighteenth century; the emergence of Keats can be noted almost to a day; later that of Tennyson. But behind this imitative expression there was an extraordinary number of cultivated, impassioned, vivid personalities. Everybody wrote—men of public affairs like William Crafts; merchants like Isaac Harby. One Manigault published anonymous novels, another was a really able scientist who brought home a great collection of natural history that is still to be seen. Still others expressed themselves through exotic adventure like Joel R. Poinsett, who found in Mexico the decorative flower that bears his name. I am deliberately jumbling periods. The spirit of the civilization of old Charleston was, while it lasted, one. From Alexander Garden—discoverer of the Gardenia—before the Revolution to Dr. Dixon Bruns of the Civil War period and to Professor Yates Snowden today, one of the marks of the gentleman and the eminent citizen has been to turn out an elegant or a stirring copy of verses at will. But the last or almost the last has been written. Only the descendants of the Sephardic Jews have shown a queer kind of vitality and have produced in the last generation and in this two writers of the shabbily popular variety—Rodriguez Ottolengui and Octavus Roy Cohen.

From Charleston "neck" to the Piedmont region

there may well come the indignant question: Is Charleston gossip an adequate account of the great, proud State of South Carolina? It is. Or shall one record the labor conditions in the cotton mills or the antics of former Governor Blease or expatiate on the lynching statistics?—I once traveled with Blease from Charleston to Cincinnati. He was going to a national meeting of the Elks. He was, with a touch of consciousness, almost of staginess, the typical leader of the democracy of the New South—ostentatiously large wool hat, dark, rather fierce eyes, heavy black mustache, gaudy insignia on a heavy watch-chain, a man who radiated or wanted to radiate a constant ferocity against the irreligious, the impure, "nigger-lovers," aristocrats, "pap-suckers," Yankees, intellectuals; a son of the soil and of the mob with a chip on his shoulder. His conversation had a steady note of the belligerent and the self-righteous. A noisy, astute yet hectic obscurantist. He might have been from Georgia or Mississippi. He despised Charleston with a touch of inverted envy. A South Carolinian quite merged in a larger and lower unity and without any relation to the specific character of the State. Finally shall one make much of the fact that though, whether through the influence of race or climate, the demands of the senses are rather exorbitant in South Carolina, the State has the amusing distinction of being the only commonwealth in the civilized world that will tolerate no provision for divorce on its statute books? In Charleston, at least, there has never been a lynching and her citizens have, at need, disregarded their Draconian law-givers. Also, they and their ancestors have created a beautiful thing

—the old city that clings to the bay. Linger in these streets and lanes and gardens and enter a few shadowy interiors beyond the deep verandas that turn to the South. A race lived here that loved dignity without ostentation, books and wine and human distinction. Its sins, which were many, fade into the past. They were always less vulgar and ugly than the sins of those who have come after.

NEVADA

BEAUTIFUL DESERT OF BURIED HOPE

By ANNE MARTIN

NEVADA to most Easterners suggests divorces, or gambling in mining shares of doubtful value on the New York or Philadelphia stock exchanges. Some, more informed, have heard of our "big bonanza" mines which produced nearly a billion dollars in silver after the Civil War, thus helping to restore national credit, and incidentally producing a crop of millionaires and adventurers, some of whom have won seats in the United States Senate. The "wild and woolly" character of the pioneer mining State fixed on her by Mark Twain in "Roughing It" still clings in the popular mind and is confirmed by most of the news that seeps through the press. Few outsiders have ever heard of her agriculture or any constructive activities, and no one with eyes can see her as anything but a vast, exploited, undeveloped State with a meager and boss-ridden population. Those who wish more information will find in reference books that Nevada began well. She was admitted into the Union in 1864 as the "battle-born State," to give President Lincoln additional support in the Senate, and with her vast domain and natural resources gave great promise. Almost as old as Kansas, Minnesota, and West Virginia, and older than Nebraska, Colorado, the Dakotas, Montana, and all other Far Western States except California and Oregon, "youth" cannot explain away her backwardness and vagaries, her bizarre history, her position as the ugly duckling, the disappointment, the neglected step-child, the weakling in the family of States, despite her charm and beauty and great natural advantages.

The casual railway traveler who has crossed Nevada remembers with wonder or weariness, according to temperament, her twelve hours of "desert" plain, her endless chain of sunny sagebrush valleys surrounded by opalescent mountains, all fertile land but valueless without water, and all without sign of water or habitation, excepting a few railroad tanks and straggling towns, or the drying bed of a river. Reformers know her as perhaps the most "wide-open" State of the West, where prize-fighting, gambling, and saloons have been encouraged greatly to flourish, and where the six-months' divorce still reigns, backed by legal and business interests of Reno. They remember her as the last Western State to adopt woman suffrage, and one of the last to accept State prohibition. She is the despair not only of reformers but of case-hardened lawyers, who must be agile indeed to keep pace with the rapid and contradictory changes in laws made every two years by servile legislatures, at the command of the selfish interests which elected them. To national political leaders she is known as a "doubtful" State, a "pocket-borough," which can be swung more easily than any other into the Republican or Democratic column, according to the amount of money used by either side. (She should therefore not be called "doubtful," but *sure.*) She is known as a State where politicians, irrespective of party, cynically combine every campaign to elect congressmen and legislatures pleasing to the "interests." These legislatures so chosen are largely migratory. Some members have been known to leave the State, pockets bulging, by the midnight train after adjournment. I recall the difficulty experienced by a former governor in securing a quorum for a special session, as many of our itinerant legislators were already far afield in other States, or in Mexico, Alaska, South America, and South Africa.

It must be admitted there are other Western States which differ only in degree. But what makes Nevada an extreme example? Why has she a larger proportionate number of migratory laborers (as of legislators), of homeless men, than any of her neighbors? Why is she the most "male" State in the Union, with more than twice as many men as women, and the smallest proportionate number of women and children? Why has she the smallest and sparsest population of any State, and why has it decreased since 1910? Why has she a peripatetic male electorate nearly half of which has vanished by the next election, with new voters taking their places who will themselves soon vanish? Why is she perhaps the most backward State in precautions against the spread of venereal diseases, the most shameless in her flaunting of prostitution and red-light districts, surrounded by high board fences, to the children of the towns? With no large cities and a largely rural population, why has she a greater percentage in her jails and prison, her almshouses and insane asylum than certain of her neighbors? How can we account for these extreme peculiarities of her industrial, political, and social life?

The migratory character of mining and railway labor has some influence, but the fundamental cause of every one of these conditions undoubtedly lies in the monopoly by the live-stock industry of the water, the watered lands, and the public range lands of the State. At first blush this may sound like saying that sun-spots cause insanity, or that there is an epidemic of pellagra in the South, of smallpox in China, or of cholera in Russia because Wall Street governs us in Washington. But the relation of cause and effect in Nevada is clear. Some may insist that her backwardness is due to her exploitation from the very beginning by the railroads; others, that the mining interests have picked the vitals from her, have taken everything out and given nothing back: witness San Francisco's and even some of New York's finest structures built largely with bullion from her "ghost cities," the Postal Telegraph and Cable system which girdles the globe by means of the Mackay millions taken from the quickly gutted Comstock lode, the Guggenheim and other similar interests still picking the bones for all that is left! True; but mere exploitation by railroads and mine owners does not account for the condition in which we find her today. Other Western States with comparable natural resources have been similarly exploited, and are not a "notorious bad example" of political, economic, and social degeneration.

The live-stock industry, established as a monopoly in Nevada under very extraordinary conditions, is responsible. It has prevented the development of small farms, of family life, of a stable agricultural population, and has produced instead an excessive proportion of migratory laborers and of homeless men, larger than in any other State in the Union. The 1910 census figures give 220 men to every 100 women. The number of married women in the State is about one-third the number of men. The number of children from six to fourteen years is less than two-fifths of the usual average in other States. Utah, for example, with natural resources not much larger than Nevada, has more than eight times as many school children. (The 1920 census figures so far received show an improvement in these proportions more apparent than real, due chiefly to the reduction of the homeless male population since 1910 by the migration of thousands from dying mining camps.) It appears that practically one-half the men of Nevada, or nearly 20,000 out of our total population of nearly 80,000, are living under bad social conditions outside the home environment, as cowboys, sheep-herders, hay-hands, miners, and railwaymen, sleeping in company bunk-houses or on the range, and dependent for their few pleasures and social contacts on the frontier towns the traveler sees from the train window. These afford a movie, perhaps, certainly a gambling house with bootleg whisky, and a "restricted district" behind a stockade, in which the women are "medically inspected" (for a price) while the men are not.

A characteristic Nevada sight, and to those who know its significance one of the most pathetic, is the large groups of roughly dressed men aimlessly wandering about the streets or standing on the street corners of Reno, Lovelock, Winnemucca, Battle Mountain, Elko, Wells, Ely, Tonopah, Goldfield, and other towns, every day in the year. They are in from the ranches and mines for a holiday with hard-earned money, and the only place they have to spend it is in the numerous men's lodging houses, gambling dens, or brothels. In our suffrage campaign in 1914 and in later campaigns we found it always possible to gather these men into a quick, responsive, and generous street audience. But a large proportion of them are wanderers, and are, of course, prevented from voting by the election laws. Of those who can vote many have most naturally no sense of civic responsibility and are easily corrupted by the political machine. If instead of the land and water monopoly by the live-stock interests for the almost exclusive production of hay, cattle, and sheep, this same land with water, now manned chiefly by "ranch-hands" and in the hay-making season by a large influx of migratory hay-hands, were subdivided into small farms for diversified and intensive agriculture, Nevada would soon have many new homes with women and children in them, she would soon have a large and growing farm population, larger towns and community centers, and greater social stability, instead of languishing on as an exhausted weakling in the sisterhood of States. But the strangle-hold of the live-stock interests continues as the cause of the mortal illness from which she is suffering, and to grasp the case we must consider some physical features.

Nevada is 110,000 square miles in area, more than twice as large as New York or Pennsylvania. Her population is 77,000, or about one person to every one and one-half square miles. Her *land* area is more than 70,000,000 acres, of which nearly 90 per cent is still owned by the National Government. The remainder is chiefly land granted by the Government to the railroad, with the exception of a little more than 3 per cent, or about 2,300,000 acres, which is reported in privately owned farms in 1920. Of this amount nearly 600,000 acres, or less than 1 per cent of the total land area, is under irrigation. The water for this purpose is supplied chiefly by Nevada's four rivers, the Truckee, Carson, and Walker, which rise in the Sierra Nevada Mountains, and the Humboldt, which rises in the northeast. The snowfall in the mountain ranges which traverse the State north and south produces in addition a few small springs and streams. These water part of the valley lands. It has been estimated that the State has enough water, if carefully conserved and used, to irrigate 2,000,000 acres, or about 3 per cent of her area. But owing to the great cost of constructing the necessary dams and reservoirs for the storage of flood waters, and the dams and ditches for its distribution, and because of waste of water by many users, the irrigated area is not increasing. According to the 1920 census it has decreased. The vital fact is that about 97 per cent of the State's enormous area has no agricultural value except as grazing land for cattle and sheep (unless water can be developed from new sources such as artesian wells), and that the National Government owns nearly all this grazing land. Uncle Sam owns it, but a few live-stock companies monopolize its use for their herds. This is made possible by the fact that the law under which government grants of school lands to Nevada were administered enabled certain stockmen to select practically all the land with water, so as to control all water available for irrigation and drinking purposes for live stock. In Nevada, unlike other States, the law controlling the sale of the millions of acres granted by the Government enabled a stockman to pick out only the forty-acre tracts with water on them. He could buy 640 acres directly, and get as much more as he wanted by using the names of relatives and employees—"dummies." The price of the land was $1.25 an acre, but only twenty-five cents had to be paid down, with long time for the balance. So a man with $5,000 could buy 25,000 acres, carefully selected in forty-acre tracts along the banks of rivers and streams, and through this water monopoly he could secure the exclusive control of a million acres of public range land as free pasture for his herds. In other States the Government land grants consisted of numbered sections according to United States surveys, and buyers could not pick out exclusively the areas with water. (The bill granting 7,000,000 acres of Government land to Nevada, which passed the United States Senate in 1916 through the efforts of Senator Pittman, was drawn on similarly vicious lines. It would have increased the hold of the land and water monopolists and large-scale live-stock producers on the people.)

Thus was fixed the strangle-hold of the live-stock interests on Nevada. A few families and corporations control nearly all her many million acres of range land (97 per cent of the State's area) through their control of the water, and own most of the watered land. Trespassers are kept off by the laws of nature, as they cannot use the pasture unless they have drinking water, or if necessary, by the "law of the range," as shown by many past conflicts of stockmen with their small competitors. With rare exceptions like the Newlands irrigation project at Fallon, Truckee Meadows, and a few other valleys early settled in small and fertile farms by the pioneers, this monopoly has made Nevada practically one large and desolate live-stock ranch. But deliberately or unconsciously its population of homeless workers has taken its revenge, as told by Nevada's overflowing jails and prison, her almshouses and insane asylum, by her lack of political, economic, and social stability, by the most backward position of all the States. No society can allow its natural resources to be monopolized and neglect its workers without paying a heavy price. As Professor Romanzo Adams points out, [1] in no other State is there such concentration of land ownership in a few families, or are there so few farmers. In no other State is the average size of farms, and the average number of cattle or sheep on each farm, so large. And in no other State are there so many migratory farm workers in proportion to the number of farms. "Nevada has from two to six times as large a percentage in prison, jails, almshouses, and hospital for the insane as certain neighboring States where farms and farm homes are numerous and migratory workers few." [2] Paupers, insane, and prisoners are largely recruited from the migratory workers. But the sorry population of her institutions does not tell the full story of damage done. Thousands more must have been maimed in body and soul, and roam free to spread the social canker, while the

[1] "Public Range Lands—A New Policy Needed," by Romanzo Adams. *American Journal of Sociology,* November, 1916.

[2] *Ibid.*

State continues to decrease in population and to deteriorate in nearly all that increases human welfare.

What is the remedy? Will the live-stock interests subdivide their holdings? Will pigs fly? The stockman's motto is, "What I have I hold," down to the last drop of water. I have seen large quantities of it overflowing the ditches and running to waste on the fields and roads of company ranches, producing a rich crop of willows and tules after irrigating the wild hay lands. Across the road were the scattered "dugouts" and cabins of settlers who under great difficulties had cleared a few acres of sagebrush land. They were struggling to "prove up" and sustain life for their families and themselves on a "dry" farm, as their entire water supply was from a well. Staring at us through the sagebrush or clinging to their mother's skirts were two or three eerie little children, timid as jack-rabbits, growing up without school or toys, in ignorance even of children's games. Sooner or later these settlers are starved out, as Nevada is literally the "driest" State in the Union (as regards rainfall), and dry-farming is hopeless. These failures please the large owners; they do not want homesteaders "fussing about," fencing the land on their own government range, and breaking the continuity of their holdings. I know intrepid settlers who have hoarded trickles from mountain streams and seepage that would otherwise be wasted, and used it to water crops on their homesteads, into which they had put years of work and all their meager capital. But they were enjoined at the behest of the neighboring live-stock company from using the hoarded water, on the ground of "prior rights." I have seen them denied its use and lose everything in court. Only their cabin home and the parched land with its withered crops were left them. The manager of this company replied to my protest: "This is *our* country, and we don't want any damned squatters and water stealers around interfering with our water and range and settling it up. We'd *run* them out if we couldn't get rid of them any other way!" However, it is generally not necessary "to run them out," as under our big-business system of government, national and State, the natural-resource monopolists, the banks, and the courts are of course in cahoots, and the verdict is to the strong.

We have in Nevada some laws that automatically keep water away from the land and the settler. On one of my campaigns I met a sturdy young fellow climbing out of a tungsten mine in the Humboldt Mountains, who told me with pride of his wife's work as school-teacher to help him in his struggle for a farm and home for their children. "This is no sort of life for a man to lead," he admitted, wiping the yellow dust from his face, and gazing off at the desert. "I've got to live on top of this mountain in a company bunk-house (and pay $40 a month extra for board) instead of having a home. We can't have it until I get water on my land. The water's there in the Humboldt River, but I can't get it." He had filed on 320 acres under the Desert Land Act, "proved up on it" by making the necessary improvements and payments, cleared the land of sagebrush, dug ditches, secured a water right to certain river waters from the State engineer, and put in a crop of wheat which sprouted well but died, because he was not allowed to run water to his ditches. Instead of the profit of $2,000 he was counting on to pay his debts and build a house, he lost several hundred dollars and all his work, and was now struggling as a miner for a fresh start. He took from his pocket a letter from the agent of a land and live-stock company owning adjoining land. It curtly refused his request for a ditch right of way over its land to his. Another company had filed a protest in the State engineer's office against granting his water right because the company "believed" a dam built at the point of diversion of his ditch from the river would back up the water and flood its land, and because his ditches would have to cross numerous company ditches and thereby prevent it "from enjoying the free use of its vested water and ditch rights." Only by winning lawsuits against neighboring land owners—and both cards and courts were stacked against him—could he fill his ditches. "And with water running to waste in the Humboldt Sink!" he said bitterly. "We fellows haven't a man's chance, and all we want is a fair show to live by our own work." He held out his large, muscular, calloused hands. "And with the Government wasting billions on airplanes and shipyards and railroads and foreign loans! We're doing some thinking for ourselves!" The tungsten mine has since shut down and he has joined the army of homeless men looking for work, while one of the neighboring land companies has filed on his water right, on the ground that he never put it to beneficial use by raising crops.

I have seen families stoically enduring life in little hot cabins in the heart of a burning desert. A well, a few scraggly chickens, a cow perhaps, and a sparse and parched field of rye or wheat were their only visible means of subsistence. The father of one of these families confessed almost apologetically: "I ain't one of these dry farmers, ma'am. I've got some good wells located and could grow fine crops if I could only get a few hundred dollars for a pump." Throughout the State I found it: on the one hand, men and women who had shown energy and hardihood and a pioneer spirit in their struggle against nature for a meager existence, asking only for water; on the other hand the Government, national and State, indifferent to the crying need for farms, homes, and jobs, doing nothing. The settlers struggle on until they lose everything, the land remains barren and unproductive for lack of "a few hundred dollars for a pump," while underground rivers flow beneath the floor of Nevada's driest-looking valleys, and undeveloped artesian water abounds. (Senator Pittman's underground waters bill, recently enacted, reserving the right to any citizen or "association of citizens" to drill for water for two years on land areas of 2,560 acres, thus securing a patent on 640 acres if water is developed, does not help the settler; as a director in one of these water-drilling corporations recently told me: "Only big companies can afford to drill and get land and water on these terms." Several companies have already done so, thus increasing monopoly in the hands of a few.)

I have seen rivers flooding their banks on their way through barren valleys which in the language of congressmen would "blossom as the rose" with the storage and distribution of this water. The Humboldt

River spreads out into a lake at one point, owing to a bad channel, and loses 300,000 acre feet in a few miles, due to evaporation and absorption. This is enough to irrigate 200,000 acres through the season, and provide homes for 2,000 families. Fertile sage-brush lands, but waterless, spread on both sides of the river for miles to the foot of distant mountains, waiting for the homemakers.

Utah has shown our bosses both in Washington and Nevada how to manage large land and water holdings for the public good. It was the policy of the Mormon church to divide good land into small farms. And Utah, with nearly equal agricultural resources, has a much larger population and greater economic and social stability than her neighbor. The Mormon church carried out this policy in Nevada, when a large cattle ranch of several thousand acres in the eastern part of the State accidentally came into its possession. It planned at once to divide it into a large number of small farms. The Mormon bishop there tells me the church was warned that the colonists would starve, as "the ranch was only fit for cattle." But the colonists came, and the land today supports two villages of more than one hundred families, which are producing diversified crops under sound social conditions, instead of wild hay for cattle at great social cost to a lot of homeless men and to the State.

What is the solution of Nevada's problem? Undoubtedly the Government should end its long neglect of its vast public domain and administer these lands as it recently began the administration of its forest reserves, but in the interest of the small settler. The

Government should extend its irrigation projects, providing credits and other necessary aid to settlers during the first difficult years, and, even more important, in coöperation with the State, should buy from the large stockmen tracts of land which control water for live stock. It should manage land, water, and public range with the definite purpose of increasing the number of small farms, of small stockmen, and range users. As Professor Adams suggests, it should also reduce the number of animals pastured on the public range by the large owners, which would of course reduce their yearly production and profit and thus lessen the value of their watered lands. Thus the natural operation of economic laws would lead to the subdivision of their holdings. But this will never be done until the people make their bosses see that government, national and State, if it is to endure, must develop natural resources for the good of all, instead of gutting them for the enrichment of a few, to the ultimate injury of all. Until it is done, Nevada's stable population cannot increase, despite the efforts of boosters' clubs and chambers of commerce. She will continue to lie, inert and helpless, like an exhausted Titan in the sun—a beautiful desert of homeseekers' buried hopes.

OHIO

I'LL SAY WE'VE DONE WELL

By SHERWOOD ANDERSON

I AM compelled to write of the State of Ohio reminiscently and from flashing impressions got during these last ten years, although I was born there, my young manhood was spent within its borders, and later I went back and spent another five or six years as a manufacturer in the State. And so I have always thought of myself as an Ohioan and no doubt shall always remain, inside myself, an Ohioan. Very well, then, it is my State and there are a thousand things within it I love and as many things I do not like much at all.

Ohio is a big State. It is strong. It is the State of Harding and McKinley. I am told that my own father once played in the Silver Cornet Band at Caledonia, Ohio. Warren G. may remember him as Teddy, sometimes called Major Anderson. He ran a small harness shop at Caledonia. Just why he was called Major I never knew. Perhaps because his people came from the South. Anyway, I ought to have a job at Washington. Everyone else from that county has one.

And now Ohio has got very big and very strong and its Youngstown, Cincinnati, Akron, Cleveland, Toledo, and perhaps a dozen other prosperous industrial cities, can put themselves forward as being as ugly, as noisy, as dirty, and as mean in their civic spirit as any American industrial cities anywhere. "Come, you men of 'these States,'" as old Walt Whitman was so fond of saying, in his windier moods, trot out your cities. Have you a city that smells worse than Akron, that is a worse junk-heap of ugliness than Youngstown, that is more smugly self-satisfied than Cleveland, or that has missed as unbelievably great an opportunity to be one of the lovely cities of the world as has the city of Cincinnati? I'll warrant you have not. In this modern pushing American civilization of ours you other States have nothing on our Ohio. Credit where credit is due, citizens. I claim that we Ohio men have taken as lovely a land as ever lay outdoors and that we have, in our towns and cities, put the old stamp of ourselves on it for keeps.

Of course, you understand that to do this we have had to work. Take for example a city like Cincinnati. There it sits on its hills, the lovely southern Ohio and northern Kentucky hills, and a poet coming there might have gone into the neighboring hills and looked down on the site of the great city; well, what I say is that such a poet might have dreamed of a white and golden city nestling there with the beautiful Ohio at its feet. And that city might, you understand, have crept off into the green hills, that the poet might have compared to the breasts of goddesses, and in the morning when the sun came out and the men, women, and children of the city came out of their houses and looking abroad over their sweet land of Ohio——

But pshaw, let's cut that bunk.

We Ohioans tackled the job and we put the kibosh

on that poet tribe for keeps. If you don't believe it, go down and look at our city of Cincinnati now. We have done something against great odds down there. First we had to lick the poet out of our own hearts and then we had to lick nature herself, but we did it. Today our river front in Cincinnati is as mean-looking a place as the lake front in Chicago or Cleveland, and you please bear in mind that down there in Cincinnati we had less money to work with than they did up in Chicago or even in Cleveland.

Well, we did it. We have ripped up those hills and cut out all that breasts-of-goddesses stuff and we've got a whanging big Rotary Club and a couple of years ago we won the World Series, or bought it, and we've got some nice rotten old boats in the river and some old sheds on the waterfront where, but for us, there might not have been anything but water.

And now let's move about the State a little while I point out to you a few more things we have done. Of course, we haven't any Henry Ford over there, but just bear in mind that John D. Rockefeller and Mark Hanna and Harvey Firestone and Willys up at Toledo and a lot of other live ones are Ohio men, and what I claim is—they have done well.

Look at what we had to buck up against. You go back into American history a little and you'll see for yourself what I mean. Do you remember when La Salle was working his way westward, up there in Canada, and he kept hearing about a country to the south and a river called the Ohio? The rest of his crowd didn't want to go down that way and so, being a modest man and not wanting to set himself up against public opinion, he pretended to be down of a bad sickness. So the rest of the bunch, priests and Indians and others, went on out west and he just took a couple of years off and cut out southward alone, with a few Indians. And even afoot and through the thick woods a man can cover quite a considerable amount of territory in two years. My notion is he probably saw it all.

I remember that an old man I knew when I was a boy told me about seeing the Ohio River in the early days, when the rolling hills along its banks were still covered with great trees, and what he said I can't remember exactly, but anyway, he gave me the impression of a sweet, clear, and majestic stream, in which one could swim and see the sand of the bottom far below, through the sparkling water. The impression I got from the old man was of boys swimming on their backs, and white clouds floating overhead, and the hills running away, and the branches of trees tossed by the wind like the waves of a vast green sea.

It may be that La Salle went there and did that. It wouldn't surprise me if some such scandal should creep out about him. And then, maybe, after he got down to where Louisville, Kentucky, now stands, and he found he couldn't get any further with his boats because of the falls in the river—or pretended he couldn't because he was so stuck on the fine Ohio country up above—it may be, I say, that he turned back and went northward along eastern Ohio and into a land of even more majestic hills and finer forests and got finally into that country of soft-stepping little hills, up there facing Lake Erie.

I say maybe he did and I have my own reasons. You

see this fellow La Salle wasn't much of a one to talk. He didn't advertise very well. What I mean is he was an uncommunicative man. But you go look him up in the books and you will see that later he was always being condemned, after that trip, and that he was always afterward accused of being a visionary and a dreamer.

From all I've ever been able to hear about Ohio, as it was before we white men and New Englanders got in there and went to work, the land might have done that to La Salle, and for that matter to our own sons, too, if we, God-fearing men, hadn't got in there just when we did, and rolled up our sleeves, and got right down to the business of making a good, up-and-coming, Middle-Western, American State out of it. And, thank goodness, we had the old pep in us to do it. We original northern Ohio men were mostly New Englanders and we came out of cold stony New England and over the rocky hills of northern New York State to get into Ohio.

I suppose the hardship we endured before we got to Ohio was what helped us to bang right ahead and cut down trees and build railroads and whang the Indians over the heads with our picks and shovels and put up churches and later start the Anti-Saloon League and all the other splendid things we have done. I'll tell you that the country makes no mistake when it comes to our State for Presidents. We train our sons up right over there.

Why, I can remember myself, when I was a boy, and how I once got out of a job and went one fall with a string of race horses all over our State. I found out then what La Salle was up against when our State was what you might call new, in a way of speaking. Why, I got as dreamy and mopy, drifting along through the beautiful Ohio country that fall, as any no-account you ever saw. I fooled along until I got fired. That's how I came out.

Then of course I had to go into the cities and get a job in a factory and the better way of life got in its chance at me, so that for years I had as good a bringing up and knew as much about hustling and pushing myself forward and advertising and not getting dreamy or visionary as any American there is. What I mean is that if I have slipped any since I do not blame the modern Ohio people for it. It's my own fault. You can't blame a town like Toledo or Cleveland or Akron or any of our up-and-coming Ohio cities if a man turns out to be a bum American and doesn't care about driving a motor at fifty miles an hour or doesn't go to the movies much evenings.

What I mean to say is that this business of writing up the States in the pages of *The Nation* is, I'll bet anything, going to turn out just as I expected. There'll be a lot of knocking, that's what I'll bet. But I'm not going to do that. I live in Chicago now and our motto here is, "Put away your hammer and get out your horn." Mayor Thompson of Chicago got that up. And, anyway, I think it is pretty much all silliness, this knocking and this carping criticism of everything American and splendid I hear going on nowadays. I'm that way myself sometimes and I'm ashamed of it.

The trouble with me is that I once had a perfectly good little factory over in Ohio, and there was a nice ash-heap in a vacant lot beside it, and it was on a nice stream, and I dumped stuff out of my factory and killed the fish in it and spoiled it just splendid for a while. What I think now is that I would have been all right and a good man, too, but on summer afternoons I got to moping about the Ohio hills alone, instead of going over to the Elks Club and playing pool where I might have got in with some of the boys and picked up some good points. There were a lot of good bang-up Ohio pushers over in that Ohio town I had my factory in and I neglected them. So of course I went broke and I'll admit I've been rather a sorehead ever since. But when I come down to admit the honest truth I'll have to say it wasn't Ohio's fault at all.

Why, do you know, I've had times when I thought I'd like to see that strip of country we call Ohio, just as that Frenchman La Salle must have seen it. What I mean is with nothing over there but the dear, green hills and the clear, sweet rivers and nobody around but a few Indians and all the whites and the splendid modern cities all gone to—I won't say where, because it's a thought I don't have very often and I'm ashamed of it.

What I suppose gets me yet is what got me when I stayed away from the Elks Club and went walking in the hills when I was trying to be a manufacturer, and what got me fired when I was a race-track swipe. I get to thinking of what that darned old man once told me. I'll bet he was a Bolshevik. What he told me set me dreaming about swimming in clear streams, and seeing white cities sitting on hills, and of other cities up along the northern end of my State, facing Lake

Erie, where in the evening canoes and maybe even gondolas would drift in and out of the lake and among the stone houses, whose color was slowly changing and growing richer with the passage of time.

But, as I say, that's all poet stuff and bunk. Having such pipe dreams is just what put the old kibosh on my factory, I'll bet anything. What I think is that a man should be glad it's getting harder and harder for any of our sons to make the same mistakes I did. For, as I figure it out, things are going just splendidly over in Ohio now. Why, nearly every town is a factory town now and some of them have got streets in them that would make New York or London or Chicago sit up and take notice. What I mean is, almost as many people to every square foot of ground and just as jammed up and dirty and smoky.

To be sure, the job isn't all done yet. There are lots of places where you can still see the green hills and every once in a while a citizen of a city like Cleveland, for example, gets a kind of accidental glimpse at the lake, but even in a big town like Chicago, where they have a lot of money and a large police force, a thing like that will happen now and then. You can't do everything all at once. But things are getting better all the time. A little more push, a little more old zip and go, and a man over in Ohio can lead a decent life.

He can get up in the morning and go through a street where all the houses are nicely blacked up with coal soot, and into a factory where all he has to do all day long is to drill a hole in a piece of iron. It's fine the way Ford and Willys and all such fellows have made factory work so nice. Nowadays all you have to do, if you live in an up-to-date Ohio town, is to make, say, twenty-three million holes in pieces of iron, all just alike, in a lifetime. Isn't that fine? And at night a fellow can go home thanking God, and he can walk right past the finest cinder piles and places where they dump old tin cans and everything without paying a cent.

And so I don't see why what such cities as Cleveland and Cincinnati have done to knock dreaminess and natural beauty of scene galley-west can't be done also by all the smaller towns and cities pretty fast now. What I'm sure is they can do it if the old New England stock hasn't worn out and if they keep out foreign influences all they can. And even the farmers can make their places out in the country look more modern and like the slums of a good live city like Chicago or Cleveland if they'll only pep up and work a little harder this fall when the crops are laid by.

And so, as far as I can see, what I say is, Ohio is O. K.

THE STATE OF MAINE

"DOWN EAST"

By ROBERT HERRICK

In my boyhood about Boston they called that part of the United States which lies between the White Mountains and the Canadian province of New Brunswick, with two hundred and more miles of fretted sea-coast from Eastport to Portsmouth — "Down East." It has been "the State of Maine" for only a hundred years, previously having been attached more or less uncertainly to the Commonwealth of Massachusetts, and it was not until 1850 that Massachusetts finally relinquished her undivided half-interest in all the Maine State lands. With its 33,000 square miles of territory (still mostly in forest), 5,000 odd streams of sufficient size to be mapped, 1,500 large lakes, 400 sea-coast islands of over a thousand acres each, and several respectable mountains—about half of all this being still in "unorganized townships," "plantations," and "ranges" without names—the State of Maine is a considerable province, almost as extensive as the remaining five States of the New England group, with but three-quarters of a million people in it. In character Maine always was and still is a province by itself, distinctive from its neighboring States. The coastwise steamers, which still ply much as they did in my youth between its river ports and Boston, bring with the salt fish, lobsters, lumber, hay, and potatoes a special breed of rugged, ungainly, stalwart New Englander. For a half-century and more "Down East" has been famous as a vacation land of romantic variety, with its roadless forests, rivers and inland lakes, Indians and moccasins, deep bays dotted with rocky, spruce-covered islands. The tail of the province running south from Portland to the Piscataqua has never been wholly characteristic, but to wake in the early morning as the Bangor boat rounded Owl's Head Light into Rockland, to see looming through the fog dim outlines of rocky coast and wooded islands, to smell the brine of cold sea water rolling clean against granite ledges was to realize that one had reached a far country, altogether different from well-tamed Massachusetts. It was much the same, if one descended from the exotic Pullman almost anywhere within the borders of the State to smell the pungent odor of fresh sawdust and cut lumber, with blueberries lying purple on the burnt pine barrens and raspberries hanging from roadside bushes. There was always, in my memory, something strong, wholesome, rugged, untamed, and romantic, about the Maine of those days, and more than most parts of the modern world, Maine has kept its native quality, moral and physical. Indeed, whatever may be left of that famous old New England, sometime puritan and always protestant, will be found today more purely and abundantly here in Maine than elsewhere. The types of faces, the habits, and the ideas are much like those I remember in the Massachusetts of thirty years ago. It is the last stronghold of the Puritan.

Of Maine's three-quarters of a million inhabitants today, five-sevenths are of native-born white stock, less than one-seventh of foreign parentage (mainly French Canadians), with only a thousand Negroes and less than a thousand Indians. Where else in the United States can be found an equal homogeneity of Anglo-Saxon blood? And in spite of the annual influx of a half-million of strangers, who have discovered the beauty and the freedom of Maine, in spite of the estimated thirty million dollars which they pay for their summer vacations, except for a thin fringe of parasitic "resorts," with their corruptions, mainly along the southern sea-coast, this great province has never turned itself into a summer boarding-house like New Hampshire. Within its ample borders, along its lakes and rivers and sea-coast, it can absorb such an enormous transient population without noticeable interference with its own proper activities. These are many, and all basic. Wood pulp, lumber, hay, potatoes, apples, blueberries, sweet corn, building stone, lime, fish—these are the characteristic products of this northern land—and one must not forget ships and sailors! Maine is prosperous. Out of its many farms and inexhaustible forests much wealth has been taken. There are few cities and none of sufficient size to have become a plague spot. Here and there are textile mills, mostly scattered in small towns, so that the industrial population has never become massed, nor a preponderant element in any community. In short, in spite of its many resources, not least an abundant water power, Maine is not developed industrially to the maximum—and may that day never come! Such wealth as it has, has largely been taken out of the soil and the sea and is pretty widely distributed. Even after the Great War and its eruptive profiteering there are, I suspect, few millionaires in Maine, and there are few miserably poor or unemployed. Rarely even in the back country does one come across a squalid farm, and I know of no slum street in its few cities. Thus as a whole in Maine there is a stable condition of comfort, self-reliance, non-parasitic occupation common in the New England of a previous generation, which makes for sturdiness, individualism, and conservatism. Maine is not so much reactionary as stationary.

That, I suppose, is why Maine has been found so often in the Republican ranks at national elections. Its people learned their political faith in the Civil War and have found no reason to abandon it, all the more as Republican tariffs look closely after Canadian competition and its long sea-coast provides ample opportunity for Federal "recognition" of one sort or another. For they still believe in high tariffs in Maine and in strictly partisan government. The State has sent to Washington such men as Blaine, Dingley, Reed, and Hale, typical perhaps of the Republican Party ideal of statesmanship not merely in Maine. But except for the fact that Maine votes in September and is therefore the subject of much earnest party solicitude, to see that her citizens continue to set a good example to other States, I do not feel that national politics plays a large part in the life of Maine. (The two matters which are most negligible in the psychology of the true American are his religion and his politics.) In State and local politics Maine well illustrates the theory that the less government the better for those governed, for the State legislature with an admirable self-restraint meets but once in two years and then only for a three months' session, chiefly concerned with game laws and road building. For the rest the famous town-meeting still flourishes in Maine, once a year at least, and the actual administration of its large, rambling townships (often fifty square miles and more in area) is left to the selectmen, who presumably give their communities as much good government as they will pay for. In a word Maine is the least-governed and therefore the best-governed American State that I know. Fortunately the prizes are not rich enough to attract heavy grafters, and there are many leisurely eyes and ears to supervise the activities of public servants.

Maine, it must not be forgotten, is an intensely individualistic community. A few of its more advanced thinkers may regret that the State disposed of all its forest lands, a precious heritage, for as little as twelve cents the acre to private exploiters, lumber companies, and pulp manufacturers, but no doubt if the question recurred today the folly would be sanctioned by popular vote, notwithstanding the fact that the income derived from these forest tracts might have made Maine a very rich State, with good bridges and roads and a modernized school system, all without cost to its citizens. But like good Americans everywhere Maine prefers to give away its natural wealth to greedy individuals and issue bonds for its public needs. The story of the looting of the pine woods is monotonously the same from the Penobscot to Michigan, to Wisconsin, and now in Washington and Oregon.

If politically and economically Maine is simple,

"stalwart" American, it should not be overlooked that the State was "advanced" in the matter of prohibition. It went "dry" two generations before the nation passed the amendment. Not quite dry! There were always zones of dryness from the well-saturated border towns to the more arid interior about the State House at Augusta. For Maine administered its prohibition temperately and intermittently, like prudent New Englanders: those who wanted to remain dry could do so without much temptation, and those who wished to drink might do so with circumspection. But the act had the support of the people of the State. It is characteristic of Maine that it believed in prohibition and tried to get it long before other States in the Union strove for this ideal. Something of the puritan tradition of discipline has lingered here into these relaxed days. . . .

The backwoods, the wilderness and the frontier, also a stern ocean, have never been far from man's consciousness in this easterly province. It is not surprising, then, that the lighter, the more suave growths of civilization are not much in evidence. Architecturally, except for a few handsome examples of old colonial to be found in coast towns like Wiscasset, Gardiner, and Portland, Maine is bleaker than its more southerly neighbors, where there has been greater wealth, ease, and ready intercourse. The usual Maine farmhouse is a strong plain affair, too steep in the roof (to stand heavy snowfalls), too heavy and angular, perched on big granite blocks, connected by a long shed with an even larger barn, equally homely. Even in the older inland towns size and substantiality count for much more than grace of line and proportion. Timber is cheap, winters long and rude, and the Maine man is not given to adornment, to prettiness. Yet perched on the hills—and I think that farmhouses are more frequently placed on high ground in Maine than in other New England States, as if to survey the approach of possibly hostile strangers—with a broad fall of plowed land and pasture and backed by heavy "dark growth," these rude white buildings have a solidity and abidingness about them which make them part of the rugged landscape. One realizes that each fertile farm is the result of a long struggle with an unyielding nature, to which generations of tenacious, strong men have given themselves. The fishermen's houses along the coast and on the many islands are smaller than the inland farmhouses, equally white and graceless, and dotted with a pleasant irregularity about the waterfront, their faces turned often to the open sea, quite negligent of the road, because from the sea comes the struggle and the livelihood. All these outer aspects of old Maine are, of course, undergoing change, being gradually overlaid with new and cheaper growths, as automobiles increase and the number of miles of passable roads. But Maine yields more slowly to new ways than other parts of the country, and it will be many a year before the "ranges" and "plantations" of the north have become tamed to the bungalow and garden hose. Meanwhile there are many "unspoiled" towns and villages, where except for the new garage the outer aspect of things is much what it was fifty years ago.

What the inner aspect is, of the life in these towns

and villages, it would be more difficult to pronounce. Culturally Maine is proud of its old New England college, Bowdoin, of its State musical festival, of its newer schools, but culturally these days America seems too much of a muchness to be discriminating about. The trains run daily from the great cities of Boston and New York, and the *Saturday Evening Post,* the Hearst newspapers, the cinema reels, and the Hart Schaffner & Marx clothes penetrate, one and all, to the northernmost and easternmost corners of the province. What Maine has "done in literature" may be read of elsewhere. Maine is not primarily concerned with æsthetics. I think it never will be. That comes like the summer visitor superficially into men's and women's minds. I doubt if many inhabitants of the State are aware today that our most considerable American poet was born and has lived many years among them.

Maine is a great example of the prodigal beauty and richness of our America. From one of its innumerable hilltops you may look across whole counties of pine and fir and hemlock, dotted with farms and lakes, across to other ranges of blue hills, and to still other far-away misty mountain tops, or to the ledgy reefs and dark salt water of its broken coast. There is a sense of space and variety and wildness in Maine not to be felt elsewhere in the United States east of the Rocky Mountains. The old province is not yet tamed and crowded. One can realize how these early adventurers felt when they sailed up to its coast out of the Atlantic—the Sieur de Monts, the Jesuit colonists, Captain John Smith, and all the others. The same

These are merely superficial [illegible] tration of Dupontism. Investigation reveals more vital and surprising saturation. Since 1906, when Henry A. du Pont broke the long legislative deadlock caused by the stubborn candidacy of John Edward Addicks and was seated in the United States Senate, the leadership of the Republican Party in Delaware has been in the Du Pont family. Since 1921, when T. Coleman du Pont went into the United States Senate by a trade with the Democratic incumbent, Josiah O. Wolcott, the Democratic Party in the State has been disorganized and divided, unable to present any adequate opposition. In addition to large holdings of real estate and the great power exercised through the explosives company, the Du Ponts have sapped in numerous directions into Delaware finance. Lammot du Pont is the largest single stockholder in the powerful Wilmington Trust Company while Alfred I. du Pont and his cousin William control the Delaware Trust Company, with its home office in Wilmington and a half-dozen branches in other towns.

Even more important in the process of Dupontization than political and industrial power—though far less understood and appreciated in Delaware—is the hold of the family upon the means of influencing public opinion in the State: newspapers, welfare organizations, and the schools. All of the three daily newspapers printed in Delaware (the Wilmington *Morning News,* the *Evening Journal,* and the *Every Evening*) are in Du Pont hands. Since 1918 a body known as the Service Citizens has become the leading —and to some extent the engulfing—welfare organi-

fir-covered islands stand sentinel before the deep bays, the same fog hangs over the cold deep waters, the same vista of hills and wide upland rises from the coast, still wild, still pungent with many mingled scents of sea and land. There is still the sense of wide, free space. There is still the wilderness for background. So life remains "Down East" a little more like what it was in the days of the forefathers, when men came to this unknown Western world to be free, to win their right to survive by struggle with nature rather than with their fellow men.

... FEUDAL FAMILY

By ARTHUR WARNER

LEGALLY adopted or wantonly kidnaped from the Sisterhood of the Forty-eight, Delaware has become the ward of a feudal family and the victim of a family feud. Of no other child of these United States is one family so closely in control; upon no other have the actions, the aspirations, and the quarrels of a single family had so profound a repercussion.

The visitor is apprised of the dominance of the Du Ponts the moment he descends from the train in Wilmington. He is driven, as a matter of course, to the Hotel du Pont. He discovers it to be part of the huge Du Pont Building, which dwarfs all other structures and contains, besides the hotel and corridor upon corridor of offices, one of the city's principal theaters. In addition to the executive offices of the great explosives company, with its numerous offshoots and graftings, the newcomer notes the existence of the Du Pont Country Club, the Du Pont Gun Club, and the Alexis I. du Pont School; he learns that there is a North and a South Du Pont Street in Wilmington and not far outside of it a town of Dupont and a fort of the same designation. The Wilmington City Directory for 1921-1922 lists twenty-eight persons or organizations bearing the family name.

... evidences of the infil-

zation of the State by grace of an annual subsidy of $90,000 given by Pierre S. du Pont. Under his presidency and under a director selected by him, the Service Citizens have conducted educational campaigns to create popular sentiment for a variety of purposes, having been especially active in promoting Mr. Du Pont's most cherished and ambitious civic project: rebuilding the public schools. The Delaware School Auxiliary Association, headed by the director of the Service Citizens, has been organized to administer a school building fund given by Mr. Du Pont. A complete reconstruction of the State's school buildings for Negroes is under way at a cost of a million dollars. The work is expected to be finished in 1923, while it is planned to expend about two and a half millions—in addition to money raised by local communities through taxation—to give modern structures to the white children.

This program is the outgrowth of a movement for better schools which has been the overshadowing political issue in Delaware for the last four years. A survey by the United States Bureau of Education in 1917 placed Delaware thirty-ninth among the States in its school opportunities. A year later the report of a commission appointed by the General Education Board showed the defects in detail. Largely as a result of this report a new school code was put through the legislature, but partly because of expense and partly because of interference with certain ancient local customs the new law became the vortex of one of the most turbid political whirlpools that has ever stirred the State, and has been changed twice since. It was the outcry against the expense of the State's school program that led Mr. Du Pont to undertake the job at his own cost.

Although formerly a member of the State Board of Education, Mr. Du Pont has nothing to do now with the administration of the schools and I am convinced that his rebuilding program is inspired by the most sincere and disinterested motives. At the same time it has given him an indirect influence upon a fundamental process in the development of public opinion —the training of the young mind—and it is charged that in carrying out his school projects underlings have used the power of his money to coerce or buy action according to their wishes. The fact that the Delaware School Auxiliary Association may grant or withhold its funds for building in the case of any community obviously gives it a powerful lever which, some say, it has not been backward in using. Its stipulation that its own architects must be employed and that school equipment must be purchased through it are also criticized. Mr. Du Pont's activities embrace not only the whole public-school system; he has also given largely to Delaware University—the only institution of higher learning in the State—among the trustees of which his friends and relatives are well intrenched.

No family in America of equal wealth has stuck more tenaciously to its ancestral home or been more closely identified with the land than the Du Ponts. Neither for administrative nor residence purposes has New York been able to lure them away. Predominantly they are still to be found within a few miles of the original powder mill which Eleuthère Irénée du Pont de Nemours, their progenitor in this country, set up on the banks of Brandywine Creek, near the present city of Wilmington, in 1802. The close identification of the family with Delaware during all this period is the more remarkable when one considers that the manufacturing establishments of E. I. du Pont de Nemours and Company have of necessity gone elsewhere, the last one in the State—the original mill on the Brandywine—having been abandoned this year.

The Du Pont family has been self-contained, clannish, and on the whole respected, if not loved, by its neighbors. The third generation has come and mostly gone without the proverbial transition from shirt-sleeves to shirt-sleeves. But for the Du Ponts the second hundred years will be the hardest. During the first century the family took little part in public life and even up to now only two members of it—ex-Senator Henry A. du Pont and the present Senator T. Coleman du Pont—have gone into politics as politics. It was solely because of a family squabble that Alfred I. du Pont took his spectacular plunge into the political pool of Delaware several years ago. Just as, until recently, the family kept out of politics, so it kept out of any business but its own. But the forces of the twentieth century which have been fusing politics with business, and squeezing both into molds prescribed by the banks, have carried the Du Ponts with them. The war, with its Midas touch, was a great stimulus. The company expanded from 5,000 to 100,000 employees and its profits bulged in proportion. For the year 1916 the company paid 100 per cent on its common stock, while in consequence of the war that stock ran the gamut from about $20 to $1,000 a share. Naturally these fabulous profits accelerated a transition already begun in the careers of the Du Ponts —from makers simply of explosives to captains of industry interested in dyes, automobiles, and a host of other products; then from captains of industry to politicians, bankers, and directors of public opinion.

The living Du Ponts who have come most into public notice are four: Henry A., Alfred I., T. Coleman, and Pierre S. All are cousins, the first named belonging to the third generation of the family in this country and the other three to the fourth. Henry A. du Pont, the ex-Senator, is the titular head of the family, receiving the first call on New Year's Day and the consideration due his eighty-four years among relatives where feudal traditions are strong. Henry A. du Pont is known as "the Colonel," while T. Coleman (now Senator) has raised himself to the rank of "the General." The title of "the Colonel" is a legitimate one descending from service in the Civil War. So far as can be learned, the only fighting front upon which "the General" has served is the sector at Dover occupied by the staff of the Governor of Delaware. It seems a bit incongruous that a Civil War veteran of eighty-four should be only a colonel while his junior adorning a Governor's staff should be a general. But when picking a title for yourself, you might as well choose a good one.

"Cherchez la femme." As already suggested, the evolution of the Du Ponts from small to big business and from big business to industrial politics has been part of a process going beyond them or their State. The unique results in Delaware are due partly to its smallness and partly to a woman—or, rather, to two women. In 1907 Alfred I. du Pont, having divorced his first wife, married again. But the Du Pont family refused to ratify the divorce and declined to receive the new wife. In some families and in some States this would scarcely have mattered. Among the Du Ponts and in Delaware it did. Retaliation and a family quarrel ensued which have been largely responsible for the orgy of vote buying that Delaware has recently experienced and the present demoralization of the Democratic Party. T. Coleman du Pont, having decided to get out of the explosives business, offered his stock for sale to the company. It was refused by the company on the advice of its president, then Pierre S. du Pont. The latter subsequently organized a pool in the family—in which Alfred I. du Pont was not included—and bought the stock. Alfred I. joined in a suit to prevent the sale of the securities to the pool. Eventually the courts sustained the arrangement, but in the meanwhile the family had become divided and the political debauchery of the State which Addicks began had been carried to a new stage. For Alfred I. du Pont jumped into politics as a means of sabotaging his opponents in the family squabble. The term of Colonel Henry A. du Pont as United States Senator was to expire in 1917. Failing in an effort to prevent his renomination, Alfred I. du Pont put an independent Republican up against his cousin and succeeded in throwing the election to the Democratic candidate, Josiah O. Wolcott. In connection with his political fight Alfred I. du Pont bought the Wilmington *Morning News* and obtained the control of several influential weeklies down State. By 1918 he had come almost, if not altogether, to control the Republican State machine. Is it necessary to add that money was burned like gunpowder in achieving these results?

But at this point Alfred I. du Pont became involved financially. Pierre S. du Pont came to his assistance, obtaining for him a loan from J. P. Morgan & Company. One of the conditions—or, at least, consequences—was the surrender by Alfred I. of the *Morning News* and other newspaper properties. About the same time the *Every Evening,* the only Democratic daily in the State, with a tradition of independence and ability, came on the market and was purchased by a brother-in-law of Pierre S. du Pont. The *Evening Journal* had been acquired a little earlier by others of the family. This publication and the *Morning News* were placed under centralized control, but for the sake of appearances the *Every Evening* was leased to a Democrat who makes a certain show of conducting it in opposition to the other two. The most immediate consequence of the Dupontization of the daily press of Delaware has been not so much to deprive the State of independent political discussion—which few communities enjoy—as to put a stop to the useful revelations that grow out of partisan journalism elsewhere. Amidst the myriad and often conflicting interests of the Du Ponts the editors of their newspapers find it hard to discuss any vital questions and are most at home when deploring, or pointing with pride to—the weather.

Now let us move forward to 1921. Senator Wolcott, elected on a fluke, had never cared for the job. He did want to be Chancellor of Delaware, the highest judicial office in the State. On the other hand T. Coleman du Pont wanted to go to Washington. His business is largely outside of Delaware—he has a string of hotels and other interests—but he has given four million dollars for a north and south highway through the State and has liberally subventioned the Boy Scouts, Consumers' League, and other organizations of Wilmington. So the strange spectacle was witnessed of a Republican Governor appointing a Republican as United States Senator while asking a Republican legislature to confirm the nomination of a Democrat for Chancellor. It was done; but against the vehement protest of one wing of the Democratic Party, that led by ex-Senator Saulsbury, the adherents of which openly charge that the arrangement was an over-the-counter cash transaction, even going so far as to name the amounts that various persons received. In any event the affair further split the already disorganized Democrats, and is the latest chapter in the political corruption begun by Addicks and continued by Dupontism—a debauchery so general and direct that, in the southern part of the State especially, farmers have come to regard their votes as a staple crop, legitimate as sweet potatoes, and to market them almost as shamelessly.

As indicating the vagaries of Du Pont journalism, it may be noted that the *Evening Journal* and the *Morning News,* which, of course, supported T. Coleman du Pont for election in November, 1922, for a full Senatorial term, at the same time condemned the appointment a year ago of Mr. Wolcott which was for the sole purpose of creating a vacancy for their candidate.

So much for the Du Ponts. Now what of the fabric of the State upon which they have embroidered their lives? Delaware is the second smallest State in the Union both in area and population. Politically speaking, one may question whether it ought to be a State at all. The fact that it has two Senators and only one Representative in Congress shows how illogical its situation is. Geographically, industrially, and socially, there is even less reason for its statehood. It is an artificial slice of the peninsula that lies between Delaware and Chesapeake bays. This region, locally known as the Delmarvia Peninsula, is an almost perfect entity in its geographical situation, its industries, and its inhabitants. But Fate has decreed that the southern tip of this peninsula shall belong to Virginia, the western part to Maryland, and the rest to Delaware. And in spite of all reasons to the contrary so it will probably remain.

This whole Delmarvia Peninsula lies only a few feet above sea level. The watershed between Delaware and Chesapeake bays is so inconspicuous that even Nature scarcely knows where to find it. Rivers that run—or drag their way—toward the Chesapeake are so interlaced at their source with those going in the other direction that they must often get wretchedly mixed. Brother and sister currents in the same rivulet may find themselves deflected by a pebble or a tuft of grass, not to meet again until they hail one another in the great Atlantic, one having arrived via the Chesapeake and Cape Charles, the other by the Delaware and Cape May. These level acres make wonderful fruit and vegetable gardens. Yes, you exclaim, the Delaware peach! Ah, but disease brought the peach orchards near to extinction several years ago; for a time peaches became as scarce in Delaware as cowboys in the streets of Chicago. They have returned somewhat, but tend to be overshadowed now by apples. Meanwhile the strawberry flourishes, encouraged by Prohibition and the seething and multiplying soda-water fountain. Some twenty million quarts are picked in a good year—at 2½ cents a quart! At least that was the pay proffered in Wilmington at the beginning of the 1922 season. It is the same as, or only half a cent better than, the rate twenty years ago when farmers were glad to sell their berries at six to eight cents a quart instead of twenty to twenty-five. The answer is: child labor. The State has a child-labor law which forbids the once prevalent employment of children under fourteen years of age in canneries, but like most such legislation the statute does not apply to farm work. Thousands of children are employed —and kept out of school in the meanwhile—to gather strawberries, tomatoes, sweet potatoes, and other products of the vast garden from which Delaware largely subsists. Without such assistance it is argued—doubtless justly—that the farmers would be well-nigh helpless. Which raises another problem.

Despite the fact that it lies on the Eastern seaboard midway between North and South, Delaware is one of the least visited of our States—one of the least disturbed by the winds of controversy, cult, and progress that roar over the rest of the Union. Thousands of persons pass through the northern tip of the State every week on the two great railway routes between New York City and Washington, but if they stop at all it is only in Wilmington. And Wilmington is no more like the rest of Delaware than New York City is like the rest of the United States. Wilmington contains nearly half of Delaware's 223,003 inhabitants, but it does not rule its State as certain other large cities of the country do theirs. It has only two of seventeen members in the State Senate and five representatives among thirty-five in the lower house. It is by no means allowed to hog the political plums, custom decreeing that the Governor, the two United States Senators, the one Representative, and other officials be passed around among the three counties of the State according to a regular rotation.

When one leaves the trunk railways at Wilmington and heads southward—as few but commercial travelers seem to do—he begins to penetrate the real Delaware. If he goes in springtime, as I did, he sees in progress a vast and omnipresent assault upon the soil, a mass attack upon the earth with plow and harrow and seed drill. Acre upon acre of pink, freshly turned ground. Peach orchards waving leaves of shiny yellow-green. Apple orchards with nodding boughs of cool gray-green. Fields lying fallow, brilliant with crimson clover and golden patches of blossoming wild mustard.

With two exceptions, Dover is the smallest State capital in the United States and one of only three having fewer than 5,000 inhabitants. Its shady streets are restful and its public square, or Green, carries one well out of the toil and moil of this twentieth century. Planted with towering sycamores, elms, and maples, the Green is surrounded by still more ancient buildings, among which stand out the Court House and the State Capitol, both of mellow saffron brick with milk-white columns, porticos, and cupolas, reminiscent of colonial days in the old South. The buildings that are not Court House or State Capitol gleam with brass plates carrying the names of lawyers sufficient for the whole of Delaware. To be a lawyer caged behind a glass door in an iron-ribbed New York office building has always seemed to me a job I should enjoy not having; but to sit behind a brass plate, put my feet on the desk, and look out over Dover Green—well, there could be worse occupations, particularly if not interrupted by too many clients.

If Delaware is little disturbed from without, it is even less so from within. Settled originally by English and Dutch stock, its population has been largely self-perpetuating with remarkably little of the later foreign infusions which have transformed or created so many of our other States. The old English law prevails in Delaware more intact perhaps than anywhere else in our country, together with the ancient legal vocabulary. Delaware still has its courts of chancery and of oyer and terminer. The pillory existed up to recent date and the whipping-post still survives, uniquely among the States. The political division of the hundred—corresponding to a township—persists, as does the levy court with its levy courtmen (the latter administrative, not judicial, officers).

Like all self-contained and ingrowing communities, Delawareans look with suspicion upon persons coming to live among them who have been so ill advised as to be born somewhere else. Sometimes years of residence can hardly remove the taint from the carpet-bagger. The head of a philanthropic society, who had come from another State, told me that after urging some action upon a public officer the latter said to him kindly but as if actuated by some great principle: "I like you, but I shan't vote for the appropriation because you're not a Delawarean."

Wilmington is the spot in the State, if any, where one would expect to encounter an eager intellectual life. Does one? On the half-mile stretch of Market Street from Christiana Creek to the Du Pont Building—the city's chief business artery—I discovered only one bookstore. Wishing to know where the others might be, I consulted the City Directory and found only one other listed for all of Wilmington! The automobile, the five-and-ten-cent store, the movies, and the pineapple nut sundae have entered Delaware with their standardized virtues and vulgarities, but of mental stimulus the State seems to produce little and to import less. A young woman in Wilmington (a carpet-bagger from New England) confessed to a liking for the newer poetry, but said she had found nobody who cared to discuss it with her. "They think my interest in it is just the eccentricity of a Boston highbrow."

Delawareans generally deplore the political corruption of their State and some look with apprehension on the growing financial ascendancy of a single family. But they are almost unanimously unaware even of the facts of, much less the danger in, the control by the Du Ponts of press, welfare work, and education. When these things are called to their attention they plead as excuse the State's poverty and backwardness, heedless that such conditions are intensified and solidified by the stifling of independence and initiative. In this, of course, the people of Delaware are not alone. They are children of a generation pathetically and universally eager to barter permanent spiritual values in return for opportunist material advantages. The Dupontization of Delaware is not a unique development. It is an advanced stage of a process under way in the United States as a whole. All along the line existing governmental organization—Federal, State, and municipal—grows increasingly impotent before the important questions of the age. It is baffled to find either the money or the intelligence to attack big problems in a big way. On the other hand the last twenty years have seen a vast augmentation of private benefaction and the establishment of various foundations the interest charges upon whose great funds are a controlling lever upon the work—and thus the lives—of thousands of men and women yet unborn. If a sparse scattering of Carnegie libraries and Rockefeller colleges is good for the rest of America, why is not the State-wide, all-inclusive educational plant promised to Delaware by Dupontism a superboon? Either Delaware is right, or the rest of the country too is wrong. We must be willing to consider a new industrial basis for society or to drift on in the direction of an oligarchy ruled not by supermen but by superwealth.

If this is to be the destiny of the Sisterhood of the

Forty-eight, then credit as the leader of a new Americanism—not blame as a backslider from the old—belongs to Delaware under the dynasty of the Du Ponts.

Meanwhile the aroma of the strawberry and the fragrance of the peach perfume the State; the Green at Dover is a tonic for fretful minds; and the potato biscuit which I ate at Lewes survives in memory as a work of art which ennobles a whole State—a deed of piety for which some woman ought to be canonized.

TENNESSEE

THREE QUARTERS OF BEWILDERMENT

By E. E. MILLER

No Tennessee orator feels he has done his full duty until he has expatiated on the State's diversity of soil and climate and its variety of scenery and resource: "A mighty empire in itself, stretching from the cloud-crowned summits of the Great Smokies to the sun-kissed banks of the mighty Father of Waters, an empire capable of yielding every product of temperate climes and dowered with every natural resource necessary to the well-being of man"—every one of us who grew up in the State has heard it time and again.

It is largely true. Nature has done her part. In the east balsam-clad mountains with the flora of New York and New England; in the west cotton fields with their billowy whiteness. Cranberries grow in the mountain bogs; muscadines and figs ripen in the lower valleys.

The population is as diversified as the topography. Back in the mountains dwell the living types and characters of Charles Egbert Craddock and John Fox. In secluded cabin settlements men and women of scant "book l'arnin' " but of keen native sense tend little patches of ground in pioneer fashion, sometimes hauling the crops on sleds from fields too steep for a wagon. Here survive the old-time hand industries—spinning, weaving, basket-making. The roads still wind up the creek beds and the ridges are crossed by foot-beaten trails. The coves are searched for "sang," and the squirrel rifle not only helps supply the mountaineers' larder, but serves at times to settle—or to perpetuate—inherited family disputes or to speed inquisitive "revenooers" back to the lowlands. With an individuality and a picturesqueness of life that should be preserved, the hill country has also a poverty that often makes life squalid and an ignorance that in many cases blurs the mental vision and stunts the soul. The problem of the mountains is how to preserve the individuality of mountain life and thought while bringing to the more backward districts the opportunity for better educational development and more profitable work.

In the old days the current of slavery flowed around the southern hill country and hemmed the mountaineers in a little continent of their own. Poor, untaught, but independent and self-assertive, they saw in the rich slave owner of the cotton country or the bluegrass lands a "furriner" with whom they had neither tastes nor interests in common. They came to hate slavery and the wealth and culture it produced. The feeling persists in the more remote districts, and to this day the mountain people have to some extent remained cut off from the rest of the world, while an ingrained conservatism has held them to the manners of life and modes of thought of seventy-five or a hundred years ago. Though closely related by blood to the dweller in the lowlands the hill man has been kept so distinct by environment and economic heritage as often to be thought a race apart. To be sure, the mountain traditions are gradually giving way, and the hill country is not all ignorance and poverty, feudists and moonshiners. Uninformed people in Boston and New York sometimes seem to think so, and then good Tennesseeans tear their hair and speak evil words.

In the center of the State, in the Bluegrass, are the remains of an ante-bellum aristocracy, a country-dwelling gentry, prosperous farmers who once raised speedy trotters and showy saddle horses. The love of them has not yet departed from the land, even though Jerseys and Shorthorns and Southdowns now graze on the rolling pastures and motor cars on the hard, white limestone roads outnumber the trotting horse a hundred to one. The Bluegrass is one of nature's beauty spots, and is loved of all who see it. Its inhabitants are not always so loved. They have a certain sense of superiority that cannot always conceal itself, and that is sometimes galling to the people of other parts of the State.

Beyond the Bluegrass lies a stretch of poorer country—the Highland Rim—and then comes the true cotton belt of tenant farming and supply stores and many Negroes, which differs widely from the Bluegrass in appearance, in its people, its habits of life and thought, and more closely resembles Mississippi or Georgia. With the mountain country of the Unakas or the Cumberlands it has as little in common as with Pennsylvania or Illinois.

In one Tennessee county the last census showed but eleven Negroes. In another there were three blacks to every white. In some sections the man who votes the Democratic ticket is looked upon with suspicion by his neighbors, in others a few lost and lonely Republicans look to the game laws for protection.

This diversity of country and population offers fine oratorical opportunities and gives the basis for a certain kind of pride, but it holds for us distinct disadvantages. For one thing, it has made smaller the unit of our provincialism; it has made us think in terms of our section rather than of our State. "East Tennessee," "Middle Tennessee," "West Tennessee," are not only fixed phrases in our vocabulary, but actual divisions recognized in our law-making. Members of our State Railway Commission, Board of Education, and Tax Commission are parceled out by legislation among the "three Grand Divisions of the State." When we established a State training school for teachers we had to establish three of them so that all sections could be taken care of. Other State institutions are similarly distributed, except the Penitentiary, which is generously conceded to the capital.

Our diversity of environment has also done much to prevent our having any definite State ideal or any State-wide enthusiasm. We have had no real State hero since the pioneer days. The list began with John Sevier and ended with Andrew Jackson. We have not had any great State figures largely because we have not had State ideals, and we have not had State ideals largely because we have not known or cared much about the very different people at the other end of the State. We inherited from the Civil War not merely a sharp political cleavage between east and west; the economic cleavage is as great. The farming in the Valley of East Tennessee is essentially different from that of West Tennessee. Certain larger problems are common, but the home-owning, self-supporting farmer in a land of mixed farming has neither the same methods, nor the same needs, nor the same outlook as the farmer of a sale-crop, tenant-farmed section. Our cities vary as much as our country districts. Memphis is the commercial center of a great agricultural region; it prospers or suffers with the prosperity or adversity of a hundred thousand cotton farms in Tennessee, Mississippi, and Arkansas. Chattanooga is a manufacturing town, looking outside the State for a market for most of its products. Nashville is the trading headquarters of a grain and live-stock farming section. There is no real State center of industry, of interest, or of thought.

We have been from the first essentially a political people. The men who laid the foundations of the State—Sevier, Jackson, Crockett—were equally ready to fight or to run for office, and what genius the State has so far displayed has been in these directions. So many Tennesseeans went to the early wars that Tennessee soon became known as the Volunteer State. Every normal Tennesseean since the first settlers crossed the Smokies has been a potential, if not an active, politician, and early in its history Tennessee became a doubtful and pivotal State in national elections. From Monroe to Lincoln it was largely what Ohio has been since the Civil War—a State which might decide presidential campaigns and which kept ready to run for President a supply of safe and sane mediocrities. Andrew Jackson, of course, was not considered exactly safe and sane by the "best minds" of his time. Neither was he a mediocrity. Nor was Hugh Lawson White, whom Jackson kept out of the Presidency, but the colorless James Knox Polk was the perfect prophecy of a succession of Ohio presidential candidates, successful and otherwise. The estimable John Bell—the choice of his own and two other States for President when Lincoln was elected—carried on the tradition of eminent mediocrity and closed his political career trying to reconcile the irreconcilable and to hold together the North and the South by keeping one foot on either side of the chasm that was widening between them.

The war brought a new type of leader. Isham G. Harris, greatest of "rebel" war governors, succeeded in dragging the State out of the Union after it had voted to stay in. When the Federal forces were closing in on Nashville he took the State funds and fled to Mexico. Soon Andrew Johnson, the anti-slavery, anti-secession Democrat—rude, untaught, ungenerous, but with an ability and a love of country not yet generally appreciated—became military governor, to be succeeded when he became Vice-President by the erratic and odoriferous "Parson" Brownlow. Brownlow was a pro-slavery but anti-secession Whig—preacher, politician, journalist, something of a genius and a good deal of a blackguard. A reward of $5,000 was offered for the capture and return of the fiery Harris, but he stayed away until a general amnesty was proclaimed. Then he returned, bringing the State money with him and soon finding his way to the United States Senate, where he served until his death many years later. These three picturesque figures form the State's latest contribution to the nation's gallery of political notables. Even they were scarcely of national stature, but since we have had only politicians of the common run. And in no other field—save for such capable and showy fighters as Sam Houston, David Glasgow Farragut, Nathan Bedford Forrest, and Alvin York—has the State ever had a citizen for whom it could even claim high rank. In art, literature, science, invention, business achievement the proudest name Tennessee can boast is far down among the minors. Our present is as our past. We have not today a writer, a musician, a painter, an educator, a scientist, an editor, a captain of industry, a lawyer, or an orator even who may be numbered among the country's best.

The little groups of our people who are really interested in literature and art and intellectual attainment and the higher things of life are lost in the mass to whom these matters are of small account. Our cities are not concerned to be beautiful; our country towns find amazing ways of achieving ugliness and squalor; our farmers seem to doubt, if indeed they ever think on this subject, that good taste and good business can live together. If we had among us a great prophet or poet or sculptor or architect most of us would care nothing about him. We do without the dreamers and idealists and do not miss them. We can manage to get along with the things we have. They fail, it is true, to satisfy us; but this is at best an unsatisfactory world.

But what is it we have that is distinctively and typically Tennessean? Let us take stock:

We have—so much do we value our present-day

crop of politicians—a fat, friendly, fiddling, fox-chasing Governor of 73, a genial soul who was a defeated candidate for the same office in 1886.

We have—so profound are our political convictions—two United States Senators, elected by the same party and largely by the same voters, voting against each other on nearly everything from the League of Nations to free seeds, yet both claiming to be true and representative Democrats, and both standing a chance of "getting by with it."

We have a deep-seated faith in our ability to elect every two years the worst of all possible legislatures, and we have, on this account, a grudge against Kentucky for beating us to a near-acceptance of the educational theories of Mr. Bryan and his fellow-scientists.

We have fifth place from the bottom of the list of States in illiteracy.

We have thousands of country children who have a chance to go to school for only five months each year.

We have county officials—mere court clerks with duties purely clerical—who receive $10,000 or $20,000 or $30,000 a year, and this despite the enactment of two anti-fee laws and an unprecedented clamor against the taxes we pay.

We have a State constitution fifty years old, which has so far protected these fee-grabbers, which prevents our getting the tax relief we clamor for, which with one voice we admit to be "antediluvian and full of grasshoppers," but which we are afraid to try to change lest worse befall us.

These are our main claims to distinction. We have more than the average number of homicides, but we compensate by having fewer than the average number of convictions. Of illicit stills, bootleggers, and law-breaking prohibition officers we have plenty, but probably no more than our quota.

We have, in short, some little difficulty in getting statistics to bear out the proudest claim we now dare seriously make—that of being a typical and average American State. Statistics not only tell us that we are a bit below the average in most things, but that every now and then we drop a notch or two in this category or that. They are so discouraging at times that we feel inclined to cry out against them as did old man Jenkins up in the hills.

Jenkins could not read or write. He owed the local storekeeper and sold him some hogs. The storekeeper figured their price, deducted the amount of his bill, and told Jenkins how much was coming to him. It was not more than half what the old man was expecting and he protested. The merchant went over the figures again, checking them off to the old man, and wound up with the trite assertion: "Figures can't lie, you know, Mr. Jenkins." "Mebbe not," said old Jenkins, as he stuffed the money into his pocket, "I ain't sayin' nothin' agin figgers, but I've allus tuck notice that liars has to figger more'n anybody else, an' I wouldn't trust no feller that I seed a-figgerin' all the time."

Tennesseeans sometimes feel like suggesting to the statistician that "liars have to figger more'n anybody else": but even so the figures only confirm our own conviction that something is wrong with Tennessee. For thirty years the State has been losing rank in population, in wealth, in agricultural and industrial development, in educational advancement, in political enlightenment. Neighboring States have passed us or gained upon us in one after another of these things. We are not living up to our possibilities and we know it. Our politicians, our newspapers, our religionists, our "successful business men" give us their same old platitudes over and over. They no longer satisfy us. We realize that they give no help, but we do not know what we need or where to look for it. So we spend most of our time milling about in circles, doubtful, mistrustful, bewildered. Our discontent with what we are is the most promising thing about us, and it as yet remains unfruitful.

Take our politics. We turn this year to our favorite election game, but we turn to it with little enthusiasm or hope. With all our plethora of politicians there is no constructive program of State improvement or State betterment offered us. We know they are trying most of all to say the things we wish to hear, that they are not striving to guide our thought to any great accomplishment, but merely seeking to capitalize our discontent and our uncertainty to their own advantage. There is with them no vision, for us no real leadership.

Here we are—a once great State that has become in every sense a very ordinary State. In 1920 one out of every eight of our citizens of voting age was recorded as an illiterate. This must mean that at least an equal number had only the most elementary education. Perhaps we do well to doubt ourselves, to fear our own political ineptitude; but surely, facing these facts, we cannot much longer fail to see what it is that keeps us on the downward grade in the scale of States.

We are an ignorant people and we are paying the penalty of ignorance. Only half a dozen States have school systems of less efficiency. In some of the poorer counties our rural schools are merely excuses for schools. Attendance laws are often poorly enforced and thousands of boys and girls have quit school barely able to read and write, some absolutely illiterate. Poorly trained teachers and low salaries are the rule. And some of our politicians are proposing to reform the school system and help educate our children by cutting down appropriations for the State University and the teacher training schools!

Up on the Cumberland Plateau lie five thousand square miles of undeveloped farming land—it lies undeveloped because it was not suited to the farming methods of earlier days and because the scattered population on it today lacks the technical knowledge to make it the great fruit and garden region it will some day become. Down the sides of the Appalachians flow, unutilized, streams that could turn every wheel of industry in the State and put light and running water in every East Tennessee farmhouse. They flow unutilized because the people who live beside them have neither the knowledge nor the capital to put them to work. A thousand hillsides that should have remained forest forever have been stripped and the soil allowed to wash away because no practical system of agricultural and forest management has been worked out for our mountain regions. Out in the western lowlands tortuous creeks wind through brush-grown fields given up by the cultivator because neither he nor the community understood the technique or the advantages of drainage.

Every year malaria, typhoid, and hookworm take their toll, women die in childbirth, and little children give up their lives to the general lack of health knowledge and public hygiene. So are our boasted natural resources wasted and our hopes for the future set at naught while we wonder what it is we need to do. "My people are destroyed for lack of knowledge."

The heart of the State is sound, but its head is muddled. A romantic history remains without any adequate telling. Daring deeds and noble lives that should have been embodied in song and story to grow into beautiful legend and inspiring tradition remain unwritten and unsung. They, too, are part of our children's wasted heritage, and the future will be the poorer for our neglect of them. Material resource or historical wealth, the failure is the same. We lack the understanding to profit by what is ours. We do not see clearly the goal we would have the State attain, nor can we bring ourselves to follow the long, hard road of endeavor and sacrifice which all who would reach golden goals must tread. The perception of the Tennessee that should be and might be is not yet in our minds: the inspiration that quickens the heart and strengthens the thews for great accomplishment has not yet come to us.

CALIFORNIA
THE PRODIGIOUS

By GEORGE P. WEST

CALIFORNIA lies wide and luminous and empty under the infinite blue between the high Sierras and the sea. Horizons are not miles but counties away, and between distant mountain sky-lines the land, lustrous and radiant in pastel shades of blue and green and golden brown, swims in warm sunlight. A physical entity seven hundred miles long and two hundred and fifty wide, California is cut off from the nearer West by a high rampart of mountains, with the sea on its other flank, while on the north its contact with Oregon lies across a wild tumble of mountains and forests, and on the south there is only the trackless mountainous desert of Mexico's Lower California. Inside these limits lies a land larger than Italy and Switzerland, as richly endowed with beauty and natural wealth as any in the world, with a climate of a semitropical friendliness that robs the mere business of sustaining life of its rigors and leaves human energy free for whatever other tasks the spirit may conceive. Within itself in stimulating variety are great deserts; noble mountain ranges where peaks of 14,000 feet go unnoticed; vast stretches of rich farming land in valleys flat as a billiard table; gentler mountains along the coast, where immigrants from northern Italy cultivate the vine or descendants of the Spanish conduct cattle ranches larger than Eastern counties; great regions in the north where mountain and valley are black with forests of giant pine and redwood, and bear lope across the logging road ahead of the infrequent stage; endless miles of glittering sea-coast where the lazy blue Pacific crashes and pours at the foot of tawny brown hills; gold mines and placer diggings in the lower canyons of the Sierras; valleys and foothills that at certain seasons are one vast flare of blossoming fruit trees; broad belts of olive-green orange and lemon orchards and of silver-green olives.

For northern Europeans made somber and astringent by a centuries-long struggle with obdurate soil and unfriendly climate to stumble upon such a land and discover it empty and waiting was in itself a dramatic episode in the life of the race. The people who call themselves Californians are not yet over their surprise. A sense of the prodigious abides with them. They are like children let loose in a new and wonderful nursery, and their enjoyment lies still in the contrast of its spacious magnificence with the meagerness into which they were born. The joy of the discoverer still exhilarates them, and stimulated and organized as their "boosting" is by the land speculator and the hotel-keeper, its swelling chorus voices also a generous eagerness to share the new-found blessings with friend and neighbor. They live in the radiance of a great destiny, which envisages the taming and the diverting of the torrents of the high Sierras, so that valley after valley and desert after desert now lying parched and empty shall become so many gardens for the culture of children and roses. The Californian of today is a pioneer in the task of turning water onto virgin soil and transforming wheat ranches, grazing land, even desert, into patinas of orchards and vineyards and truck-gardens.

But only the map-makers and politicians still think of California as an entity. In its human aspects it is sharply divided into north and south. There is San Francisco and there is Los Angeles, each with a million people within an hour's travel. Between the two stretch nearly five hundred sparsely settled miles of mountain and valley and desert, and a spiritual gulf wider still. These two communities *are* the State, in a cultural, sense, and they are farther apart, in background and mental habits, than New York and San Francisco, or Chicago and Los Angeles. For ten years there has been a movement to write southern California with a capital S. Its people are as different from the older Californians up San Francisco-way as Cromwell's Roundheads were different from the Cavaliers and the seventeenth-century successors of Falstaff. It is a difference of origins.

San Francisco's beginnings have been sufficiently celebrated. In an epilogue to "Two Years Before the Mast," Richard Henry Dana describes in diary form a visit to San Francisco in 1859. Here, set down more than sixty years ago, are observations that remain true of the city of today. "It is noticeable," he writes, "that European Continental fashions prevail generally in this city—French cooking, lunch at noon, and dinner at the end of the day, with *café noir* after meals, and to a great extent the European Sunday—to all which emigrants from the United States and Great Britain seem to adapt themselves. Some dinners which were given to me at French restaurants were as sumptuous and as good, in dishes and wines, as I have found in Paris."

It is a picture of the one pioneer American community where Puritanism was never permitted to intimidate the gusto and the zest for living of healthy men. Dana meets "a man whom I had known, some fifteen years ago, as a strict and formal deacon of a Congregational Society in New England. . . . Gone was the downcast eye, the bated breath, the solemn, non-natural voice, the watchful gait, stepping as if he felt himself responsible for the balance of the moral universe! He walked with a stride, an uplifted open countenance, his face covered with beard, whiskers and mustache, his voice strong and natural, and, in short, he had put off the New England deacon and become a human being."

Thus Dana in 1859—and still today the north holds all that is natively and distinctively Californian. It faces San Francisco, and celebrates the Argonauts of forty-nine as New England the Mayflower Pilgrims. It is a lusty, cosmopolitan community that has drawn its later increments of population largely from Ireland and northern Italy, and that maintains with undiminished gusto the Good-Fellow tradition instead of the Puritan. It cherishes a romantic, conventional æstheticism, drinks wine habitually, despite the Eighteenth Amendment, feels a vast tolerance toward weaknesses of the flesh, nurses a sense of the great world, a feeling of kinship with New York and Paris, a contempt born of utter ignorance for Chicago and the Middle West, a touch with the Orient, a love of the sea, a quick eye for the picturesque and the romantic. It loves fêtes and pageants and froths with uncritical sentiment at the slightest provocation. There is a regard for the past such as you will hardly find in Boston. "The days of old, the days of gold, the days of forty-nine" live again in the imagination of every school-child. Yet this San Francisco which holds an undisputed eminence over the older California belongs rather to the world and to the sea, which pierces the coast here through the narrow straits of the Golden Gate, between steep cliffs, and spreads out then into a bay of vast extent. One arm of it runs south for twenty miles and leaves between it and the sea a mountainous sliver of land with San Francisco crowded onto its northerly tip. The city's half-million live on wind-swept and seagirt hills, now drenched with fog, now bathed in a sunlight that is opalescent and sparkling and bracingly cool in reminiscence of the sea-mist that here never quite surrenders to the California sun. They live for the most part in the innumerable downtown hotels and apartments, or in solid blocks of wooden houses and tenements, standing flush with the sidewalk, painted white or gray, ugly with scroll-work. Here and there through the town a cluster of charming houses in Italian renaissance cling incredibly to some steep hillside and look sheerly down over the red-brown roofs of gray tenements to the blue Bay. But the city would be hideous if its streets were not forever marching up sheer hillsides or plunging down from dizzy heights to the flashing sea, so that the poorest Italian on Telegraph Hill knows the imminent glory of far-flung waters and encircling hills, and breathes clean winds from afar.

Contrast and surprise lurk around every corner, and

the city's people are sensitive and untiringly appreciative of every beauty, every contrast, every grotesquerie. They love their city as a man loves a woman of many moods and surprises. And the town is incurably bizarre and exotic. Cool trade winds blow down its streets every summer afternoon, and toward five o'clock a fleecy white billowing sea-fog, chill, eerie, palpable, drifts eastward over its hilltops, hugging the land, bringing the feel and smell of the sea like a presence. It throws a glamour over the cheaply built wooden tenements, mile after mile of them. It makes of summer evening interiors so many cozy havens from its chill and sinister mystery, and accounts in part for a café life that for generations has been normal and habitual. People of every race and nation meet on an equal footing in the restaurants and on the streets. For San Francisco belongs to Europe and the Pacific Islands and the Orient and Latin America and the wanderers of the sea as well as to California.

Chinatown is now adored by a people who stoned Chinese a generation ago, only to discover, after the exclusion act had removed them as an economic factor, that they are a singularly honest, humorous, and lovable folk. The Japanese might be more popular if the large Japanese colony weren't so colorless. Perhaps we should be touched and flattered by their eagerness to discard everything Oriental and adopt every Western banality of dress and custom. It would take a Freudian to explain why the intensely proud, nationalistic Japanese should do this while the Chinese persist in their own ways. San Francisco owes its Oriental flavor to Chinese who came before the exclusion act, cr were born here, or smuggled in.

For the rest, San Francisco is distinguished by its startlingly radiant women with their superb health and their daring color; by its swaggering workingmen; by its rowdy and disreputable politics, nourished by an underworld that remains institutional and arrogant in spite of prohibition; by the imminence of the sea and the life of ships; by its dozens of odd characters, past and present, such as the monkey-house bar where an old man in a plug hat sold liquor amid the chattering of birds and beasts from the Pacific Islands—a long-vanished phenomenon that is yet somehow eloquent of the town today.

Here, in this district about the Bay, is the California of Bret Harte, Mark Twain, Joaquin Miller, Charles Warren Stoddard, John Muir, Robert Louis Stevenson, Frank Norris, Ambrose Bierce, Edwin Markham, Henry George, Gertrude Atherton, Henry Morse Stephens, Gelett Burgess, Lincoln Steffens, George Sterling, the Irwin boys, Jack London; the California of Stanford and California universities; the California of the Vigilantes, Nob Hill, the Big Four of the Central Pacific; Abe Ruef and the graft prosecution; the Mooney case; the California of Hiram Johnson, Fremont Older, William Randolph Hearst, David Starr Jordan, Herbert Hoover.

San Francisco has always been a favorite with those who rail against a Puritan and regimented America. Yet it might be instructive to our legions of young people who indolently blame Puritanism for everything banal to come and live for a time with these anti-

Puritans of the Golden Gate. They would find the Good-Fellow tradition as stifling in its way as the Puritan, and harder to escape. There is a celebrated club in San Francisco the very name of which is a protest against Philistinism. It admits writers and artists without fee, and proceeds then to kill them with kindness. It has blunted more than a few men of first-rate talent by acclaiming them to the clink of glasses, drowning them in an easy and bibulous success, censoring in them any impulse to self-expression not compatible with the *mores* and taboos of the Good Fellow. Each year it presents an elaborate masque in blank verse in a noble grove of giant redwoods. Words and music are written by members, and the most successful business and professional men of the town compete for part in the cast. The plays celebrate friendship or portray the burial of care. Usually they are rather conventional and dull, full of "What Ho!'s" and "Who Is Without?'s" but the members sit through the performance with a touching religious fidelity, proudly conscious of their rôle as patrons of the arts and further assuaged for the tedium of the performance by a warm hazy alcoholic glow. For all that it is a brave and handsome enterprise. But when Witter Bynner, sojourning in California and admitted to membership, signed a plea for the release of political prisoners, the heavens fell on him and there was such a club row as reverberated for days in the newspapers of the town.

Yet it is hard to be critical of a town where George Sterling is as popular as Edgar Guest in Detroit; where a tiny Spanish galleon with golden sails, set in the center of a public square between Chinatown and the Barbary Coast, commemorates Stevenson's sojourn, where successful business men even pretend an enjoyment of the arts. Many young people here are without that hard-boiled quality, that contemptuous sophistication, which blights so many American youngsters of the prosperous middle class. The minority that has escaped the cultural sterility of a nation that worships salesmanship is perhaps a little larger, in proportion, among native Californians than among Americans generally.

But because Puritanism never did prevail here, one misses certain advantages of the Puritan temperament. In the East young people find it exhilarating to make their rebellion. There is passion and iron in it. California youngsters miss some of that thrill. They grow up in a society congenial enough to seduce them. Where good fellows are not barbarians there is a tremendous temptation to be one. In more than one respect living in California is like being happily married to a very beautiful woman, a placid, maternally wise, mentally indolent woman of the classic tradition, whose mere presence allays restlessness by making it seem gratuitous and a little ridiculous. In California one worries and squirms for fear one is not worrying and squirming enough. It is not only the need of a market that sends creative youngsters scampering to New York. From a California hilltop, much of the eager striving and rebellion afoot in the world get to seem mere stridency, much of the hard discipline of creative effort so much senseless drudgery.

Nor must anything here set down show San Francisco in too rosy a hue as a sparkling oasis in an America, in a world, that seems so often these days the desert of this metaphor. What Dana's outnumbered New Englanders could not accomplish in the fifties has been, to an extent, accomplished by the leveling and regimenting processes of our industrial civilization, so that here as elsewhere men and women go about too much as though listless and driven, as though bound on the wheel. And a nationalism that in this one of its effects seems suffocating and unnatural brings San Francisco within the workings of the Prohibition amendment, where its Latin spirit flutters, crippled and bewildered, like a bird in a church.

Not so the wide region at the other end of the State that calls itself the Southland. Wine was never honored in this heaven on earth set up and maintained by the great Mississippi Valley as a dazzling reward for thrift and piety. Southern California is an amazing achievement in colonization, an achievement not of California but of the Middle West. It stands there flaunting its testimony to the wealth and the overflowing population of what was yesterday our Middle Border. They discovered it when the first trains rolled westward over the newly completed Santa Fe and Southern Pacific in the eighties. It lay empty before them, except for a few negligible and benighted Spanish Americans. Real-estate speculators and health-seekers and the elderly retired came first. They were mostly New Englanders of modest savings, confirmed in their Puritanism by a generation or two of hard work and drab living in the Middle West. And they were not to be seduced by anything in the air of California or the ways of its shiftless caballeros. Among them there was no turning of backs on the familiar. They brought their household gods and all their mental baggage with them, and set them up in California without missing a prayer-meeting. They accepted the mountains and the sunshine as their due from God for being thrifty, Republican, Protestant, and American, but they did not neglect to give thanks regularly at the churches which they promptly erected. Most of their social life still centers about these churches, which remain amazingly untouched by any profane idea or discovery that has come into the world in the past hundred years. Of the New England that flowered in the great Unitarians, in the Abolitionists, in Phillips Brooks, in Thoreau, in William James, there is scarcely a trace.

The preëmpting by these people of southern California, a land drenched in sunshine and fragrance and sensuous, languorous beauty, is poignant irony. Contemplating one of their towns, with its trim bungalows and shrewd Yankee faces and many churches, it is easy to conjure up the ghostly figure of an ancient caballero, sitting graceful in his saddle under the moon, a brown-paper cigarette in his lips, long tapaderos brushing the ground, the moonlight glistening on the heavy silver trimmings of his bridle, gazing scornfully, wonderingly, sadly down from a hilltop over the electric-lighted rectangles of these victorious aliens. In a short generation they have wiped out a Homeric society of Latins and Indians and replaced it with a Gopher Prairie de luxe.

To write thus of the Yankee strain that predominates for the moment in rapidly changing southern

California is to fall into the literary habit of the hour. Some day, as the drubbing continues, those of us who come of that stock will feel a pricking of latent pride, a call to arms. And we shall find, then, and reaffirm in new terms, certain brave victories for the human spirit, certain unique conquests of happiness and even of beauty. Probably we shall always feel that they were bought at a frightful price of suppression and perversion, a price demanded not alone by the racial heritage of northern Europeans, but also by the hard conditions of pioneer American living. But the victories are real. They are to be seen today in southern California, where the orthodox American genius has proved itself not merely acquisitive, but creative as well, by bringing into being towns and countrysides that in homes, and schools, and gardens, and in every sort of community enterprise show a taking of thought, an intelligent care, a vast competence, a striving for a kind of life from which, if the free and diverse and inquiring impulses are banished, so also are the ogrish and the sensual. One may not disregard the community taboos. But by regarding them one may feel the community enveloping one in a kind and neighborly and even gracious concern. Out of the agglomeration of diverse and unoriented elements that make up southern California came, a decade ago, the major impulse behind most of the political progress associated with the six years of Hiram Johnson's governorship. True, it was in essence the orderly and moralistic impulse of comfortable, privileged commoners intent on putting down the heathen. The same people seemed in 1920 utterly satisfied with Mr. Harding. They destroyed the corrupt, generous, disreputable old railroad machine that had ruled the State for forty years. But they jail radicals and squelch labor organizers with more gusto still, with the same pious resentment once detected by the writer in one of their typical individuals, a retired farmer, who had discovered a cat that didn't belong there under his garage, and forthwith brought out a shotgun with moral and sanguinary intent.

Along with the elderly and the moderately prosperous who represent the virtue of the Middle West, the climate has attracted a vast assortment of odds and ends of humanity—poor souls in sick bodies, victims of all manner of starvations and suppressions and perversions. Every weird cult and -ism flourishes on the patronage of these pitiful refugees. Large areas of the community are stamped with shoddiness—the shoddiness of "folksy" real-estate men who station forlorn women on the sidewalks to hand cards to passers-by, or who advertise free turkey dinners at the opening of their new additions; of worn-out farmers and their wives from the prairie States who move about blinking in the unaccustomed sunlight and take refuge in their churches; of a horde of petty venders and mountebanks who prey on them. Bible Institutes flourish, and the thousands who flock to them are aroused to excitement by the reaffirmation of such doctrines as the second coming of Christ. Here, too, have come in increasing numbers the camp-followers and veterans of such professional sports as baseball and boxing and automobile-racing and of less reputable trades, so that Los Angeles is acquiring an underworld and a half-world of startling proportions, which shades into the lower reaches of the movies.

That serpent crawled into this garden unnoticed, tawdry bands of adventurers from "the show business" who took up quarters at third-rate hotels, twelve or fourteen years ago, and began making "Westerns." Today there are ten thousand actors alone in and around Los Angeles, including all who are listed with the central casting bureau from millionaire stars to drug-addicts used for "atmosphere" in plays of the underworld. The movies spend hundreds of millions a year for salaries and materials. They have profoundly changed the tone of Los Angeles, a sprawling, formless city with an underlying population of Middle Western villagers, and their influence reaches into every home of the Southland where there are boys and girls. In Hollywood, Puritanism out of Iowa lives neighbor to this demimondaine of the arts.

But California, like any youngster, is chiefly interesting for what it may become. As they go about the State and comprehend its natural resources, men of any imagination at all are able to foresee here a great society. Other States no older have already begun to "settle down," but here the seventy-five years of American occupation have made only a beginning. Development has been slow because a fuller use of soil and climate has waited always upon finding and conducting new water at enormous expense, and upon adapting tropical or semitropical plants at the cost of endless experimenting. No decade passes now without an excited planting of hitherto neglected acres to a new fruit or nut or a new variety, discovered usually by some obscure putterer in experimental gardens maintained by the State or Federal Government and then promptly exploited by shoals of land salesmen. And ceaselessly, in the high mountains, first engineers and then workmen concentrated in great temporary camps perform prodigies of tunneling and damming to get more water for irrigation and more hydro-electric power for the cities and for pumping more water still from the beds of the valleys. Instead of the four millions who inhabit the State today, every Californian confidently looks forward to the time when there shall be twenty or thirty millions, and these visions are shared by the disinterested and the skeptical, by such authorities, for instance, as Dr. Elwood Mead. This sense of a great future is a challenge to every citizen with an instinct for State-building or social engineering. (One uses terms hateful to the individualist, who indeed will find it hard going for a long time to come in a State where even tilling the soil requires organized community enterprise in getting water and in marketing its peculiar crops.) The future is a challenge, equally to the conservative and the radical, each of whom wishes ardently to build the greater community according to his pattern. Today California is eminently a child of privilege, the largess of its climate and soil increased at the expense of the rest of the country by means of high tariffs that give its growers almost a monopoly and so keep half a dozen delicacies off the tables of the poor. The benefits are promptly capitalized in land values, so that citrus and walnut orchards bring as much as $5,000 an acre. Unimproved land fit for tillage is held at $200. Nearly as much more is required to prepare it for planting and irrigating, to provide the minimum in equipment and living quarters, and to sustain life until the first returns. It is a situation that has already checked development and made of fruit-growing or farming of any sort a rich man's game. And the tariff corrupts the State's participation in national politics, by making of its congressmen so many log-rollers in collusion with special privilege everywhere.

One thing California has achieved already: a body of water law, in statutes and decisions, that establishes the principle of beneficial use as a condition to possession, and that decides as between users in favor of the greater number. And this year the private control of hydro-electric power by half a dozen great companies is being challenged by the influential and widely supported sponsors of an initiative act substituting State development and operation—a socializing of this vital necessity that may be safely predicted for the near future even if it is defeated this year. There remains the land. A constitutional amendment limiting tenure by the single-tax method, in accordance with the principle of beneficial use, received a quarter of a million votes in 1916. It has been more decisively beaten since then. If one were not hopeful, if one did not cling to the belief that it is too late in the day, one might foresee California becoming another Italy, the Italy of a generation or so ago, with beggars and an aristocracy. The beggars it would be easy to manage, in time. It requires more imagination to see our land speculators, with their Rotary badges and Elks buttons on belted khaki coats, metamorphosed into anything corresponding even dimly to the Italian aristocracy. To prevent that sort of thing there are a fair number of local H. G. Wellses—such men and women as are now pushing the Power act—with a generous following. And, far off, new winds are blowing, and gently, oh, so gently, stirring the minds of the people of the Golden State.

WISCONSIN

A VOICE FROM THE MIDDLE BORDER

By ZONA GALE

SHE said: "When we come to Wisconsin forty years ago we drove the ninety miles from Milwaukee and settled here in the woods. We didn't have a plow. We didn't have a ham. The neighbors lent him an ax and a saw and he begun. And now we've got this eighty we're on. And the three forties next we give the boys for wedding presents. They ain't all paid for yet. Ours'll be ours, though, before we die." She and he are seventy-odd, made of brown horn and cord. To them living means their "eighty."

A north-country townsman said: "My wife and I have adopted two children and she wants to take another. I laid aside above two thousand last year and I tell her to go ahead—nothing like music in the home." And in another mood: "I tell you, a man's got to do something for somebody else. Down and out, is he? Family sick on his hands? Put me down for a tenner."

After the sixties, such was the State drama: New Englander, Scandinavian, German pioneer or son of a pioneer paying for his eighty; or as prosperous townsman saving for his home. Here and there a voice asking or pledging remedial aid. Farm, business, home, school, drone of legislature—and a crust or a coin for the uncompensated. Beyond farm and town were the crash of falling forests, clink of new-spiked rails, detonations from the iron counties, and the occasional cry of a bewildered Red Man. All on a background of shadowed grain and colored lakes and glossy pasture land.

Also there was a lullaby titled: "Do not do so-and-so lest capital be driven out of the State." In a word, the drama and refrain of the old individualism. Already forgotten were such stirrings as the coöperative settlements of the forties and the Granger movement; and already aging was that young party of protest at slavery and secession, the Republican Party, born at Ripon, Wisconsin, in 1854, and christened in the Capitol Park at Madison.

Until the nineties. Then came La Follette. His story is one of the great romances of Wisconsin. His battles have now been fought in State after State but in Wisconsin it was pioneer ground and principally a one-man conflict. It was news to the people that they had not a representative government because of the convention system. It was news to the farmers and manufacturers and home-owners of the State that they were paying double the taxes paid by the railroads. It was news that in reporting gross earnings the railroads had not counted a million dollars annually in secret rebates. Spectacular collection of taxes on these rebates, abolishment of the whole rebate system, imposing of equal taxes at State valuation on holdings, and then rate regulation to prevent payment of increased taxes by increased carriage cost; and at last the Railroad Commission itself, following an earlier and abortive commission—all these came to Wisconsin through the one-man center of energy who could fill other men with conviction and teach them the peril in which their government labored. Rocking up through the black prophecies came the laughter of the State when the Railway Commission books showed for the first five years of its operation a two-million-dollar reduction in rates but an increase of 18.45 per cent in net earnings of the roads of the State against 18.41 per cent increase in net earnings for all the roads of the nation. The other public utilities, soon shepherded into the commission, outran that record. Capital simply could not be driven out of the State! Meanwhile the first full primary law in the United States had been written into the Wisconsin statutes.

Yet the story of the struggle to defeat this legislation is one of the saddest in Wisconsin records. The whole story of the opposing lobbies has been told in La Follette's Autobiography and shows that Monte Carlo stages nothing more devastating than do the committee rooms of the Capitols.

For a time Wisconsin lit new peaks at every legislative session. The commission idea kindled a flame then new to our traditionized vision: that the determining of conditions of certain relationships on a basis of legal precedent is fantastic and must be replaced by administrative interpretation on the basis of present economic and social fact. Followed a statute said in 1911 to be the greatest piece of labor legislation in the United States, the Industrial Commission to administer the new Workmen's Compensation Act and all other labor laws—the first instance in the country of the

State assuming to control and regulate health and safety of the workers. Tax Commission, Dairy and Food Commission, Free Library Commission, State Insurance Department, State Banking Department for bank inspection, and Immigration Bureau of the Department of Agriculture (with a Chicago office) now all contribute to the humanizing of the State machinery, to the stressing of human values in organized living. The Wisconsin Idea. The last commission, the Market Commission of 1919, to teach farmers to grade their own goods and market their own products and organize in coöperative groups, is designed ultimately to do for agriculture what the Industrial Commission does for industry. And to do more than that.

Not that coöperation in a quiet way has not already had growth in Wisconsin which passed one of the first coöperative laws in the Union. Perhaps it is by spiritual inheritance from those five coöperative communities of Owenites and Fourierites—the Wisconsin Phalanx, Hunt's Colony, St. Nazianz, Spring Farm, and the Utilitarian Association which had early dreamed their dream of relationship and died of institutionalization—that in 1917 there were in Wisconsin 1,536 coöperative creameries, cheese factories, produce companies, live-stock shipping associations and stores, besides 803 mutual telephone companies. These are soil for the flowering of that inevitable great growth so slow to root in America.

"Poor Wisconsin! So burdened by administrative commissions that the tax-payers move out of the State." One hears that occasionally from an editorial pen, a pen descended from that quill which used to be afraid of driving out capital. The answer which that pen will best understand is that not one dollar of the general property tax touches the Wisconsin commissions or boards or departments, for these are supported by the corporation taxes. (Railroad taxes, for example!) All the Capitol expenses are worth pausing over. The legislature of 123 members costs $373 a day and has eighty-eight employees who are in the classified civil service. This sum is one-third that which some States pay smaller legislatures having two score more employees politically appointed. Of course by political appointments the commissions might be sabotage-ed, as is said to be happening now in New York State.

One hears occasionally too that Wisconsin is losing its progressivism. It is true that during the three administrations preceding the present, Wisconsin rather stood still. But nothing of importance was repealed. Indeed Wisconsin was the first State to ratify the Nineteenth Amendment; and to pass the Equal Rights Bill by which women are given equality before the law, with the safeguarding too of the protective legislation "which they now enjoy for the general welfare"—the eight-hour day and minimum-wage laws. The revolutionary rights to enter into equal partnership with her husband, to sue and be sued if she must, to make contracts unaided, have her residence declared to be where she actually lives, and to receive employment even though married are all insured by this radical bill. By it lichened centuries of the old English common law are dropped. Can anybody say that the State is not progressive still?

Meanwhile something else had been happening in

Wisconsin. A mile down a Madison street from the Greek dome of the new Capitol ($2,000,000, the dome alone cost, we tell you, and we add that the Governor's reception-room is a replica of a room in the Doge's palace; but for the Doge we give no reason) stands an institution which makes every Wisconsin tax-payer either a psalmist or a prophet of peril. He ought to be a poet, for there is, we concede, nowhere in America a lovelier campus than that which lifts from Lake Mendota. Inscribed on a stone near its highest hall is that declaration of freedom made by the regents who had just tried Dr. Richard T. Ely for "economic heresy":

We cannot for a moment believe that knowledge has reached its final goal or that the present constitution of society is perfect. . . . In all lines of investigation . . . the investigator should be absolutely free to follow the paths of truth wherever they may lead. Whatever may be the limitations which trammel inquiry elsewhere, we believe the great State of Wisconsin should encourage that continual fearless sifting and winnowing by which alone truth can be found.

This cry of Tomorrow, adopted as a plank in one Republican State platform, is of course not always lived up to by Capitol or university. Of late the halls of the university have been denied for the public appearance of the editor of the *Nation,* of Scott Nearing, and of Kate Richards O'Hare, who were obliged to speak somewhere else in Madison on those occasions —Mrs. O'Hare at the Capitol. And within five years both the faculty of the university and the State legislature have, not quite unanimously, formally censured Senator La Follette for his opposition to the entrance of the United States into the World War. But the dream is there and Wisconsin has had for that dream two wings, one political and one educational. Dr. Richard T. Ely's "curious new individualism, that the State is a necessary good whose duty is to preserve to men opportunities which they deserve and profit by" did as much for the young as progressive legislation did for the elders to make men socially conscious and to give them a right attitude toward public affairs. Dr. John R. Commons and Dr. E. A. Ross (the latter fresh from two boycotts of his own for "economic heresy") sifted and winnowed in political economy and sociology "on the hill," while La Follette and others sifted and winnowed at the Capitol; and Frederic C. Howe sifted and winnowed at large. In those days were many giants. Some of the giants still survive.

Then McCarthy. "I, a wandering student, seeking knowledge, came knocking at the great gates of the University of Wisconsin and it took me in, filled me with inspiration, and when I left its doors the kindly people of the State . . . gave me a man's work to do." The "man's work" was for one thing the Legislative Reference Library. For what was the use of progressive legislation if the new statutes were so loosely drawn that they failed to express the will of the people? And what was the use of expressing the will of the people if there were no trained servants to carry it out? McCarthy saw democracy failing at its source; legislators with ideas of public service thwarted because they could not find out how other States and nations handled those ideas; unscrupulous lawyers drawing up bills purposely unconstitutional; the openly recognized scheme of jokers; the farmer or grocer or country lawyer faced unprepared with the making of laws on every phase of life; and expected to vote on two thousand bills at a session. He came with his idea of a Legislative Reference Library. They laughed at him; much later they took him on sufferance in the attic of the Capitol; very early they introduced a bill to abolish him; then they accepted him. The idea has been adopted in State after State and at Washington—though at Washington they are slowly strangling the library by failure to make it appropriations. These two tasks which "McCarthy of Wisconsin" set for himself—the improving of statute law and the improving of public administration, so little spectacular, so ripe for drudgery, are of the fabric of Wisconsin, present and to come. Some day his Society for Training for Public Service will not exist merely on paper as it does now; and the extended functioning of administrative experts may lead to nothing less than his idea of a new equity.

Also McCarthy's touch is on the continuation-school laws—entrance into industry not dependent on age alone but on completion of eighth grade, part-time attendance obligatory up to *eighteen* years, and such schools required, with State aid, in towns of five thousand. And on the University Extension program which serves its thousands in spite of the reactionaries' slogan of: "This university-on-wheels business has got to stop." And McCarthy's trail led by the farms and through one administration the State Board of Public Affairs was transformed into a rural agency studying, with the university, European marketing systems, State loans to farmers, coöperative credit. The Marketing Commission was his dream. His death two years ago was as little a death as ever a man died. He is still saying about the Capitol his careless: "Well, it's something where there was nothing."

Something where there was nothing. But there must be soil. And even with leaders like these, preaching that democracy and representative government are never won to keep, how was it that Wisconsin proved such favorable soil for progressivism? They were the camera, but who made the plate? The plate was made by the spirit of liberty stirring in northern Europe in the late forties. In Scandinavia, Germany, Ireland, Poland, Belgium, Switzerland. In political refugees. In Carl Schurz and the revolutionists of 1848. Intellectual brothers to those of the New Englanders who would still have brewed tea in Boston harbor. And it was spiritual brothers to the Brook Farm folk who now founded those little coöperative commonwealths whose ideals, reinterpreted, recur among us like a motif. Migrant to America, they read a pamphlet printed by immigrants to say that Wisconsin, then just admitted to the Union, had a constitution favorable to a Free State and that here only a year was required for citizenship. But the whole northern Mississippi Valley was peopled with such immigrants.

"Not a plow . . . not a ham . . . they lent him an ax and a saw and he begun. . . . I laid aside two thousand last year. . . . Something for somebody else. . . . Careful lest capital be driven from the State."

Yes, all that followed. Farm and business, home and

school, caution, conformity, economy, and a charity crust for the uncompensated. The old individualism, drama and refrain. But beneath the fine old individualism slept the stuff of the pioneers, patriots who had not been afraid to mention it when their country was wrong. And when the cry for representative government reappeared not as a political slogan but as an economic and educational program something ancient, it seems, woke in the flesh of their children. "I have never doubted," said La Follette, "that, once the people understood, they would reclaim their government."

Something where there was nothing. A proper attitude toward public affairs. A torch brought by the pioneers and held by President John Bascom of the university, patiently urging the service which education must pay back to the State. One of his pupils was the late President Charles Van Hise, who held the torch for a while. Another pupil was La Follette.

What else of Wisconsin? Always there is the still background of that stretching acreage of farms. And it isn't that $234,000,000 worth of milk was produced in the State in 1920; or 307,000,000 pounds of cheese and 95,000,000 of butter in 1919; it isn't this (though we like thus adroitly to get it in the conversation). It isn't that the university agricultural school has bred pedigreed grain with which it won the world's championship in 1910; or made corn and all kinds of fruit grow up Lake Superior way; or that it has brought research contributions to soil testing and marsh draining; or discovered five of the six tests used everywhere in dairying. It isn't these, after all. It is that the university and the Capitol *care*. That they are not serving the hand-picked alone. That they touch the people's life as it is lived. The Wisconsin Idea. The University Idea. And here it is, from Major Edward Fitzpatrick of the present Wisconsin Board of Education: "Wherever spirit grows by mysterious contact with spirit, in the passion to make knowledge serve human needs, there is the essence of the University Idea." No wonder that this board has lately become a social planning department and that there is now being outlined a State-wide educational program to make the progress of Wisconsin a course consciously planned for a decade to come.

Among the unacademic educational forces in the State should be named the Socialist Party with Victor Berger. Not only because, anonymous on the statute books, is many a measure which the Socialists urged years ago and saw others pass; nor because for years the Socialists have successfully governed Milwaukee as they do now, but because of their general service to the State in quickening the social consciousness.

What else of Wisconsin? A progressive Governor, renominated on a platform which includes the abolishing of the secrecy clause in the income-tax law; and in Governor Blaine's hands are figures and names which show that $1,500,000 in income-tax returns have been held back from the State in the last six years by certain corporations—and the work of auditing is barely begun. No wonder that for the first time in the political history of Wisconsin the Old Guard, the stalwart Republicans, are calling themselves "independent progressives," or "constructive progressives," or just progressives for short. "The sheep in the clothing of what he used to call a wolf," says an earnest wag.

And what else? A unique geological background of thrilling revelation and a rich Indian and French and Jesuit tradition. Thousands of acres of forest reserve—now that millions of the northern giants have been felled. A State Conservation Commission and a "Lovers of Our Native Landscape" preserving woods and granite cliffs and waterfronts—now that some of these waterfronts already bear a general resemblance to the burning ghats. A labyrinth of little towns with pathetic Main Street lists inscribed with names of boys fed to the old, old Minotaur. A mass of the people still living the lives of the sixties—individualists, as we say "egg and bird" ("Fine citizen. Tends exclusively to his own business"); turning a languid or a suspicious or an alarmed eye on social legislation ("Social or Socialist, what's the difference?" And, "Don't 'civic' mean keeping the saloons shut?"); with women of three generations awake and aware of these dawns, pioneer suffragists or undergraduate utopists; and with other women repressed, overspecialized to housework, and that pendulum swinging to daughters neither repressed nor specialized. All the tawdriness of the sad scramble for pleasure in rides and reels, with hard-favored recreation halls and desultory pageants of commercial floats as our chief form of art expression. But also the schoolhouses open for non-partisan non-exclusive assembling of the people and this mandatory on all school boards. And the Wisconsin Players, a laboratory for the youth of the State to try themselves out, without cost, in the arts of the theater.

A Milwaukee Art Society with a permanent exhibit by Wisconsin artists, an exhibit taken out in the autumn to the county fairs. A State Music Federation. Stephen Babcock, inventing the fat test for milk and refusing to patent it. A poet, William Ellery Leonard, whose voice and vision are for "the prophets of the New, until the few are all." John Muir's homestead. Ole Bull's house as the executive residence. Bill Nye's own town. Edna Ferber's laughter and Hamlin Garland's devotion celebrating the Middle Border. The home of Ringling's circus—and when of late Al Ringling died the legislature adjourned and (in the neighboring town where he began his show business with one dog in a crate) attended his funeral. Everywhere stir such revaluations as that, furthering sympathy, furthering reality.

In brief, the well-known human being, wistful that life be physically and spiritually beneficent to him and even to his kind. And lifting through the mechanism of government and education the Wisconsin spirit saying so that it is actually audible: "Your hope is the State's task."

But McCarthy's words are best: "Well, where there was nothing there is something."

MICHIGAN

THE FORDIZING OF A PLEASANT PENINSULA

By LEONARD LANSON CLINE

On the great seal of the State of Michigan, under the woodsy emblems of elk and moose and sunrise over the water, is the legend "Si quæris peninsulam amœnam, circumspice." If you seek a pleasant peninsula, look about you. There is something pastoral, Arcadian, daisy-and-cress about it. It chimes a gentle angelus. It smells of warm milk in the pail, of new hay in the loft. And one can fairly see the Michigander, sturdy and kindly rustic, standing bare-headed at his hospitable threshold, gazing with a smile of pure and simple content at the hills and flashing lakes and meadows brimming with toadflax and brown-eyed Susans.

Actually, it is with quite different sentiments that the Michigander looks about him. If he is a farmer he glooms at his fields, wondering why the devil his son, who has gone to Detroit to work in the factory, doesn't write, and where in hell he can get help for the harvest. If he is a salesman he grins with glee at the billboards stuck up in front of pleasant views wherever paved highways lead; and then, driving on, he ponders whether to go to Yellowstone for his vacation or to Atlantic City. If he is a mechanic he never looks about him at all unless he is on his back under the hood of the car.

Some day some convention of salesmen will agree to a much more appropriate coat-of-arms for the new Michigan. It will picture the lean cheeks and the death's-head smile of Henry Ford, in the halo of a spare tire, flanked by chimneys and flivvers on a ground of soot. Underneath, in place of the stately Latin, will be inscribed the more salesmanlike legend: Always in the Lead.

And yet, Michigan is a pleasant peninsula, or peninsulas, for there are two of them—the only State in the Union boasting a spare part. It is a land of undulating hills, spendthrift in wild-flowers. Save for desolate stretches of cut-over timber land trees abound. On the east lies Huron, on the west Michigan with its yellow dunes, and on the north Superior—blue waters, cold and beautiful. Inland along the courses of many streams are little lakes and ponds estimated at from five thousand to fifteen thousand in number. The older residents love Michigan for these things, but the new find reinforced concrete more gratifying to their eyes; and the new constitute the State.

Before them, in the latter part of the last century, Michigan stood for nothing. It was at the end of its frontier period, with the first impulse wasted and animation low. In 1820 there were less than nine thousand persons in the State. Timber in the Lower Peninsula, copper and iron in the Upper, started an avalanche of immigration. When the forests soon gave out, those with transportation in their pockets departed, leaving a dozen cretinoid towns huddling around the ruins of their mills, gaping dully at the stumps and naked hills. In 1900 Michigan had a population of 2,420,982, of which more than one-fifth was of alien birth, including large settlements of Poles, Scandinavians, Finns, Germans, Dutch, French, and Italians—in short, a typically American mid-Western State in respect to its foreign-born. The Michiganders were a people without identity, without community of purpose or past, without tradition.

Then Ford.

In twenty years the population swelled to 3,668,412, the increase being almost wholly in the southern cities. Detroit became four times as large as it had been, Lansing four times, Flint eight times. And Michigan is coming to stand for something: mechanics, factory methods, salesmanship, in life as in business, for the two are one.

The Fordizing of the State is not yet complete. Toward the north there is a great deal of bitterness, not unmingled with envy, at the growing domination of Detroit. Nevertheless the thrill of new vigor shoots into every flaccid limb of Michigan. Highways poke like scalpels into the moribund towns of the timber district, and leave garages like new thyroids to give alacrity and bustle. As you come south the cities more and more take on an air of newness, of hardness, of thin varnish, faking up what passes for prettiness, lending themselves to the salesman's glib rehearsal of modern improvements. In Detroit at last you find the consummation of the salesman's ideal.

In the residence districts there is block after block of two- and four-family flats, as alike, as cheap, as ephemeral, as quantitatively produced as the Ford to which they owe their presence. Each has its skimping lawn in front, its back-yard with clothes-lines strung from the stoop of the house to the bleak little flivver-sized garage on the alley. Each is shinily decorated, equipped with laundry chutes, toilet extras, French doors, glued-on ceiling beams in the dining-rooms, gaudily painted glass chandeliers suspended by brass or nickel chains, and built-in bookcases that serve as depositories for anything but books. These dwellings satisfy Detroiters because their desire is not to find something different, but something just like So-and-So's. And what difference does it make that in the winter a stiff gust may blow the carpets from the floors, or that in summer a drenching rain may loosen the ceiling, or that the prepossessing big brick hearth won't draw, or has been built without any means of removing ashes? In the spring one sells one's house and buys another. These places are built not to be lived in, but to be sold. Good salesmanlike dwellings.

In matters of government modern factory methods have been applied generally. The new Detroit quickly adopted a new charter. It replaced the old 42-man council with one of nine members. The old council had at least a sense of humor. The new is grim, sacrosanct, with a Sunday-school tidiness in its habits, but not appreciably more honest or more efficient. The Detroit Citizens' League brought in a crew of energetic young men who have been several years now modernizing the city departments. In spite of a display of innocent political energy closely modeled after Henry's own, the millennium is still bashful.

A new municipal court has been created, and deals rapidly and severely with such miscreants as the excellently organized police can catch. The juries here are no longer random affairs; the panels are chosen from a select list of the ministers, the leading salesmen, the eminent figures of the community. Detroit is proud of the long sentences given its criminals and the proportion of convictions in the total number of arrests. Yet in spite of so many ways to discourage it, banditry slugs its dozen a day, at noon or at midnight. Banditry is particularly bold in Detroit. Naturally the salesmanship ideals here gleam most splendidly and lure on most temptingly to steal. One must wear silk stockings and drive a big car; one must build one's chimneys as high as Ford's, whether for patented roller-bearings or blackjacks; one must satisfy that craving which originates in the habit-forming narcotic of fifty miles an hour.

While the noonday bandits are hunting down paymasters and shooting bank clerks, the dining-rooms in the hotels are serving cheap collations to the Rotary clubs, the Lion clubs, the exchange clubs, the conventions and confraternities of salesmen that serve Detroit's noblest purposes. The Elks are gathering in their imposing new home for the business men's lunch, gobbled between snappy rehearsals of new tricks to catch prospects. And the workmen in an enormous pit are laying the foundations of the new Masonic temple, to be built at the cost of millions of dollars, probably the most grandiose temple of the bib-and-tucker brotherhood in the world.

No doubt about it, Detroit is coming to be a city sweet to the eye and satisfying to the intelligence of the salesmen and mechanics who inhabit it. Sublimated peddlers, "get-it-across" advertising men, and other hundredpercenters look on their work with a smile of perfect admiration. Proper credit is also due the real-estate agent swaggering in the glory of his new title of realtor, proud of the miles of pleasant woodland he has turned into "subdivisions" with sidewalks and lamp-posts but no water, trees or houses. Salesmanship it is that makes the prospect visualize a "home" in this "development" for so much down and so much a month.

And if one of these boosters is selling you his city, he may ask you, after dinner, whether you like music. "Don't think our city hasn't got anything but factories," he says. "If you're a highbrow you can find lots in your line. We got the best orchestra in the world, with this . . . now . . . Gabrilosky for conductor. We got an art museum owned by the city. We got the most beautiful public library in the world. Say, let's take in a concert!" And with a guffaw and a clump on the back he hauls you off to Orchestra Hall.

Detroit really has a remarkable collection of paintings, old masters as well as new, and ground for an imposing museum is being broken on a site across Woodward Avenue from the Library. Its Orchestra has its own auditorium, one of the most charming in the country. But these things are the outward and visible sign of an inward and spiritual salesmanship. They are a gesture, like the carnation on Mother's Day in the buttonhole of the man who has not written home for twelve years. The Art Museum and the bulk of its collections were given to the city. A few thousand dollars are appropriated every year for acquisitions.

But in order to get the money it is necessary to argue that pictures increase in value and are most profitable investments. The Orchestra has a deficit every year, and the public is asked to subscribe because as the jazz-adoring salesman tells you it will be a wonderful advertisement for the city. It is a fact that if Gabrilówitsch played the music his patrons beseech him to play his programs would be choked with Tostigoodbyes.

As for the Library—the luxurious new building is displayed to visitors—but its staff so far hasn't had much success in selling a taste for books to the natives. Detroit is the worst book market among all our cities of anywhere near its size. Good publishers will not advertise in the local papers because they sell no books. Detroit reads Eddie Guest.

Eddie Guest, the great intellectual product of the new Michigan! No doubt about the sincerity of that acclaim. He is extolled again every week as poet laureate of the State. His poems are taught in the public schools seriously as literature. He has proved his salesmanship by collecting the leavings of the bonbon bacchanalia of Eugene Field and peddling them. Detroit loves him not only for his sentimentalism but for his success and the way he can turn off four or five stanzas every day of his life. Henry Ford, too, stands as one of the great philosophic forces of the new Michigan. After the disaster of the peace ship this homme-dieu got him a new Rosinante in the *Dearborn Independent,* and tilts weekly at windmills, routs flocks of sheep, and otherwise advances the cause of salesmanship. "It's like Bryan's *Commoner,*" sighed a melancholy dissident; "only commoner."

After them come the diplomats: the Ambassador to Japan, who has served as Republican sales manager in Michigan and enjoyed some success; the Secretary of the Navy, a lay figure; the junior Senator, Mr. Newberry, who demonstrated his salesmanship recently in a most convincing way.

There is another prophet in Michigan whom the community has come to regard all the more highly since a sixteen-story building bearing his name was put up. He is a five-and-ten-cent-store magnate, and naturally a violent prohibitionist; Commissioner Haynes named him as national head of the league for spy service in the homes of friends. Not long since the papers printed a little story touching upon this man. Some unfortunate had been arrested for shoplifting in his five-and-ten-cent store. It turned out he had swiped some whisky glasses. This was eminently good salesmanship. It was about as good as that of the other leading Michigander who generously volunteered to lend some of his mummichog underlings to swell the numbers in an august patriotic parade, to make the parade bigger. He supplied them with banners advertising not the serious matter being commemorated but his own private business. Just what the occasion was has slipped my mind; I think now it was in token of respect for Michigan's dead in the war. But the memory of those dairy ads is as clear as yesterday.

The nearest thing to the sublime in Michigan is the Ford factory. See it at dusk some October afternoon, from a distance away, a vast squat looming monster, glinting a shrill blue light from its windows into the shadows, gibbering, ominous. Out of the tall chimneys drifts black smoke. It smuts one's nose and collar, and the soot of it cakes over one's imagination and is too heavy for wings.

In its glooms and glares the young Michigander labors and plays. He plays hard, and drinks his whisky without a chaser. The national prohibition commissioner has declared Detroit one of the driest cities in the country. That shows only what a good salesman of prohibition he is; for Detroit is saturated. Or perhaps he has been deceived by the seeming of sobriety in the new Michiganders. They go to church dutifully, and listen to panting harangues against rum, by salesmanlike ministers who have carried out the Coney Island idea in religious advertising to remarkable perfection, adorning the house of the Lord with illuminated revolving crosses and other kewpie bangles. Once, when an Episcopalian minister ventured to express a belief that wine was not entirely evil, his brothers of the cloth were permitted to heap on him the vilest abuse, with hardly a single voice lifted in his defense. After church, however, the new Detroit goes home to bottle its last brew. It has given numerous members to the society against the prohibition amendment, but not one of the wealthier topers has been willing to let his name be used as local head of it. In New York and Philadelphia there were men courageous enough to be leaders. The big men of Detroit have been quite candid in their refusals. It would hurt their business. It would be bad salesmanship.

Anything for a sale. Success is indicated in the one maxim, Never let go of a prospect. The young business man is the most agreeable person in the world, in your company. Though your hobby be Sanskrit, philately, billiards, whisky, or venery—the demijohn or the demijane—he will learn it. He defers to your opinion with unctuous eagerness, and offers himself to do valet service for your spinster cousins. You find him in your church Sundays, seeking the prominence of the front seat and bawling his hosannas. One of them boasted to me that it took him a year once to land a sale. But he cheerfully wallowed in the dirt his prospect was soaked in, and put the deal across. Then he was ready to change his religion, with conscience serene, to that of another.

Sunday afternoons Detroit gets in its car and goes riding. The car whenever possible is not a Ford. That would not be big enough for the salesman. His idea is to sell Fords and ride in a Packard. And on his Sabbath outings he drives fast, taking the same straight, flat roads week after week, the roads everybody else takes. When he gets home he squints at the speedometer to see if he has had a good time; how many miles has he traveled?

The population of Michigan has doubled in the past twenty-five years, but you perceive little difference in the beautiful northern lake districts, the wooded shores of Lake Huron, the solitudes of the dune country along Lake Michigan, with its living pictures exquisite as the most sensitive Japanese print. It was my pleasure to spend seven summers on Portage Lake, and in that time the only new cottages were put up by visitors from Illinois, Wisconsin, Ohio, even New York City. Yet the Long Island shores hardly offer more than does Portage Lake. Railroad communications with these northern places are little more developed than they were before the boom. Recently the Detroit & Cleveland Navigation Company announced the suspension of its summer steamship to historic old Mackinaw Island, at the head of Lake Michigan. I am not sure that the line actually was suspended, but certainly it has not prospered. And yet twenty years ago there was plenty of traffic on these boats, northbound from Detroit. The pleasantness of Michigan is virtually ignored today. But what can one expect? When the salesman goes vacationing he wants a boardwalk, a dance hall, a roller-coaster, and a brass band, something big, loud, and gaudy.

From a high place—from the colossal new General Motors Building, an Acropolis of salesmanship; from one of the towering structures that are beginning to loom up from the ruins of old mansions above the trees of Washington Avenue and Grand Circus Park—one can almost see Ann Arbor, thirty-five miles away. The Blackman of the new Michigan, that jigs in the wind every morning on the top of Henry Ford's chimney, looks about him and sees it. Sometimes he points that way, with an empty gesture.

Here Michigan plays its sweetest charms. The little city basks on its hills, under its elms and oaks. The Huron River, most gracious stream, curves past, slipping through a park-like country for miles. There is no Niagara here, nothing to make one gasp, but a delicacy and intimacy and loveliness that one returns to always with a gentle exaltation and thrill of release. Here stands the University of Michigan.

The State has not been ungenerous with its appropriations. The last legislature set aside several millions for the expansion and improvement of an already excellently equipped institution. Some big men are on the faculty. But the liberal minds of Michigan are subject to nightmares. If the Blackman sees what they are up to, they get fired. For the university, controlled largely by the same interests that put Truman Newberry in the Senate, is administered by an elected board of regents who are therefore the jumping jacks of triumphant Republicanism. Salesmanship reigns. Courses in business administration are being built up at the expense of courses in intelligence and feeling. One learns at Ann Arbor to judge one's aspirations by the way they jingle.

Not many years ago the editor of the campus paper prepared a series of stories showing unsanitary conditions in the water supply. These the authorities would not permit him to print. Their argument was, as he reported it, that the stories might scare prospective students away from the university. They might hurt sales.

Only from time to time a few of the young people in this great university bolt their classes in economics and salesmanship and learn greater verities out in the pleasant hills of Michigan. They are scolded in the classroom and sneered at on the campus. They are not invited to Detroit as guests of the alumni club, which brings in football coaches and players to make speeches, and undertakes as its principal object to get good high-school half-backs to matriculate at Ann Arbor. They are not enough to give the University of Michigan any tradition at all of literature or art or idealism, or anything but salesmanship and business ability.

In the past the university won fame by her football team and her College of Dentistry. For the present, as is quite appropriate in the university of the new Michigan, she seems content to produce more mechanics and salesmen.

The bachelors and masters of arts from Ann Arbor will sell other people things they themselves would not use. They will get rich, and build big houses which they will decorate with dried starfish and souvenir gew-gaws from summer excursions. They will continue to thrill over the *Saturday Evening Post,* and believe the sumac a weed, beauty a pinwheel. And whenever they pass the Jim Scott Memorial Fountain they will pause to admire.

This, the most costly, most magnificent, most prominently situated memorial in Michigan, is being slowly constructed at the foot of Belle Isle, that beautiful park lying in the middle of the Detroit River. Seventy-five acres is being reclaimed from the stream. There will be a great basin 1,200 feet in length, filled with leaping jets of water. Over it will soar a white shaft, dominating all the waterfront of Detroit, saluting every ship that enters the harbor.

And who was Jim Scott? A man who made some money, and died, bequeathing to Detroit the sum of $500,000 on condition that it be used to erect a monument to his memory. A few voices shrieked in protest, crying that Jim Scott had never done anything people wanted to remember, that he knew perhaps too well the distinction between a straight flush and two pairs, that beside this Jim Scott project Camembert would have no odor but a faint fragrance of lilies. But Michigan, the new Michigan, was staggered by the bigness of $500,000. It accepted the bequest.

Jim Scott never bothered about his fellow-men when he was alive. On his deathbed he thought it was time. And he sold himself to them. Around his monument for years and years to come the Sabaoth of Michiganders will shuffle, gawking, and they will ponder here the great lesson of salesmanship.

LOUISIANA

(MADAME DE LA LOUISIANE)

By BASIL THOMPSON

A CLEAR and unimpassioned visualization of so unique a commonwealth as Louisiana becomes a complex and disquieting performance, especially when your raconteur is a native son not wholly lacking in sentiment toward his delightfully volatile soil-mother. Native-born Louisianians, Kentuckians, and Virginians, unlike native-born Georgians, Arkansans, and West Virginians, must of necessity retain some sly regard for the romantic, historic, and traditional foibles of their several *terræ matres*.

Madame de la Louisiane fairly screams romance. At once piquant, naïve, effete, blasé, and bumptious, she presents to her sister commonwealths more or less the same aspect that Mam'selle Nouvelle-Orléans, her capricious daughter, exhibits to her staider cosmopolitan brethren. Though her glitter, her arrogance, her superficiality, her little *minauderies* are beyond question, beneath the veneer one glimpses her true personality—elusive, coy, droll, if you will, but very real, quaint, colorful.

Madame de la Louisiane is woman and mother. Regard her thus. Only as woman and mother may one detect her authentic gesture—her history, sentiment, tradition, her odd little quirks of character. She is, moreover, "a woman with a past." But she is, too, a mother humoring the whims of her favorite child, Mam'selle Nouvelle-Orléans. Her whole life whirls about this elder daughter, whose manner and insouciance are inimitable; whose fame and dark beauty have gone the world around; who is not, despite all her extravagance, ever anything but herself. Let us consider her *en fête, en costume de bal,* arrayed at her best—as one should always consider lovely woman.

It is February. The air is crisp, clean, invigorating. You have just had an absinthe in the "Assassins' Den" of the Old Absinthe House. Monsieur Cazenave, on learning you are down for the Mardi Gras from Hoboken, Kansas City, or the Yukon, unbends graciously. He concocts for you an absinthe, cool, milky, satisfying. Your gullet titillates deliciously. You have another, this one frappéed by way of change. For the nonce, Mr. Volstead is relegated to the limbo of the unborn. You sip your drink dreamily, reminiscently. Shades of Paul Verlaine and Jean Lafitte! Where are you? Parnassus, Paris, or Nouvelle-Orléans? The last indubitably.

The hoot of horns, the cries of masqueraders intrude from the street below. It is Mardi Gras in New Orleans in the year 1922. There must be some mistake. You are dreaming. You are drunk. "L'addition, M'sieu?" Your reverie is disturbed. The bill settled, Félix, the garçon, offers you hat and topcoat. You are out in the street—Bourbon Street at the intersection of Bienville. You walk toward Canal, surrounded by a riot of color and sound. The deliciously treacherous absinthe seeps into your brain. The day is rich, glorious; the air, tonic; the people, mad, young, wanton. . . .

A masked girl in cotton tights bumps into you. "Pardon, M'sieu," she laughs and is away. A ten-year gamin, in Charlie Chaplin make-up, notes your abstraction—"Hey, Mister, come out of it! Git in the push." He supplies the push. You are aroused. You look about eagerly, excitedly. You nudge your friend. You ply him with innumerable questions. "Rex" is making down Canal Street. Bands are playing. Club galleries gleam with pretty frocks and faces. A storm of confetti bursts upon you. The Carnival colors are everywhere. Buildings, windows, galleries, signs, banners, the people themselves blaze with color. It is a vital, an electric pageant, veritably charged with passion, imagination, beauty, madness. . . .

A slight picture. Ineffectual, if you will, but where else in all America may you glimpse it? And Mardi Gras Day is but one day in the year, and New Orleans but one section of Louisiana. None the less it is this carnival spirit that pervades New Orleans, and it is this New Orleans spirit that pervades Louisiana. Louisiana is New Orleans and, by the same token, New Orleans Louisiana. This despite great sugar and cotton plantations, the rice and sulphur industries, the oil fields, the timber lands, the salt islands, the big game preserves, the State Capitol at Baton Rouge the "city" of Shreveport, the insane asylum at Jackson, and the protestations of upstaters.

Perhaps it were not amiss to rehearse here somewhat of the history of this *soi-disant grande dame* among States. Parenthetically one begs your indulgence a space wherein Madame's past is, one trusts, tactfully, if not entertainingly, reviewed. In speaking of a lady's past, however, it seems not gallant to become personal lest, by the token, one also become odious. Thus shall be given over, for the time, Madame's femininity as such and her origins sketched in the broad, impersonal, though, be it confessed, lack-luster manner of historiographers.

Aboriginally *locus* La Louisiane was a body of water, a geological sea. More late, a prehistoric dwelling-place for amphibious brutes, where primitive peoples built shell mounds to climb upon in high-water time. These mounds excavated today betray a certain native art, evidenced in rude bowls, earthen vases, stone implements. Later the Indians: some indigenous, like the Attacapas; some nomadic, probably from Mexico, like the sun-worshiping Natchez tribe; in all five or six groups, living each a community life.

The early roads of La Louisiane were waterways. The pirogue, a sort of canoe built for four, was means of transit from bayou to river and river to bayou. Wild fowl and buffalo served to victual the winter season. Fish and local crustaceans sufficed the summer. Fruit and nuts, notably the pecan, were plentiful. Corn was planted. Rice grew naturally. With nothing to do, with no need to go anywhere, with labor done by the women (days that are no more!) it was usually too warm or too rainy deliberately to make war, so even fighting, a pastime in the "Canetuckie" country, could not cajole these pre-Caucasian Louisianians out of their native indolence.

But the forest stillness of the swamp country, just

below the mouth of Red River, was soon broken by the clanking armor of Hernando de Soto's men. Moscoso buried De Soto in the waters of the Mississippi, and with the remnant of his conquistadores floated on a raft down past the site of Nouvelle-Orléans, putting out upon the Gulf of Mexico. The Spanish were not then seriously impressed with the somber, moss-grown wilderness of this future American commonwealth, and so did not formally include it except as an extension of Florida.

A century or so passed before Père Marquette and the merchant Joliet, followed by Robert, Cavalier de La Salle, and Tonty of the Iron Hand, came down the river from Canada. The Fleur-de-lys was raised at the mouth of the Mississippi. The country, the entire valley from the Alleghenies to the Rockies of the West was, with much ceremony, named La Louisiane, after *le grand monarque* Louis Quatorze and his Queen-Mother, Anne of Austria. Thenceforward, we have recorded the familiar story of Louisiana.

After pioneering discoveries by La Salle came settlement by Iberville at Biloxi. The French King sent over ships and soldiers. Hardy men and women followed to hew wood, draw water, and procreate. In and about were the omnipresent Jesuits, lending first aid to the sordid lives of a people whose very existences depended on daily exertion and innumerable hardships. The story of the province of Louisiana—a French colony five months' sail from France; barely known to exist by the people of Europe; moving slowly onward; filling its requirements to the best of its abilities; taking lessons from its Indian neighbors in fishing and providing food; waiting ever for encouragement from the King—this chapter in the history of Louisiana was but one of desperate effort to survive flood, fever, and famine. Yet stout hearts prevailed and another generation was gradually born—the Creole, so dubbed in France. Here upsprang this new American breed, scarcely aware of the Fleur-de-lys, breathing the air of "freedom" and "liberty" along with their brethren —bird, bear, and Indian.

A ship came over in 1766 bringing from Europe a new Governor and a new flag. The King of France had handed over to his cousin, the King of Spain, the colony nominally cared for since the days of John Law. After the Mississippi Bubble had burst, the Province de la Louisiane ceased longer to interest the Court of Paris. The Creole at last had something to break monotony. He revolted. Cutting the hawser that held the Governor's ship to the levee, he sent word by the same ship as it floated to the Gulf that, "We, the people, if no longer subjects of France, elect to be subject only to ourselves." Strange that a declaration arrived at in Mecklenburg and Lexington some years later should have been born down in the forests of the delta, stillborn, if you will, for the revolting group was executed in 1769.

Cession of Louisiana to the United States in 1803 affixed to the young republic more territory than all it had until this time possessed. From a chain of States on the Atlantic seaboard, whose farthest west was then the Ohio country, Oregon, Texas, and California alone remained to complete the vast bulk that forms the United States today.

If the condiments that go to make up the type now known as American depend on quantity and proportion of Caucasian blood, this Latin strain as diffused through the French and Spanish Creole forms a nice balance to the Swede and German of the West, and the New England and Virginia strains of Anglo-Saxon. Most persons should know, by this, that the Creole is Latin-American, a white man, and not, as sometimes vulgarly believed, *café au lait* French mulatto. In Louisiana the Creole is white. He is the direct descendant of the Spanish and French pioneer. The term in its original connotation implied a colonial Frenchman, one born in the colonies. But there are four distinct varieties of Frenchmen in Louisiana: the Frenchman, born in France, the Creole native of French descent, the San Domingan Creole, and the Nova Scotian Acadian or Cajan.

This Cajan is worth a word. In the Teche country—southern Louisiana—he preponderates, speaking a peculiar dialect or patois quite at variance with that of the Creole. In the towns of St. Martinsville and New Iberia this emasculated lingo is almost the common tongue, certainly *la langue de famille*. It is estimated that some fifteen hundred Cajans of those expelled from Nova Scotia settled in Louisiana. They now number one hundred and fifty thousand or thereabouts and for the most part adhere to their native speech. Of course, the Cajan and the Creole must not be mentioned in the same breath. The Creole is, in his kind, a cultured though somewhat decadent type; the Cajan, in his, a crude, ingenuous one. An interesting fact in connection with the French-speaking people of Louisiana is the publication, at the present time, of several purely French papers scattered over the State, and in New Orleans of two weeklies: *L'Abeille*, the earliest existing journal printed in the Mississippi Valley, and *La Guêpe*. These titles are not without significance but one cannot help but feel their sting has gone.

But I digress. When Louisiana came under American dominion in 1803 it included a great variety of new citizens, the majority French-speaking, but all apparently eager to gain identity and cut away from European traditions. The battle of New Orleans proved an excellent baptism. From that time on until the Civil War a gradual Americanization took place. The Confederacy failing, Louisiana was to be born again. This time the process included the customary "sackcloth and ashes." Reconstruction, slavery abolished, brought the individual white man into action as an entity. He, of course, has remade himself, and recently, when our latest American army assembled, looking down the line there seemed but one composite face. Gray veterans of previous wars would indeed have had a difficult job to pick out the grandson of Johnny Reb—Cajan, Creole, cowboy, cracker, Hoosier, and New Englander, all looked alike.

Louisiana today! One pauses and ponders, withal a bit ruefully, Louisiana today! "Mais où sont les neiges d'antan?" Master Villon's cry, sounding down the ages, bemouthed and hackneyed as it is, was not more pat in his application than it is to the subject in hand. Where are the leaves of yesteryear? Where are the Louisianians of the past? The buccaneers, pirates, filibusters, scented quadroons, gentlemen duelists, starched Creole ladies, lordly planters, sugar barons, and impeccable barristers—the odd fish, the aristocracy of pre-Civil War days? Where are the clubs, the cotillions, the liqueurs, the fine old customs and courtesies of the past? What has become of Madame Macarty and Dominique You; Maspero's Exchange and the Théâtre d'Orléans; the Baron and Baronesa de Pontalba; the Carondelets? Where are the haunts of Lafitte, Humbert, Pêpe Llula, Croghan the Sandusky hero, Lopez, Walker, Walt Whitman, and Lafcadio Hearn?

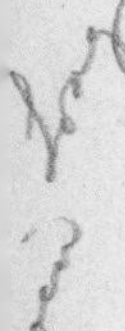

What remains? A deal. The life, the spirit, the essence of Louisiana, what are they but heritage of the past? Louisiana is a Catholic State and New Orleans is a Catholic city. When we say Catholic we mean none of your invading, upstart, alien populations. The Catholic church is part of Louisiana, bone of her bone, moss of her oaks. Bigotry, that so afflicts some of our Southern and perhaps some of our New England States, is little known here, unless perhaps in the extreme north where pioneer "red necks" from South and North Carolina, Tennessee, and Georgia came in to settle. In southern Louisiana and New Orleans there is little intolerance, but an intense spirit of rivalry between the Catholic and Protestant elements, the rivalry of each trying to outdistance the other in the social, economic, and educational race. This last accounts perhaps for the recent gratifying reduction in Louisiana's illiteracy. By Government census of 1910 she was rated the most illiterate State of the Union with 23.9 per cent of her population unable to read or write; but the census of 1920 shows a reduction of 7.1 per cent as against 1.7 for the whole country.

That Louisiana has produced little or nothing in the creative arts is a fact that can't be blinked. In poetry (quite amusingly) Adah Isaacs Menken—burlesque queen, "intimate" of Dickens, Swinburne, the elder Dumas, and Gautier; wife of Heenan the prize-fighter, "Orpheus C. Kerr" the humorist, and a brace of less noted husbands—despite her obvious extravagance and lack of technique, for sheer dramatic interest tops the list. The Menken legend is certainly the most delightful in the literary and theatrical history of the State. In music the older heads cry up L. M. Gottschalk—a composer of ante-bellum days. In fiction George W. Cable, who has treated of the Creole in satirical vein, is as yet unchallenged. The Cable novels certainly rank first in the old-guard fictional output of our State. Then we have Grace King, not so much novelist as raconteur, charming in her kind. And then Professor Brander Matthews! who according to a native "has forsworn his birthplace after acquiring honors at Columbia University and environs." Our historians are sturdier. To Charles Gayarré goes the crown. His "History of Louisiana" has almost attained to the distinction of a classic. The late Dr. Alcée Fortier ranks perhaps second, though François Xavier Martin is conceded the sounder student.

Still, in the creative arts Louisiana has produced little or nothing. True, Walt Whitman, Lafcadio Hearn, Eugene Field, Degas the painter, and others sojourned, found inspiration for and accomplished some of their finest work in New Orleans. Yet where is our poet? and where our painter? and where our novelist? excepting the early Cable. And this in one of the most inspirational atmospheres in America. Sherwood Anderson, writing in a Southern magazine, says: "I proclaim New Orleans from my own angle, from the angle of the Modern. Perhaps the city will not thank me, but anyway it is a truly beautiful city. Perhaps if I can bring more artists here they will turn out a rag-tag enough crew. Lafcadio Hearn wasn't such a desirable citizen while he lived in the 'Vieux Carré' . . . I am in New Orleans and I am trying to proclaim something I have found here that I think America wants and needs.

"There is something left in this people here that makes them like one another, that leads to constant outbursts of the spirit of play, that keeps them from being too confoundedly serious about death and the ballot and reform and other less important things in life."

The nomenclature of Louisiana, too, tells the story. The place names of New Orleans, the names of the parishes, rivers, bayous, towns, plantations, evince an imagination not perceptible in less Latin sections of the country. The old Spanish and French Creoles, men of sentiment and invention, named their thoroughfares and their mansions with the same feeling as they did their sons and daughters. Instance some of the place names of New Orleans—Elysian Fields Street, Madmen Street, the Rue des Bons Enfants, Mystery Street, Music Street, the Rue d'Amour, Virtue Street, Pleasure Street. There are streets named for the nine muses; for the great poets, musicians, philosophers;

oddly named streets such as Craps (which pastime, by the by, had its incipiency in New Orleans), Bagatelle, Tchoupitoulas, Prytania, Lotus, Ophir; streets after saints, battles, generals, heathen gods and goddesses —streets with *names* not numbers or commonplace associations!

And the nomenclature of the rivers and the beauty of these rivers—the dark glamour of the Tchefuncta, the misty languor of the Bogue Falaya, the Ouachita, the Atchafalaya, the Vermilion. . . . And the mysterious bayous—Goula, Lafourche, Teche, Barataria. . . . Here I pause. The uncanny remoteness, the quiet, the peace, the sort of primal witchery of this little "no man's water" just out of New Orleans stings the blood like Veuve Clicquot or malaria, as you will—poisons you into forgetfulness. And the parishes! (Not "county" as in all the other States.) Here are some: Acadia, Concordia, Tangipahoa, Avoyelles, Terrebonne, Lafourche, Calcasieu, Plaquemines, Rapides, Natchitoches, and many others as odd and sonorous.

Some years ago New Orleans earned for herself the metronym, "Paris of America." As Louisiana has been dubbed the Pelican State, the Armchair State (not out of tenor with the whilom proverbial lassitude of its people), the Boot State, et cetera; so New Orleans has been termed the Crescent City, the Pageant City, et cetera; but "Paris of America" sticks and will so long as American "liberty" and that child-like, festive, emotional temper of its citizenry permit. We are, those of us who are acclimatized, an emotional love-loving people. Though we are not by one-third or one-fourth of French descent, we have nevertheless subconsciously taken on habit and attitude of the Continental.

Thus New Orleans supported a legalized tenderloin long after the custom was taboo everywhere else. The restaurants, cafés, and cabarets of "befo' de war" (the recentest fracas, of course) exhibited an atmosphere distinctly un-American in every respect. Garçons were garçons and not waiters. The proprietor, Madame or M'sieu, cooked the meal. Politeness itself was smiled upon. Men grew tipsy in a perfunctory sort of a way that annoyed no one, not even themselves. An evening at the cabaret followed the burlesque show or the opera and the local cabaret lights sometimes seemed to outdo the imported performers. "Storyville," so named in honor of Councilman Story, who arranged the matter, bloomed, boomed, and wassailed. Even "the dollar women" smirking from their "cribs" seemed not unhappy—in the old days. Row upon row of them in bright-colored shifts ogling, leering, wheedling: "Come in, bébé . . . be a nice boy . . ." The larger "houses"—Arlington's Palace, Piazza's, Lulu's, and the rest—loomed disdainfully above these lesser fry. One pictured as he passed the great mirrored salons; the old "madam," white-haired, powdered, spotless (in the laundry allusion), the paint-smeared, puffy-eyed girls, and the "professor." Tom Anderson's at the one corner, Toro's at the next, the Tuxedo a block in, and so on—in the old days. A filthy mess perhaps, a dunghill of disease and immorality, but have we entirely done away with it? Driven it out? Can we? One wonders. Stamp it out in one place, it pushes up in another. Legislation is all very well and good, but legislation is—legislation.

What else? A state, viewed as the bird flies, very like any other State; fertile, well-tilled; combed with farms and factories; quick with gross, bustling, active humanity—typical one hundred per cent Americans, dulled by commerce and competition, deadened to romance and tradition, alive, apparently, but to covet and profit: hardy, stupid spawn, molelike, ferreting out existence. All of course according to one's slant. But what differentiates Louisiana, say, from Georgia? History, traditions, romance—the past.

Though Louisiana as a State today is very like any other State, New Orleans as a city today is very unlike any other city. For New Orleans, despite the recent ravages wrought by post-war propaganda, the Eighteenth Amendment, blue-sky laws, and modern office buildings, came through almost unscathed. Her identity, her individuality, her cap-and-bells quality seem as droll and native as ever. In fact, a sort of renaissance is now transpiring in her heart. The "old town" or French Quarter is being renovated, represerved to its former uniquity. Buildings toppling in ruins are being touched up much in the manner of Leonardo's "Last Supper" with sometimes, alas, like results. But the spirit remains, the old buoyant spirit of pristine times, and the Place d'Armes flanked by the Pontalba buildings, the Cabildo and Cathedral with its Presbytère, still remain to memorialize the Vieux Carré of the *ancien régime*.

Where in America will you find cheek by jowl examples of architecture that include the best traditions of the French Renaissance, the Spanish—Moorish and Colonial—as interpreted by a ship carpenter, and a pot-pourri of gaudy exotics, stemming from God knows what countries and eras? The rhythmic arts—music and the dance—have always had a home in this "Venice of the Gulf." The opera was here in 1796, before the birth of Chicago and San Francisco. And when New York had but a paltry two hundred thousand population, Nouvelle-Orléans was a sophisticated city with cabarets, coffee houses, bathing parties, dueling bouts, gallantry, and sportsmanship. The horse race, "two forty on the shell road," originated on the old driveway past Metairie to Lake Pontchartrain.

If present-day Louisiana has any claim to an individuality, a color, a note of her own, it is lodged unmistakably in this sport-loving, sun-loving, unquenchable spirit which was and is New Orleans. Mistress of chivalry, cuisine, and the dance; cosmopolis of legend, caprice, and motley; the Columbine of the cities —New Orleans!

IOWA

A MORTGAGED ELDORADO

By JOHAN J. SMERTENKO

IT is the boast of Iowans that one cannot cross the State's boundaries at any point without realizing that here is a land of plenty as different from its neighbors as the plains of Canaan from the fields of Gomorrah. Everywhere within these borders is fecundity, wealth, and solidity. The stranger is at first amazed and eventually bored by the unrelieved regularity of bumper crops, trim wire fences, pure-bred and well-fed live stock, huge barns and silos, smug and freshly painted homes. And if he is surprised at the country, he must indeed marvel at cities and towns which have no slums, no ramshackle outbuildings, and no decaying genteel quarters. Virtually the only signs of the poverty that one habitually associates with urban life are the red, superannuated freight cars which house the Mexican road-builders. Farm and factory, church and dwelling, school and library partake of the heavy, formidable air of prosperity which is Iowa.

Statistics—and Iowa "boosters" revel in statistics—bear out this impression of general well-being. According to the latest United States census report Iowa leads the nation in the value of her horses and hogs, of pure-bred live stock, of farm machinery and farm property per farm; she has the greatest number of poultry, of pure-bred hogs and cattle, of autos per capita—one to 5.5 persons—and of telephones on farms; she excels in the production of eggs, corn, and oats. Her road system, railroad facilities, her dairy products and packing industry are among the first in the country. She has coal, water-power, and lead mines, foundries and lumber mills; she produces enormous quantities of cereals and canned goods, cement and bricks. In short, Iowa is self-sufficient in most of the necessaries of life and is creditor of all other States in many of them.

Still, today the farmer groans. When he is articulate, he reviles the railroads, the bankers, the commission merchants, and all the other agents that stand between him and the consumer. He seems to be the only Iowan who is not convinced by statistics. In his nightmares the corpulent cow which is Iowa to the passengers of the through train looks as lean as the kine of Pharaoh. And at the end of each year he experiences a mirage: his fields, his farm, his crops, and his cattle fade to a blank page on the credit side of the ledger. His computations lead him into blind alleys and his remedial legislation does not remedy. Then he curses again his pet enemies and also the land which is a deception to the eye, even as the fair body that hides a cancer.

But this contradiction is a recent experience. Twenty years ago it was unknown and before that inconceivable. The first settlers found a land which waited but the turn of a plow to uncover its golden riches. Their reports of the "strike" sped eastward, and soon the farmers who had used up the shallow soil of New

England, the pioneers of the Middle Atlantic States who had found the cheap lands of the Northwest Territory equally unproductive, and the poor whites who had been forced out of the South by slave labor fell like locusts upon the virgin prairie, clean and level as a playful ocean and just as inexhaustible. Thus for thirty years after the first permanent settlement all roads west seemed to lead to Iowa. From the mountains of Kentucky and Tennessee, from the forests of Michigan, from the clay of Virginia and the sands of Ohio, from the mines of Pennsylvania, the orchards of New York, and the coast of New England came the seekers of a farmer's Eldorado. At the end of this period, 1870, Iowa's 1,194,752 inhabitants exceeded the population of Michigan, which had been settled 150 years before. The numbers of burrowers in black loam had doubled, trebled, or quadrupled within each decade.

There are certain features of this million which cannot be overlooked by those who would know contemporary Iowa. Chief of these is the fact that no Northern State has ever had so great a proportion of original settlers from the South. Though there is a general impression that New Englanders settled Iowa, the earliest census shows that there were as many immigrants from Tennessee as from all of New England; there were more from Virginia than from Tennessee, and more Kentuckians than Virginians. Even as late as 1850 the Iowans from Southern States outnumbered the immigrants from New England almost six to one. By 1860 the influx of Yankees had changed this proportion to a little more than two to one in favor of the South but the Southerners still held most of the political offices, dominated State and local legislation, threw the State's sympathy to pro-slavery views, and generally fought all "Yankee notions and for'ard movements." And during the Civil War they were strong enough to attack companies of Northern soldiers training in the State. How much they contributed to the making of Iowa is a mooted question of doubtful importance. Both important and certain, however, is the fact that the Iowan of today is in the fullest sense an American; in his veins is mingled the blood of practically every Colonial. On the other hand, there is probably less foreign blood in the Iowan than in any other native of the Middle West. Few States in America have been settled with as small a percentage of foreign-born. For so uniformly rich was the soil that nothing remained here for the land-starved European who in other Middle Western States was permitted to take the leavings of the natives.

And finally, it is vital to record that the settlers were of a definite and uniform character. Though the three streams of our westward movement conjoined in this State, the ambitious, the adventurous, and the lawless elements passed on. By virtue of her protected frontiers and peaceful Indian settlement, her monotonous and heavy tasks, her stable and rising wealth, Iowa appealed more than any other State to the cautious, prosaic, industrious, and mediocre. Here, at last, is the synthesis of an American agrarian type like the yeomanry of England and the peasantry of Russia. Here, too, is the answer to that rebellious song,

When Adam delved and Eve span,
Who was then the gentleman?

For cultural tradition and leisure are necessary to the making of gentlemen. The first Iowans do not possess; neither can they develop it, inasmuch as the second is contrary to all their standards of right living. He who has met the pathetic, puttering creatures known as retired Iowa farmers, or retired Iowa anything, with their tool sheds and truck gardens, their bees and their Fords, their uncompleted real-estate deals and their worthless auction bargains, will thereafter find cosmic disturbance in the flutter of a leaf and universal significance in the movements of an ant. Yet this is all the leisure they know in "Ioway," and even this is reserved by public opinion for those who are on the grayer side of sixty.

The result has been justly called a dull, gray monotone. With the exceptions of a thinly disguised immorality and a spiritless church affiliation, rural Iowa —more than a million souls—has no interests beyond bread and butter. The movie and the pool room, the church social and the high-school entertainment are the amusements of town life. And the sophisticated city has its stock-company comedies, its lodges, its card parties, and its dances. There is really no community life in the State—neither folk-gatherings by the lowly nor common enterprises by the élite. And no one has been able to rouse this people to a participation in any creative expression of the commonwealth.

"But," cries the indignant Iowan, "look at some statistics. Man alive, just examine a few unbiased census reports! We have 'the highest percentage of literacy, 98.9, of any State in the Union or of any equal area in the world.' We have more schools, urban, rural, and consolidated, and a better school attendance than most anybody. We have libraries and museums that can accommodate thousands more people than use them. There are women's clubs that study lite'ture, poetry, music, and furniture, and all that sort of stuff. We get lectures and concerts and readings galore. We're among the first in city planning, in State music contests, and in community dramatics. And there's no State west of the Mississippi that can show more culture than we've got—that's a fact!"

All of which is perfectly true. And so, out of their own mouths are they confounded. They confuse literacy with education — witness their extensive primary-school system and their privately endowed, undernourished, and mendicant academies styled colleges. They mistake the social activities of a few liberated housewives for the cultural expression of a people—thus they visualize art as a half-dozen much-mispronounced, expensive, and authenticated masters; they understand poetry in terms of syndicated "people's bards" and leather-bound sets of undying and uncomprehended "classics"; they make the acquaintance of music in an annual enthusiastic meeting with an operatic banality. Their best theater is a child of the drama league of Chicago; their folk-songs are creations of Broadway; their epic theme is a misguided cyclone.

Descendants of New England stock, proudly conscious of what is expected from their heritage, are frankly perturbed about this condition. They plead the State's youth and they blame the South. "What can be expected of a State that has barely outlived her first hodge-podge and irrelevant laws, that is still unmindful of the work of her historical society?" they ask. Again they say: "The preponderance of Southerners in our early days formed the deadweight which still holds Iowa's eagle close to the ground." The South — autocratic county management which supplanted the intimate, democratic township system of New England; implacable opposition to the growth of governmental power through the fear of taxation and of encroachments on personal liberty; vigorous resistance to education at public expense, which is still reflected in the dearth of significant institutions of collegiate rank; and, above all, impenetrable indifference toward civic and social questions, which has been a most effective barrier to progressive legislation—the South, then, and all the backwardness that the word connotes is held responsible for the Iowaness of Iowa. And undoubtedly a good deal of energy has been wasted in combating Southern lethargy which might have been used in furthering New England ideals. But we need not look farther than Kansas to see what Iowa might have been with less dominant Southern influences—instead of the mulct law, outright prohibition; instead of a hopeless, languorous sanity, a militant puritanism.

Despite their comfort in flattering figures the Iowans manifest an unmistakable inferiority complex. Their jealous watch on the "Who's Who" for a proper representation of State celebrities, their far-fetched and persistent claims on the nation's great ones in the fields of art and literature, politics and finance, their furtive emulation of other States in publicity-giving enterprises, good, bad, or indifferent, are obvious signs. During the war it was this sense of inferiority rather than praiseworthy zeal which was responsible for an unabashed and militant system of extortion in Liberty Loan drives. At the head of this violent effort for glory was, appropriately enough, the father of Hanford MacNider, the American Legion commander who has so violently demanded a bonus.

* * * * *

It is a curious coincidence that the fleeting observation-car impressions of the traveler and an equally superficial perusal of statistics should lead to the same conclusions. And thus Iowa's well-being is in danger of becoming a truism. Not one in a thousand sees that the goodly apple is rotten at the heart or suspects that Iowa's troubles are caused by something other than periods of national depression. As elsewhere, there is constant talk of a greater prosperity toward which Iowa is supposed to be moving as inevitably as the Mississippi flows to the Gulf. In their slight knowledge of both, the orators of popular causes are fond of comparing the river and the State. They seem equally placid, equally slow-moving, equally intent on one direction.

There is an analogy, to be sure, but a totally different one. For he who has plunged beneath the surface of the river knows there are countless currents, springs, and whirlpools that pull upstream and to either side in obedience to hidden forces which can stem even the downward flow of waters. So it is with Iowa. There is the old, broad current pulling to the West, depositing its rich burden of superannuated farmers at "Loss Anjelees." There is the phenomenon of former feed-ers now either dry or drawing sustenance from the main stream—pioneer trails, again peopled, but the people headed in opposite directions. There is a boisterous rapid in the *Iowa Homestead,* an agricultural weekly which is the source of liberal power in the State. There is a cool, clear spring, the Des Moines *Register,* one of the most honest, thoughtful, and fearless dailies in the country. There is a Pierian spring at Grinnell whither flock the thirsty after knowledge. There is the vicious, seething whirlpool of a Greater Iowa Association that every so often sucks down some weak or foolish victim. And there are fine, deep, quiet backwaters—these peaceful colonies of Quakers at Oskaloosa, of Hollanders at Pella, and of religious communists at Amana.

All this is to be seen in the stream of Iowa life. And close observation discloses more—discloses that the seven times seven years of plenty are past, and that the lean years have come upon the land. We see that one of the purest landholding communities in the world has been transformed during the past thirty years into as bad a tenant-farmer State as any north of the Mason and Dixon line. Even the statistics that are so dear to the Iowan heart support this view, though one must glance beneath the surface of census columns.

The first signs of this momentous change are evident in a study of population. In the decade of the sixties Iowa's numbers increased 96.9 per cent while the whole of the United States showed a growth of 26.6

per cent. During the following decade the State's population rose 36 per cent as against 26 gained by the nation. By 1880, however, the peak of Iowa's growth had been reached. Her most desirable land was taken up. She no longer showered welcomes on the immigrant. In the next ten years her numbers mounted 17 per cent; the country at large increased 25.5 per cent. And thereafter Iowa falls farther and farther behind the national expansion, until, in 1910, a period of unparalleled prosperity in the State, there is an absolute as well as a relative decline in population, a loss of 0.3 per cent. In the last decade there has been a gain but still 6.8 per cent below the national average.

Again, as early as 1890, began the exodus of enriched farmers to southern California. (Few have realized the extent of this migration; some idea may be obtained from the fact that at the annual picnic in 1920 more than 40,000 Iowans gathered at Los Angeles.) In the main, these farmers sold their land before leaving, but on terms which eventually proved worse for the buyer than any form of rental. It is then that Iowa achieved the distinction of having the most valuable farm land in the country—a reputation which did much to bring about a greater increase in land values than that of any other State. Speculation, with its consequent overvaluation, was inevitable, and the ridiculous prices of three, four, and five hundred dollars per acre were paid in the feverish anxiety to plant a stake in this Eldorado. The pioneers or their descendants, on the other hand, could not resist the temptation of selling. They found a hysterical mob of bidders who were convinced that Iowa land would be worth any price they chose to set on it and who were incapable of realizing at the moment that even the richest soil has a definite limit of production. The land was sold. Then came the reckoning.

Now this land-boom phenomenon has been recurrent. The last, started by the war and ended by the recent industrial depression, was the most intense, the most vivid, and the farthest-reaching in its results. The reckoning came quicker and is therefore more apparent. When the process of deflation set in, it was found that a majority of the transactions were "paper sales," bought with a minimum of cash payment and a maximum of mortgage, the interest on which—much less the principal—could never be gleaned from the land. By and large, the sellers were content, for this interest was greater than any income obtainable from rentals; but the purchasers quickly came to realize that they had become debtors in perpetuity.

What wonder that they grin sardonically today when the Iowa Chamber of Commerce proudly publishes the fact that there are 124,375 farm owners on the two hundred thousand odd farms in the State! The figures are meaningless; true to the records, yet false to the actual conditions. But these very figures, taken in sufficient detail, further reveal the situation. They show that the two counties which have the highest percentage of farm owners stand fifth and sixth from the bottom in a table of land values, whereas O'Brien and Lyon, which have the greatest percentage of tenants, rank twelfth and thirteenth among the ninety-six counties in the value of their farm lands.

This corroborates the suspicion that only the poorer soil is tilled by the so-called owners; the more expensive farms are rapidly reverting to the original possessors and are being worked by tenant labor. Thus mortgaged owner and broken tenant sweat to pay the increased bills of Iowans in southern California.

Important as this is in the life of Iowa, it gains still greater significance as a presage of national development. With the exploitation of our virgin resources goes the loss of individual independence and the growth of economic slavery. Elsewhere this exploitation has meant stripping of forests, impoverishing of soil, exhausting of mines, and draining of oil wells. In Iowa it is summed up in the one word mortgage. Her resources are almost intact but the fruit of that land and the labor of her people are eaten by strangers.

"Go West, young man, go West," said Horace Greeley to a poor theological student. And the young man settled in Iowa, founded a town, helped build a college, and accumulated a modest fortune. Today if he made his way there, he could not supply the pettiest pulpit at starvation wages. Today it is more likely that the Iowa farmer's son will seek a church or shop or field in the East or farther West in an effort to pay off the mortgage, to stave off the day when another "owner" must turn tenant. Perhaps a dramatist will one day portray the tragedy of this act, the poignant sorrow of those who relinquish this yellow slip of paper, empty symbol of ownership, and return to till the soil on shares.

This tragedy is being enacted everywhere in the State. The attempts to forestall it are now political history—a history of transformation. Standpatter Senator Kenyon turned leader of the agricultural bloc and passed measures of relief that shocked the "interests." The boss-ridden Republican Party of the State turned out its regular candidates and elected in Kenyon's place Colonel Smith W. Brookhart, friend of the *Iowa Homestead* and avowed liberal, who is characteristically described by the small-town press—and not a few of the "college" presidents—as a "socialistic and anarchistic Bolshevik." The people turned a deaf ear to the radical-baiting of the Greater Iowa Association, and flocked to the meetings of the Nonpartisan League which a few years ago was unable to gain a foothold in the State. Local measures passed recently are in harmony with the new spirit, and students in college economics classes no longer vote unanimously to have Marx's "Communist Manifesto" barred from the shelves of the public libraries. Everyone demands reforms. Reactionary Iowa is insisting on measures as drastic as the Interstate Commerce Commission which its Senators brought into being during an earlier crisis.

Lest those who think that radicalism and idealism go hand in hand should grow unduly optimistic about the "soul of Iowa," let me state at once that there is no spiritual background, no generous purpose in this reform movement. The appeal to black, or rather, red magic for relief is hardly an omen of better days. Never was Ellis Parker Butler's motto for his State,

Three millions yearly for manure,
But not one cent for literature,

more pat. Seldom has a people been less interested in spiritual self-expression and more concerned with hog nutrition.

Nevertheless, neither the increased materialism, nor the astonishing new-found radicalism, nor the bounty of nature can avail much in the present situation. The luxuriant Iowa scene will remain as little changed, as deceptive as ever, but the aspect of the future is bleak indeed. What might have been a landed gentry must now become a burdened peasantry. Another land flowing with milk and honey must now feel the yoke of iron. Another set of prophets must sound lamentations. Perhaps a new spiritual life lies in this bleakness; perhaps the Mississippi will find its folk-songs more kin to the minors of the Volga than to the empty clangor of Broadway. Perhaps the farmer of Iowa will be first to follow the peasant of Russia in freeing his land from the yoke. Is not his sentential motto: "Our liberties we prize and our rights we will maintain"?

MASSACHUSETTS

A ROMAN CONQUEST

By JOHN MACY

IT was at Commencement in Cambridge, more than twenty years ago. A multitude of us loyal alumni was lifting its voice in "Fair Harvard." Beside me stood a handsome young man in the garb of a priest, whose clear Irish baritone struck pleasantly upon my ear through the mass of noise.

Till the stock of the Puritans die.

My neighbor was psalming with unconscious heartiness and representing in his own comely person a new era in the oldest intellectual stronghold of the old Bay State. The Puritan was beginning to die. He is not dead yet in Massachusetts and he survives vigorously in the new New England, the Western States. But a generation ago he was losing grip and his hymn was coming true in a way that the author had not intended nor foreseen. A boy with an Irish name was captain of the football team. There had been scandalous and rebellious talk about the hold of boys from Back Bay families and saintly schools upon the crew and the baseball team. At about this time Dr. Eliot, then president of fair Harvard, observed, in one of his frequent shrewd moments, that Massachusetts is a Roman Catholic commonwealth. The stock of our forefathers was visibly losing power. It was losing in religion, in politics, in education, in business.

I hold no brief for any race, creed, party, or other condition of servitude, but merely note facts, especially changes and developments. When Dr. Eliot observed that the codfish commonwealth is dominantly Roman Catholic, he made the observation, we may be sure, with a bland freedom from prejudice. The fact is there. Let us consider it. The most potent clergyman in Massachusetts is William Cardinal O'Connell. But there is no sign of a successor to Edward Everett Hale or Phillips Brooks. Add together the "orthodox" Congregational churches, which are the traditional godly center of all Massachusetts towns, the right and left wings of the Episcopalians, housed in The Advent and Phillips Brooks's Trinity, the Unitarians of old King's Chapel, where once worshiped the intellectual aristocracy of Boston, and all the other Protestant, nonconformist sects, such as Methodists, Baptists, and the rest. The Catholic Cathedral dwarfs them all—that is, as a spiritual institution. I once heard a member of the Clover Club, composed of Irish Roman Catholics, many of them brilliant and delightful, and probably prolific, say that the time was near when a Baptist parade would be impossible in the streets of Boston, partly on account of lack of material and partly on account of interference. The Clover Club thrives. The Papyrus Club is dead. And the Saturday Club of the elder New England wits and poets died so long ago that one has to think of it in terms not of decades but of generations. If it existed today there would not be anybody to belong to it.

Roman Catholic does not mean Irish, in Massachusetts or anywhere else, even in Ireland. But if the two terms do not register exactly, if in Boston and the surrounding mill cities is a large population of Italians, Canadian-French, Portuguese, Poles, who are spiritually subject to the Celtic-American cardinal, nevertheless Irish and Catholic are roughly synonymous in the Bay State. And non-Roman Catholic does not, in an age of slackening interest in religion and of wavering demarcations of faith, mean either Puritan stock or any one brand of nonconformity. The Protestant forces are scattered, lukewarm, and blurred. Consider that the First Church of Christ Scientist is about halfway between Brimstone Corner and the Harvard Medical School. If you want to start a sect, start it in Massachusetts. Other States will take it up later. Any dark-skinned individual with straight hair can initiate a new creed in the Back Bay with no other equipment than the dermatological—with pleasure for all concerned and profit to himself. But alone among all diverse groups Irish Catholicism marches triumphantly on.

Politically Massachusetts still plays an important part among her forty-seven sisters, and she has acute private troubles. Nothing can be proved but much can be suggested by contemplating three of her sons who represent her wisdom in the national government. We shall not argue about the party politics of any of them but shall view them as expressions and examples of interesting social conditions. First there is the senior Senator. Mr. Lodge is an aristocrat by birth and training. Perhaps he has never had a great thought. Without question he is neither a Sumner nor a Hoar, but at least he has not for fifty years written or spoken a bad sentence. If he had not given up to politics what was meant for mankind he might have been a distinguished historian and writer of essays. His introduction to the autobiographical "Education" of Henry Adams is a neat bit of writing, worthy of Adams himself. He carries on the traditions of a State which in times past has sent men of letters to all the capital cities of the world, including Washington.

The junior Senator is David Ignatius Walsh, a graduate not of Mr. Lodge's fair Harvard but of Holy Cross, a member not of the Massachusetts Historical Society but of the Irish Historical Society of America. He was a small-town lawyer and seems to have no literary ambitions. For two years he was Governor of the State. He does not belong to the Boston political rings, and his public life has been clean. However that may be, it is safe to predict that he will be succeeded by many of his own race and kind. There will be no more Lodges. That breed is passing.

Above these two learned gentlemen from Massachusetts sits Calvin Coolidge, Vice-President of the United States, Calvin Coolidge of Northampton, born in Vermont and not, distinctly not, of the Boston Coolidges. They are on the boards of directors of great trust companies. The highest fiduciary position attained by Mr. Coolidge was that of president of the Nonatuck Savings Bank of Northampton. How he got to be Governor of the State and Vice-President of these United States is one of the inexplicable jokes of politics. The three men, the two Senators and the

Vice-President, may be easily placed. Mr. Lodge is the aristocrat, well bred, well educated, with literary talent. Mr. Walsh is the successful small-town Irish lawyer, inclined to progressive ideas, not brilliant but with sufficient command of words not to make a fool of himself, inherently a democrat, and growing with his public experience. Mr. Coolidge is the yokel, neither of the blue-blooded aristocracy nor of the red-blooded invasion. He neither represents staid tradition nor brings insurgent progress. I have lived among New England farmers and I have read or heard many specimens of what is supposed to be the Yankee manner of speech from Hosea Biglow to "The Old Homestead" and "Shore Acres." Mr. Coolidge's diction outdoes caricature and parody but has no trace of the shrewd humor of the soil. It must grate on Mr. Lodge's exquisite Boston ear.

There are two men in the political-legal life of the nation of whom the more enlightened citizens of Massachusetts may be proud. How often you find in the dissenting minority of the United States Supreme Court Justices Holmes and Brandeis! Were ever two men of such different origins and traditions linked in the interests of liberalism and humane interpretations of law? The one is an aristocrat with blood as blue as the bluest vein in the fine hand of the senior Senator (it was, I think, Judge Holmes's father who first applied the term "Brahmin" to the Boston swell); and the other is a Jew, whose appointment to the Supreme Court made members of clubs writhe in their leather chairs, not because he is a Jew—he had been accepted socially—but because he had dared to attack State

Street and the New York, New Haven & Hartford Railroad. These two men are almost always together on the same side, the minority, the beaten, the right side. And both are citizens of a State which is assumed to be the heart of conservatism, of reaction, of the safe and sane. There is matter for reflection in this pair of colleagues. They are in a sense the living survivals of the best New England tradition, of independence, of intellectual courage, of *noblesse oblige* applied to public service—an indication in their disparate origins that the blood-stream is not the channel through which the faith is perpetuated.

The legal profession of Massachusetts has always had a reputation for wisdom and integrity. I once heard a Boston judge say that the decisions of the Massachusetts courts carry weight in England as compared with the decisions of the courts of other States or even of the United States courts, and I think he quoted Pollock as his authority. I am not sure. I merely noted the judge's remark as showing the pride which exists in Massachusetts, and probably in all Atlantic States, in having the approval of Englishmen, and also as showing the great respect, no doubt deserved, in which judges and lawyers are held.

Not long ago the legal profession of Massachusetts, or rather a small part of it, was under fire. Long-standing and well-intrenched corruption in the district attorney's office in Suffolk County, and an infection therefrom in the neighboring Middlesex, was at last brought to the bar of judgment. An elaborate system of extortion and blackmail was revealed and the offending district attorneys were removed from office and disbarred. Now this state of affairs had long been current and generally known in the State. But inextricably bound up in it were the threads of religious and racial antagonism and prejudices. The central figure, the district attorney of Suffolk County, was the "Supreme Advocate" of the Knights of Columbus and hence probably the most conspicuous Catholic layman in the State. This had played no small part in the immunity generally credited to him and his ring. His safety was axiomatic in the whispering galleries of non-Catholic Massachusetts. That he was found guilty by a unanimous Supreme Court of which two members were of his own faith calls for no encomiums, but merely a solid satisfaction that the prophets of peril were again proved wrong. On the other hand the conviction was apotheosized into a religious martyrdom by a group of his friends and a very considerable Catholic following—despite the two Catholic judges, his replacement as district attorney by another Knight, and the Protestantism of his fellow-malefactor in Cambridge. The Catholic following was sufficiently strong to secure for Pelletier the Democratic nomination for the office of district attorney from which he had been removed; and the Democratic nominee for Senator, Mr. W. A. Gaston, a former president of Boston's leading bank, did not repudiate his fellow-candidate. But the voters in this overwhelmingly Democratic district did and so ended a nauseating episode.

The tinder-box is ready for the irresponsible match-thrower. The burning of a convent in the fifties is still street-corner campaign material. The use of public funds for parochial schools is a constantly recurring issue. That they have not been voted in 80 to 90 per cent Catholic Boston would indicate that this religious group is not more than any other politically a unit, nor, as is charged, clay in the hands of its hierarchy. Of course State support may come and will, if the resident "Prince of the Church" has his way. The political cleavage is, generally speaking, along religious lines. Protestant Democrats are for the most part isolated iconoclasts, individualist dissenters, whose part in the State's party politics is wholly disproportionate to their numbers. Social cleavage is even more marked though it is diminishing. But there are still many business firms which exclude typists and office boys because they are Catholic, and owners of estates to whom their gardener's faith is more important than his work. This is of course resented by the Catholics, whose most effective response is their steady increase.

The signs of this increase are obvious in the daily press, which in no other metropolitan city so extensively chronicles the four-corners gossip and the personal item. The County Kerry Associates are holding their annual ball—with the Mayor, or perchance even the Governor, leading the grand march. The St. Joseph's or Sacred Heart parishes are busy with their whist or other entertainment. The Cardinal has dedicated a new church or chapel with Celtic monsignori in attendance, filling specialized sacerdotal and, to the native, exotic-sounding functions. The Irish are everywhere. "Take for granted in talking with anyone that he is a Catholic unless you definitely know the contrary" was the advice given by a Boston newspaper editor to one of his reporters. Boston is filled today with O'Brien and Fitzgerald and Murphy "Squares" named after the boys who fell overseas—and the square which once bore the name of Edgar Allan Poe now bears the name of Matthew Emmet Ryan. And many communities, like South Boston or Dorchester, the summer resorts around Nantasket, or Brant Rock further south, are as homogeneous as the villages of Tipperary. If they are more slovenly they are perhaps more joyous than the habitats of the inbred Bakers and Davises on the Cape, of the Litchfields and Turners of Plymouth County, of the Lanes and Pooles of Cape Ann. If these more recent Americans sometimes mistakenly and stupidly abuse their new-found strength in applying their Index Expurgatorius code to debar from public libraries works on the Spanish Inquisition or the novels of Zola theirs is but a slight transformation of Puritan zealotry. When the trustees of the public library of Brookline, stronghold of the elder respectability, exclude Professor Chafee's scholarly "Freedom of Speech" on the ground of "radicalism," what consistent grounds of protest against newer forms of obscurantism remain for these suppressors?

I have referred to the Boston newspapers, which deserve one more word. In the scandal involving District Attorney Pelletier and others the editors began unctuously rubbing their editorial palms and congratulating Boston and the commonwealth on the housecleaning—after it was all over. For years every cub reporter had known that all was not well, and many of them with the crusading enthusiasm of youth and decency burned to bring out the facts. Boston editors, if they stay Boston editors, are not made that way. At least not since the days of the late Edward Hazen Clement, who despite restrictions and his inhibitory environment gave the *Transcript* much of the quality which made it the best-known Boston newspaper in the country at large. The rest of the press, unless we except the *Monitor*, which is national rather than local, exhibits the dress and cultivation of a boom mining-town. Of it no less an expert than Jason Rogers, publisher of the New York *Globe*, says in his book "Newspaper Building":

I don't recollect whether the *Post* is responsible for leading nearly all the other Boston newspapers into big black type on the front pages and the playing up of really trifling items beyond news of world-wide interest or not, but I think so. . . . The fact that some small preacher in Lynn slipped from the strait and narrow path is bigger news from the Boston newspaper standpoint than almost any ordinary first-page news in other newspapers throughout the country. Likewise the Boston papers of large circulation follow the erring village pastor and erring mill-worker clear up into Maine or New Hampshire. On the surface of things it would seem that there was a fine opportunity for a first-class, honest-to-God morning newspaper in Boston. . . .

There is such a fine opportunity for real newspapers in Boston, but there will not be one if we concede the truth of Chester S. Lord's dictum that a newspaper cannot be greater than its editor. A newspaper need not be a moral crusader, and its chief business may not be to reform a naughty world, but, in the face of long-continued social blood poisoning those papers did nothing, did not even call for the facts. It was the Attorney General, assisted by respectable and indignant members of the bar, who took the lid off the unsavory Pelletier mess. But no newspapers in America—and the standard is not high anywhere—do less than those of Boston to encourage common, ordinary decency in public affairs. They start nothing, but live in timid subserviency not only to the greater economic and denominational powers but to the pettiest wire-pullers, to the cheapest advertising bullies. The editor of the *Herald,* which pretends to be the organ of the cultured—in the jargon, "the quality medium"—once remarked that the modern newspaper was essentially an advertisers' broadside, and its editors were merely hired to fill in the chinks between the advertisements. But even under this conception which dominates Boston journalism the possibility for improving the filling is immeasurable. To find a paper which tries, or in times past tried, to work for the good of its local community, the State, the nation, and the universe, one has to go to Springfield, the home of the *Republican,* an individual and beautiful community, notably free from political scandal, with a fine and justified civic pride.

This suggests that Boston is not the whole of Massachusetts. It is both more than the State and less. It is more than the State because it is the business capital of all New England and it is a national financial center second only to New York and equal to Philadelphia and Chicago. It is the citadel of "protection" and privilege. In the capitalization of the West, the building of railroads, the exploitation of mines, the developing of the textile industries, Boston money was, and is, potent. Boston has no Rockefeller, no Carnegie. But the aggregate wealth in the stockings both of old families and of modern upstarts is tremendous. Nor should we omit mention here of the considerable and fruitful profession of trusteeship—the handling of the estates of defunct industrial pioneers—which nowhere has been more firmly established. That the third and fourth generations are frequently unable to take care of the copper deposits, paper or spinning mills developed by their energetic forbears; that they ride the hounds, or live abroad, or sometimes form innocuous connections with the bond houses, indicates that the older stock has not merely been driven out by more fecund newcomers. The old race has of itself been petering, and not a few of its occasional atavistic scions sensing its atmosphere of dry-rot have of late gone elsewhere to seek fortunes founded on their own abilities. Even the children and grandchildren of the recent Abolitionists have faded into complaisant and insignificant conformism. That last and greatest chapter of the contribution of Massachusetts to America has melted into past history. The Union Club still has the tradition of its founding—otherwise it is scarcely distinguishable from the slightly more effete Somerset. Uninspired and static—that is Boston today. Who can adduce tangible or visible evidence to the contrary?

Boston is less than the State because the smaller cities and towns, especially those of the western part of the State, have a character or characters of their own. The eastern cities are Boston, even though they preserve their municipal entities. The region from Lowell to Fall River may be considered as a vast industrial city, interspersed with lovely bits of country, which are rapidly becoming a vast suburban garden. To the west there is something different. The difference may be slight and I do not know how to express it. There is all too little difference between small American cities. But as William James's friend the farmer said: "There's mighty little difference between one man and another, but what little there is, is mighty important." If you consider that Massachusetts is so small that measured on the map it would look like a mere county of a Western State, and that in an age of communication the distinctions between neighboring communities are being obliterated and State lines are artificial, then you will expect to find the diversities between the eastern and western portions of the little commonwealth faint and hard to define. Yet they are mighty important, if you can capture them. I think of Massachusetts as jammed in between her neighbors, separating them and sharing their natures. Lowell and Lawrence, although near Boston, are like New Hampshire's industrial cities, like Nashua on the same Merrimac. Brockton, Fall River, and New Bedford resemble Pawtucket and Woonsocket in Rhode Island. If I suggest that Pittsfield is like up-State New York, it is not wholly because the General Electric Company has also a plant in Schenectady. It has one in Lynn. Yet Pittsfield is liker to what lies across the line than she is to her sister who lives on the Atlantic coast. Is it not said in this community, where county pride exceeds State pride, regional affection, and patriotism, that "the best thing about Berkshire County is the chain of mountains to the east which shuts it off from the rest of the State"?

Perhaps we put too much emphasis on cities. But Massachusetts is, for America, thickly populated, and the passage from town to town by train or motor is almost imperceptible. The rural life is changing, it is changing character and changing hands. It is changing character because the old village is becoming a small manufacturing town or suburb of a manufacturing town, and the smoke of the mill blows over the fields. I have known many old Yankee farmers but few young ones. Those who turn the sod now and make market gardens in the east and tobacco fields in the Connecticut Valley are foreigners who know how to work and make things grow. The native has not been entirely supplanted, but the tendency is that way. The Yankee farmer is disappearing in Massachusetts, going into business—or getting to be Vice-President of the United States. The most beautiful farms are the playthings of gentlemen who live in Massachusetts or who come to Massachusetts in summer. And Tony or François does the work.

In the villages and small towns you see a State road, sometimes in need of repair but usually good. It runs past a pretty common. Facing the common are stores, bank, church, movie theater, and a few old houses, some of which are run down, some of which have been spruced up by new owners or by heirs who live somewhere else but take a pride in the old place; in some of them the heirs, as pathetic as Hawthorne's Hepzibah, are trying to make a living by a tea-room where tourists are fed nothing for a big price. A factory district. A splendid estate, either the old house made over or a new, not altogether successful Italian villa. One of the stores is still owned by Ezra Chapin, who has been town clerk for thirty years, but he is being put out of business by the Greek or Italian grocer on the other corner. The post office is dingy, the church is good, thanks to Wren and a defunct race of carpenters who built both churches and ships, the "libery" is not offensive, the soldiers' monument is a fright, the trees on the trim common are gorgeous unless the beetles or the moths have completely routed the local tree warden and the State commission.

And so to the next town, which is much the same. But it is not always the same. There is diversity within the compass of this tiny commonwealth. If you happen to have been under the delusion that Boston is Massachusetts and that Harvard and Bunker Hill are intellectual and historical Boston, you may be disabused of that idea at odd turns of the road; by the thrill that follows one's glimpse of the gentle dignity and beauty of Williamstown and its college; of Greenfield, of Leicester, of old Salem, of Sudbury, or the quaint charm of Deerfield, of Ipswich, of Marblehead, of Duxbury, of Provincetown, of Newburyport. None of us knew until recently, because it is a recent structure, the beauty of that excellent building which Boston College has erected on the hill overlooking the city. The State is full of learning, at least of visible signs of the effort to learn, Amherst, Williams, Tufts, Wellesley, Smith, Clark, Holy Cross, Boston College, Boston

University, Technology, Mt. Holyoke, Wheaton, and others. No State has more conspicuous educational institutions. And every small town provides in its own high school, or by arrangement with a neighboring town, free instruction in preparation for any college. Colleges and college education as they are today need not be taken too seriously, but I insist on the number and variety of the colleges in Massachusetts, because while the other States were developing their own institutions, perhaps greater and better, they always looked to Massachusetts for education, common and preferred.

Then, with all this equipment, is Massachusetts intellectually decadent? In some ways she is, but decadent from the standards which her own people set. Boston is, as Mr. Herford said, the abandoned farm of literature. But not in literature alone. In all the arts, in all intellectual matters Boston, once the Athens of America, is stagnant, moribund. The *Atlantic Monthly* is the sole heritage of the vanished Pericleans.

One reason is that young people of talent follow a tendency, already cited, which is both social and commercial, to move to New York, much as Englishmen seek London and Frenchmen seek Paris. The migration does not greatly matter, for it makes little difference where a man of talent lives. And it seems that the intellectual life of Massachusetts is not quite exhausted by departing sons and the declining vigor of the native stock. For note this, making due allowance for the fact that there is immigration as well as emigration and for the general fallibility of statistics: in the Geographical Index of the latest "Who's Who"

New York occupies twenty-seven pages, Massachusetts is second with ten, Pennsylvania and Illinois are third with eight each. And the rest are also-rans. If I have seemed a bit severe at times with the Massachusetts that I have known and loved a generation, it is, I repeat, in relation to values of her own erecting, to ideals of her own creation, to the visions and hopes and aspirations she herself has inspired. It is not by the standards of Mississippi or Arkansas that one judges Massachusetts. Come back to her from afar and there is a clean orderliness, a wholesome stability, a familiarity with the coinage of culture—in short, a civilization, which is as a high plateau to Middle Western flats and Dixie swamps.

The intellect of a community is its great interest, its human value. But God, the God of the Puritans, was active long before the Puritans, or the Indians, or the Irish, or the Italians. He happened to lay out, not as a commonwealth but as a landscape, one of the loveliest corners of His footstool in the small strip of land which is now by man called Massachusetts—the North Shore with its rocks, the South Shore with its sand, the Berkshires on the west, the Connecticut Valley, and all the tumbling hills and gentle smiling little corners in between. It is not so rugged and vivid as the more mountainous and still wild States to the north. Connecticut is a bit softer. The Bay State, most of which is not on the bay, lies between, the heart of New England. God made it so, and man has not yet unmade it.

ALABAMA

A STUDY IN ULTRA-VIOLET

By CLEMENT WOOD

THE Spaniards marched raggedly into Alabama before 1540, and then blundered on. The French fortified Twenty-seven Mile Bluff on the Mobile River in 1702, and in that neighborhood they have stayed. English traders of Carolina bored into the valley of the Alabama River in 1687, and radiated and settled throughout the four-square richness of the State. They found almost infinite variety: Florence perched upon its palisaded bluegrass plateau, Dothan drowsing in the sluggish shadows of palmettoes, Livingston crowning the fertile western muck of the Black Belt, Opelika baked in the sandy eastern lowland. There were no igloos and icebergs, no grand canyons, no fire-breathing Popocatapetls; but there were hill and valley, river and Gulf coast, chill uplands, baked midlands, lush tropical lowlands: a land superbly endowed to be an abiding-place for the soul of man. These English traders dragged over the Blue Ridge with their wagons, floated in flatboats down the Tennessee to Muscle Shoals, and pushed on packhorses to the bottom of the State; they overflowed along Gaines's Trace and the Natchez Trace in the north, and the "Three Chopped Way" in the south. Not only traders came: planters pushed behind them, with their household goods and Negro chattels. In 1820 the Negroes were nearly a third of the total population; in 1870, they constituted 47 per cent; in 1910, 42½ per cent. In the eleven counties in the Black Belt, Negroes compose more than 75 per cent of the population; "free and unterrified white Anglo-Saxon Democrats" constitute the remaining quarter. In ten of the upper mountain counties there are practically no Negroes. It was these counties that gave birth, in 1860, to the stillborn proposal to form a neutral State to be called Nickajack. They went with the South in the end; and the problems arising from the commingling of colors are theirs, as well as Alabama's, and the South's, and the nation's.

Alabama is the center of the sisterhood of Southern States: Montgomery was therefore the first capital of the Confederacy. Topographically these are the most fertile States in the union; if we are still to judge a tree by its fruit, mentally, spiritually, they are the most sterile. What is true of Alabama is largely true of Georgia and Mississippi, of Tennessee, the Carolinas, Florida, northern Louisiana, and Arkansas. It is perhaps more true of Alabama than of any of these. Hers is a static sterility; observing the stubborn medievalism that possesses her merely, one may well credit a surviving saurian in Patagonia. For years there was one Darwinian—in Alabama argot, "atheist"—on the faculty of the State University; the fact, in spite of the professor's popularity, was a whispered scandal. Darwin to many Alabamians is Lenin and Landru in one, assuming that they have heard of either or both. The State is saturated with a provincialism that prefers the *Demopolis Gazette* to the New York *World,* and the Capitol at Montgomery to Notre Dame. This may be due to shrewd common sense; as a hoe is worth more to a field hand than a Stradivarius could be. It is a land where G. K. Chesterton's ideas would be considered advanced; none but an Alabama radical considers advancing them.

Alabama has the largest production of pig iron among the States, and the third highest percentage of illiteracy. She is fourth among the States in the production of cotton, and one of the heartiest encouragers of child labor. Apologists for the State point to the drain of the Civil War, and the anguish of Reconstruction: both of these were by-products of the vaster blight of slavery, whose price the State is still paying. Her story is the story of Romulus and Uncle Remus, the white man and his darker brother. In the old story, the autocratic city-builder slew his brother; this facile ending was only in the fable. Alabama is still looking for the answer to the questions: What will she do with him; and what will he do with her? There are other problems as definitely hers as this one; but, since it is the most important and the least understood, the others must be ignored, with mere acknowledgment of their existence.

An after-growth of slavery—that is Alabama today. And slavery, as Helper's "Impending Crisis" decisively established, is the most costly form of industrial organization yet devised. "If slavery continues," a Southern representative admitted in Congress, "they will soon be advertising for runaway masters, instead of runaway slaves." "Free" Negro labor has not served the State better; although free Negro labor might. How many throughout the Union know—how many Alabamians guess—that the average value per acre of farm land in Alabama dropped from $11.86 in 1860 to $8.67 in 1900? A more recent figure might show again an upward trend; but the decline was the product of the first forty years' wandering in the wilderness of black emancipation.

The Negro question permeates every phase of Southern thinking. It wakes with the Southern white, walks with him, keeps him from sleep; it is never absent from the Southern black. It drugs Alabama's educational system. How can it be otherwise, when a typical Black Belt county spends $17.35 on each white pupil, and ninety cents on each colored pupil? It determines Alabama's economic thinking. The per capita wealth of the Southern white is $885; that of the Negro, $34, or one-twenty-fifth as much. It splits the labor movement. Shall Negroes be admitted to unions, and how; and if not, what about strike time? Long before the country hit the camel trail, it saddled prohibition on Alabama and the South in the attempt to divorce the Negro from the intoxication of gin. It retarded woman suffrage. "Would you want your wife and daughters to be forced to jostle Negro washwomen, and worse, at the polls?" This, by the way, was typical American political logic; since Negro men are as prominent at the polls as Eskimo pies in Hades. It may retard any general exodus from Alabama to Heaven, at least until the unsullied Anglo-Saxons are assured that the Negro there will know his place. And, speaking of the unsullied Anglo-Saxons, the catch phrase applied by rural Southern statesmen to their white audiences, the mind directly recalls that the Negro problem affects the sex life of the whole South. White women shiver at its feline menace; white men arm and klan against it, even while its siren voice hums a constant invitation; Negro women smile with satisfaction at it, or, more rarely, shrink from it; Negro men watch it, sometimes reach an arm over the wall for its forbidden fruit, and sometimes burn for it.

"What is the solution to the Negro question?"

"There's only one: amalgamation." The man who said this to me was then an Alabama congressman, conservative, non-alarmist, who still stands high in State and nation. "But, above everything, don't quote me! My political life wouldn't be worth that, if you did. . . . You see," he continued, "it's going on now. . . . All the time. It always has. Read your statistics on the increase of mulattoes. It's a pity that it's the lowest elements of both races that unite; but . . . it's going on."

How far was this congressman right? A few scattered facts may materialize the problem. A Democratic candidate for governor was speaking at a rally in Montgomery, some twenty years ago. He finished his set speech; an excited man rose in the rear of the hall, shaking a lean, accusing finger at the orator. "What about your family of black bastards, Governor?" The distinguished Alabamian came forward to the challenge, and pointed an index finger straight at his questioner. "I've raised 'em, and educated 'em, and made decent, law-abiding citizens of 'em; and that's a damn sight more than you've done for your black bastards!" There was wild applause at this; the interrupter was thrown out. The story spread from end to end of the State; the candidate was elected. Spoken like a true white Southerner; for the ethics of old-time Southern chivalry included this treatment of the black race.

In what other section of the Union could a man have been elected to public office, after such a confession?

In slavery, a state of concubinage between the master and comely slaves was permitted. The master was owner of the bodies of his slaves; cannot a man do what he will with his own? There are those who state that certain strong-minded white mistresses played the same game, as a fitting payment to their catholic spouses. Certain leading white men had two families, the white and the near-white; in certain places this was done openly, until the cousins on the right and the left sides recognized the relationship. There was a State senator who was half-brother to a Negro door-tender at the Capitol—a Negro so light that visitors mistook him for the white brother. In slavery, it was to a large extent the better class of each race which intermingled. For years, in both races, the drift has been away from this. In many circles the white man who has a colored mistress thereby has lost caste; the better class of Negroes no longer admit to the circle of their peers the Negress who is a white man's by-wife.

And yet, the mixing continues. There are still the double families, in scattered locations. There is still the case where the white woman accepts a Negro lover. For instance, the Varner case, in North Carolina last year, which filled columns in the surrounding newspapers. A prominent white man took frequent business trips out of the city. His neighbors observed that a wealthy colored man of the same city, named McRary, visited the house in the husband's absence. They all knew McRary; he was said to be the son of a distinguished white resident and a Negress—the only son of the white man, who had been educated in exclusive Northern schools and one of the leading universities. When they saw McRary frequent the house, these neighbors warned Varner. He laughed at them; such a thing could not be possible. They determined to act, since he would not. One night, when he was away, a lookout reported that McRary was within. A cordon of white friends surrounded the house. The Negro saw them, retreated to the cellar, hid there all night. At dawn, convinced that he could not outlast the watch, he emerged. The whites let him go, after making sure that he knew of their presence. The husband, Varner, brought suit against the Negro for one hundred thousand dollars, charging him with intimacy with Mrs. Varner; it is said that it cost the Negro forty thousand dollars to settle the suit. Mrs. Varner sued her husband for support; a jury of her townspeople returned a verdict against her. Two features make the case interesting, although untypical; the local prominence of the parties involved, and the fact that the Negro was not manhandled by the crowd. He was explained as a cultured and wealthy Negro; these two facts earned for him a respect that lifted him entirely out of the low regard which is the usual lot of the Southern Negro. These two facts should be suggestive when the matter of lynching, and possible preventives, is considered.

Sporadic cases are reported where white girls of good family become intimate with their colored chauffeurs or other servants. There was one case in Birmingham less than ten years ago, where the daughter of one of the wealthiest white men in the city gave birth to a mulatto child, three months after her marriage to a white man of good family, the putative father being the family chauffeur. The matter of course was hushed up. During two years the writer, as judge of the Central Recorder's Court of Birmingham, came into close contact with superficial symptoms of the condition. A number of cases came before him, during this period, concerning white women arrested with Negro men; in all the cases the parties were found guilty. Last year newspapers carried accounts of an alleged Ku Klux Klan flogging near Birmingham, of a Negro man apprehended with a white woman. When such cases occur among the better families, science may dismiss it as akin to the perverted; since the tendency of sexual selection on the part of the woman is to choose a mate higher in culture than herself. With lower classes of white girls, the situation is altered. In more than one mill town the white mill girls are more popular with the Negro bloods than girls of their own race. Four Northern Negro men arrived in such a village a few years ago. They addressed a Negro cabman: "Can't you get us some girls, uncle?"

"W'ut you prefers—white or cullud gals?"

"You don't mean to say you can get white girls . . . here in the South?"

The cabman returned in an hour with four girls, clerks and salesgirls, all white. This naturally is hidden, and is often unsuspected, in the South. As a contrast, in the Negro colony of Harlem, in New York City, certain white girls associate openly with Negro men.

Among white boys of all classes there is much of this denial of the color line. This is less in the cities, and more in the country: for the cities offer white prostitutes, and in the rural districts loose white women are scarcer, or more difficult of approach, than Negro girls. The condition at the State University is not untypical. It is located in a small town, Tuscaloosa, with few slack white women; and the Negresses are "easy." More than a dozen of the writer's classmates and intimates at this institution have explained to him that their first direct sexual experience had come with one of the willing Negro girls; the prevalence of the relationship there was a byword. The State agricultural and mechanical college at Auburn is said to have at present an ethic the opposite of this. Mixture with the Negro girls—in Auburn—is banned; as a substitute, a number of the students motor to ———, where a Negro girl student known to the collegian meets him with enough girl friends to accommodate the college boys. Around an industrial center like Birmingham white boys of all classes are known to mix with the Rosedale Negresses across the mountain, or with the maids and washwomen living in Brown's Hill, Tittlesville, Scratch Ankle, Buzzard Roost, or some other Negro Fifth

Avenue. During the war development of the nitrate plants at Muscle Shoals, at the north end of the State, no color line was drawn. A steamship, the *Paducah,* twice a week took four-hour trips up or down the river. This allowed the workers—Mexicans, Porto Ricans, Northern transients, as well as natives—to drink, gamble, and enjoy hasty dalliance with the female occupants of the twelve cabins on board. Some of the women were white, some black; the proportion varied. As many as thirty or forty men would stand in line for the accolade of access to one of these cabins. On the short walk from the Shoals to Florence or Sheffield, it was the usual thing for a white man to be solicited eight to twelve times, about half of the women being colored.

When it comes to Southern white men of the better families, it must be remembered that in slavery many men openly cohabited with Negro mistresses; now as a rule only the boys of college age do this. The practice has shrunk from an accepted custom to a wild oat. But the mixing is not confined to boys today. There are certain white men, usually not from the better classes, who live exclusively with Negro mistresses, or who maintain families in both races. It is told on good authority that in one town the long-suffering white wives met in indignation, and delivered the ultimatum to their husbands that they must choose between their white wives and their black mistresses. The husbands refused to leave the mistresses.

The white woman occupies a peculiar position, in thus sharing her man, not with an equal, but with one who in her eyes is little removed from the animal.

How does she react to the situation? For one thing, she denies that it exists; just as the white man, until he becomes confidential, denies it. The generation of the white mother of yesterday and the day before—I speak of the so-called higher-class women especially—was so saturated with that forthright denial of life and its truths that we call Victorianism that she did not know of the dual racial experiences of her men-folks; that she would not hear of them, and can say little concerning them. Such a woman led a life sheltered and remote, even as compared to the Northern white woman of the same period; she kept to her bedroom, her kitchen, her parlor, and had no eyes and no ears for what happened in the servants' quarters. But the men knew; and the Negroes knew.

It was—it is—a life of strange inconsistencies, of eerie contradictions. There is the stream of unsullied Anglo-Saxon blood; there is the casual byword that no Negress has virtue. There is the denial that the races intermingle to any extent, with laws and klans to extirpate the odd case; there is the fetish that loose morals among Negro women protect the purity of white girls. Everybody knows that it is, and that it isn't. It is like life in the fourth dimension, which the mathematicians tell us touches our familiar three dimensions at all points, and yet is wholly intangible. In the fourth dimension we can enter a sealed room, do what we will, and leave it, without having once disturbed the walls or the windows or the seal on the door; in the fourth dimension we can turn the apple Eve picked inside out, extract its substance, then return it until it appears as before. It is in this impossible and omnipresent world that the Southern whites and Negroes dwell. Perhaps it would be apter to say that they inhabit a world illumined by the light rays beyond the violet of the spectrum—rays invisible to the eye, but more active and, wrongly used, more maleficent than the visible. These are the rays of powerful chemical action; they scar the photographic plate exposed to them, and share certain qualities with the dynamic Roentgen or X-rays, which penetrate through the garb of flesh to the bone beneath. They are rays that cure —or kill. It is in this infra-twilight world, never seen, yet always just at hand, just beyond the corner of the vision of the eye, that the races meet and mingle. It is no shrinking violet of a world: it is a land of gusty and pernicious forces, driving furtively to their perverted, unrecognized matings. If there is a remedy for this beside the torch of the lyncher, it can only come when the hidden happenings have had turned upon them the more powerful X-rays of common knowledge and common counsel.

We have spoken of that postulate of Southern white thinking, that a Negro woman has no virtue. The Southern white man today knows only the lowest type of Negress, the type largely in the majority. More than two hundred thousand Negro women work in Alabama; almost as many workers as the Negro men. Seventy-one per cent of these are field hands, and 26 per cent domestic servants. The white man comes in contact with these, and generalizes his denial of virtue to the race from them. But there is a growing class of cultured Negro women, sheltered from the Southern white, of whom this is increasingly incorrect. The truth lies at some distance from the casual byword. The low-class Negro woman attaches little value to her chastity; and in accepting a white lover, she obeys the deep biological law that woman chooses a mate superior to herself. This slackness is not confined to the Southern Negro girl; there is much of it among white mill girls, perhaps the largest low white class in Alabama. In certain parts of South America, white mothers of this class openly offer their daughters to men, white or black, who are wealthy. Miscegenation today has its roots in slavery; and in slavery the master had, not the feudal right of first night, but the right of all nights. Something of this psychology clouds the Alabama air.

Worst of all, from the standpoint of the white man's welfare, there is, in the South, apparently no acceptance of responsibility in such a relationship, on the part of the man. The Negro girl, it is said, has no legal recourse. The law in certain States recognizes no such thing as a bastardy proceeding of a Negress against a white man. The very intimacy is outlawed; no rights may spring from it. It is no wonder that the Negro girl is easy game; there is no closed season against hunting her. It is easy for the white man to accept the relationship; he assumes no risk. Illegitimacy is always an anomalous relationship; but elsewhere there is a recognized stigma on the father. This abnormal freedom from responsibility is true only of the South. As long as it continues, we may expect this furtive tasting of the flesh-pots of Ethiopia.

The case of the cultured Negro woman is rather apart from the others. She is sheltered from all Southern white men, as far as may be; yet her problems come too. The wife of a Negro doctor, quite well-to-do, confided to a friend: "I would never dare tell my husband or brothers half of the things white men say to me. Whenever I enter a store, the clerks make insinuations or outright proposals. . . ." No comely girl of this class escapes solicitations from white men. One Negro father sent his daughter North to Columbia University to separate her from the attentions of a white admirer. The man followed her to New York. Such a woman, in the main, is sheltered; she is never safe. Advances come to her; there is little law to which she can appeal, if a white man invades her home. It is at the risk of his own blood that her husband dare even lay hands on a white man to protect her. Grandfathers had been lynched for protesting against mistreatment of their young colored granddaughters. The situation of the Negro husband, father, or brother, under these not infrequent occurrences, is a hideous dilemma: dishonor or death are the proffered choices. And there is always the threat of the black hour of a race riot, started by some isolated breath of white lust.

What is the status of the breathing product of these alliances between the races? Is he white, or black, or both, or neither? He is really both; but man itches to checkerboard the universe, and pigeonhole everything as this, or that—never half this and half that. It hardly irks him that what he calls the laws of nature are against him; let the legislature pass a law that it is day until 5:59 p. m., and night the next second; and all will be well. Is there any problem our American Solons cannot and have not solved? The legislature of Texas has decreed how long sheets must be, the Assembly of Maryland has fixed by ukase the length of women's skirts, the Houses in Pennsylvania have banned a cinema kiss beyond thirty feet or so, and prohibit a scene showing a mother sewing on baby clothes, before the baby is born: the element of surprise in life must be maintained, at any cost! By a majority of one, the Kentucky legislature recently decided that Darwin was right, and that man evolved from the animal. A million years' slow incubation of the wonder of life could have been changed by a switch in the vote of the tobacco-chewing gentleman from Alfalfa County. We will know the truth about Einstein, and the potency of ectoplasm, when Albany acts, or Washington acts. It is interesting to see what the law says of the children of the dusk. Edward's "West Indies" declared that in the Spanish and French West Indies there was no degradation of color beyond the quadroon. In Virginia, before 1860, a colored person was one who had a fourth or more of Negro blood; in Carolina, an eighth or more. The Louisiana law was stricter; no amount of white blood could emancipate the offspring of a slave. A Louisiana war legislature considered a bill to legalize marriages between white and black, and rejected it; later her law defined the white man living with a Negro woman as a vagrant. The law in many Southern States defines as a Negro one who has one-eighth or more of African blood; but the census enumerators since 1790 have followed the popular conception which classes as Negro all persons known or believed to have any admixture of African blood. All such persons are subject to the discrimination of Jim

Crow cars, Jim Crow restaurants, Jim Crow theater balconies, and to a social standing that means ostracism in its kindest hour.

These things are known to Southern white men, and are beginning to be known to white women; but they are not advertised. These things are known to the Negroes; but, as a race, they are not yet vocal; and, as a race, it might be incorrect to say that they oppose the mingling.

"What is the solution to the Negro question?"

"There's only one: absorption." The man who said this to me is one of the most prominent of American Negroes, who has made his mark in political, philanthropic, and artistic life. "Nor can I say that I object to the solution; but I wish that the process might be consummated on more equal terms, and with more dignity to the Negro race."

The leading thinkers of both races may be near agreement as to the probable end. And the dignity will insensibly come; it had already come, remember, in the North Carolina Varner case.

If this were all—this crazy-quilt of racial intermingling—it might not be worth while to put it down on paper. But this is not the half. The great misfortune is not that there are mulatto children in Alabama; it is that Alabama, the State itself, is the offspring of two races, united so furtively and blunderingly that she is immeasurably the loser by her joint parentage. The mental and spiritual sterility of the land has been catalogued with devastating impertinence by H. L. Mencken, and stated by others. Two-fifths of the population are stigmatized as inferior, and kept illiterate;

their every effort at individual and racial progress is obstructed and bitterly contested. The races are in daily contact; and each is affected by the contact. The Negro is elevated by his association with the white; and the white is correspondingly degraded by his association with the Negro, in the low stage of culture at which he is kept. The white imparts to the Negro something of his outlook on life and its problems—an outlook lifted and corrected by contact with the progressive thought of the world. The Negro imparts to the white his ignorant, superstitious attitude on the same questions—an influence that is not recognized, that may be scoffed at, but that takes root and grows to noxious height. Let us not have this or that benefit, lest the Negro share it. "Inasmuch as ye have done it unto one of the least of these——" Alabama is both races. If she forgets this, the cost to herself will be desolating.

This cost she is paying: and it is not a small thing. What is the State's—or the South's—contribution to the absorbing world of science, that handmaiden of man in his progress from beasthood? What is the State's—or the South's—contribution to music, to drama, to sculpture, to painting, to literature? Where are the State's, and the South's critical reviews, publishing houses? Some slight answer might be made to all these questions. But Alabama leads the States alphabetically; and it is time she awoke from her lotus doze, and accepted man's responsibilities, out of which grow man's achievements. It is easy to follow the old ruts, to keep alive old attitudes of hatred, prejudice, ill-treatment; it is hard to think, to weigh courses and adopt the stranger, fairer way: but this is the price of full living. That land does not prosper, half of whose citizens are kept from wisdom, and in economic, mental, and spiritual poverty. That land cannot speak her word, nor sing her song, when half of her tongue strives against the other half, when half is paralyzed and half is not, when half is bound and half is free.

And when has good counsel brought forth sweet fruit? Are there any teachers but the lash of experience, and the red scorpion of time?

SOUTH DAKOTA

STATE WITHOUT END

By HAYDEN CARRUTH

THE way of a serpent upon a rock seems broad and distinct compared with a parallel of latitude or longitude. I remember some years ago a friend showed me that every time I went to the post office I crossed latitude forty-five north. I had not been aware of it. He pointed out the exact place, by a tree, and ever afterward I found myself stepping high when I passed over it, bound not to trip. But a State that must depend on these artificial map decorations for its boundaries is unfortunate. How shall it know itself? How develop individuality? Perhaps it can, but it will take time. Of course I am thinking of South Dakota, which, except for a few miles in two corners, exists only because it is a certain distance north of the Equator and west from Greenwich; and the Equator is imaginary, and I have my doubts about Greenwich. Enter it from north, south, east, or west; nothing from the sky, or the soil, or the people, or their houses will call to you that *this* is South Dakota. Over endless prairie you come. Over endless prairie—you go on.

Let me pretend that I am living in South Dakota, as once upon a time, and may be addressed: Journeys End, Rose Bud Prairie, Near the Bijou Hills, Sentinel Butte, S. D. But though feigning of residence is easy, the assumption of birth in South Dakota may scarcely be.

No, not here; but in southern Minnesota; between the same imaginary latitudinal lines and of a longitude not so much nearer Greenwich, with the same Indians, and the same blue sky and wild flowers, and the same weather.

There was a map; it was truly of a size, and half covered one wall. It was large, still it covered These United States only so far as one hundred and four degrees and a few odd minutes of longitude; so the scale was ample. It was printed on extraordinarily heavy paper, of a rich yellow-brown tone, one-third of the counties were of a soft pink-red, and another third of a mild blue-green, leaving the last third to the mellow parchment of the paper. That is, the older States bore this embellishment of county, but Kansas and Nebraska, the latter probably and the former perhaps, still Territories, had only a few square counties heaped up in the eastern parts, as a child would make a block pile; but the Indian Territory and Dacotah (as the map had it) showed no counties at all. I found more pleasure in Dacotah than in anything else on the map; it was near enough to be not unattainable; there I traveled, fascinated by a vast region three hundred miles long and fifty wide edged with map-makers' mountain fringe, called Table Land; another half as large with the enticing name of Coteaux des Prairies; with the names of different Indian tribes scattered carelessly here and there, and above all else, to the northwest, a great region of Unexplored Country. When this map of maps was made I know not; probably before the Civil War or early in the conflict.

I went to Dakota (came, I mean) in the early

eighties, while it was a Territory, and still one, the North and the South, but hostile. Many changes had occurred from the old map. The Rivière au Jacques had become, by way of the James, the Jim. The beautiful Table Land had been found not worth putting on the newer maps, the Coteaux des Prairies had suffered the same fate. Where were Spirit Hill, Butte de Sable, Dead Colt Hillock, Hole-in-the-Wall Mountain, and, above all, The Lightning's Nest? Many enticing names had gone, but a few others had been acquired, as Charles Mix and Bon Homme for two adjoining counties, and, in the Black Hills, Deadwood, beloved of the authors of the dime novel, by recent analysis shown to be our only true American literature. You enter the picturesque Black Hills region through Buffalo Gap, and leave it by way of the Cheyenne River, Grindstone Butte, the Bad River, and Fort Pierre; at least I did—on horseback. But Old Harry's, Blue Blanket Island, Dog's Ears Butte, October Cache, and Bear-in-the-Lodge Butte are gone.

Perhaps without further delay I should confess that I shall not give many statistics, so dearly beloved of our State, such as that if all the cows in South Dakota were placed end to end they would reach to the moon, and leave one to jump over. But who would believe this, cold, provable fact that it is, allowing the modest estimate of seven feet and four inches to each cow? Nobody. So with a thousand other facts about our glorious State, which I with painstaking care have collected. Who would believe what I could tell of our production of wheat and corn, of cattle and hogs, of butter and eggs; of gold? The facts are too tremendous for human consumption; the simple, smiling truth becomes a figure of fright. I shall pass it all over in detached silence. You, of course, saw recently in the newspapers that South Dakota stood next to the top in the percentage of drafted men found acceptable by the medical examiners in the late war. It is not my fault that this fact was made public. Only Kansas was ahead of us. But I shall make no triumphant references to our products, our resources, our intellectual achievements, or our virtue.

But there is one thing of which I must speak pridefully, perhaps boastingly. I do so the more boldly because it is never mentioned in praise of this or any other region. On it the Boosters are silent. Along our rivers, about our lakes, among the mountains of our southwest corner, there is much beautiful scenery of the conventional type, which receives due praise; but all States have the regulation scenery. We have the Prairie. We have it to a greater extent and in more beautiful guise than any other State. The Prairie, level or gently rolling, is the earth we inhabit brought to its highest point of perfection; it is the world ordered, arranged, settled; the world at peace; the world kind, thoughtful, brooding; the world passed beyond the treachery of the sea, the clamor and savagery of the mountains; the earth with its other half, the sky, above us and about; the world open, frank, constant, giving man to look about him and to know his littleness or to exult as a god; the Prairie is the world in its calm, serene, beautiful old age, meditative, unhurried, unafraid; approaching Nirvana. To know the Prairie friendly-wise, above all to know it as mother, is to feel "the exceeding beauty of the earth."

There is no other place where so fully may be realized the immensity of the earth as in the midst of the Prairie. There we know our earth for what it is, and turn our faces to our sky, and know that we are part of all. The Prairie is clothed by the universal grass, and beautified by the flowers that are fitted to it, the pasque flower of spring, the wild rose of summer, the goldenrod and wild sunflower of autumn; the sky is a deeper blue, the clouds a more glowing white than anywhere else; at night there are the stars. Every spot on the Prairie is a High Place whereon may be offered sacrifices to Truth and Beauty. The Prairie is but the desert watered, and, as hath been said, "The desert is of God, and in the desert no man may deny Him."

And with the prairie there is what may be called an attribute even more important for the progress of mankind: the Wind. Above, "Messer Sun" of the hymn of Saint Francis of Assisi; below, and part of it, "Brother Wind." The prairie is static, the Wind dynamic. The prairie nourishes thought—the Wind demands action. The Wind of the prairie is a long, long Wind. It comes not by fits and starts, but steadily, as the sun moves across the sky; it is the eternal calmness of the prairie in motion. There are no gusts, no pauses; if you are without you cannot hide from it; you can breast it, overcome it, but you cannot avoid it. And there is no sleep like that companioned by strains "rung by the running fingers of the wind."

It cannot be denied that our Wind on occasion momentarily oversteps the bounds. It is as a test at the end of the school term. Even then it is beneficial, with its lesson in forethought, resourcefulness, mind against matter. Great Pan stamps his foot in The Lightning's Nest and the proudest citizen retires to his cyclone cellar.

But we who are at school in the great Academy of the Wind have our vacations. In October, usually, the winds are hushed; the sun floats big and red in the hazy sky, the land is a cloth of gold and purple, gossamer streams lazily on the wandering airs, and alone, on a little uprolling of the Immensity, you may catch the faint tones of far-off fairy music—"tired bells chiming in their sleep"—Pan again, I dare say, in gentler mood, perhaps this time at Spirit Hill with his pipe and the little animals, his friends, about him.

What is the effect of all this beauty upon the dweller in South Dakota? No effect is discernible. There are our sunsets—for they are beyond compare, a prairie sky being the only canvas adequate for this daily miracle, making it the marriage of heaven and earth, celebrated with a mighty harmony on Nature's color-organ; well, there it is—what about it? When the farmer sits down to milk his cow of a summer evening he turns his back to the sunset. . . . But the cow sees it. Maybe through her milk a little of the sunset may somehow touch the youthful members of the family. Certainly in time the effect will come, since no man may escape nature. Our "intimate contact with wind and sky" must touch our physical nature first. Our world has been too new, we have had too much to do. Before we were settled and had things put to rights the distracting recent inventions jumped at us. We brought the bicycle with us, "high," perhaps, but still a "wheel." Candles we never knew; electric lights were ours before we harvested the second crop. We lisped in telephones, for the telephones came. Then ensued the motor-car, and we had no solid tradition of ox-teams to help us withstand the shock. We saw that they were created for our benefit. We have yet to discover that a man may not own a motor-car and still be respectable. But it cannot be denied that to be able to call the doctor twenty miles away over the telephone, and have him dump himself at your door from his car within an hour, is a privilege not to be surrendered. The way of a motor-car on the prairie is one of swiftness. In time past distressing stories have been told in this country of life on the great central plains; especially for women; of its drabness, of resulting depression, insanity. The holy anchoret would probably find a telephone in his cell an affliction, with tradesmen calling up about the overdue payment on his last hair shirt; but it has brought needed companionship to the plainswoman. And now there is radio.

South Dakota is the heart of the prairie region of North America. Take a pair of compasses and on your map set the legs to cover six hundred miles. Plant one in the middle of South Dakota and swing the other around, and in your great circle, twelve hundred miles in diameter, you will have the prairie, nipping the Rocky Mountains a bit, to be sure, and missing some plains to the north in Manitoba and Saskatchewan and to the south in Oklahoma and Texas; but mostly you'll have your prairie inclosed in your imaginary line—as good as anybody's imaginary line. And South Dakota in the exact middle of this great plain of the world should be its very heart and soul, and is. It finds itself the essence of prairieism. Perhaps, after all, there are more negative than positive qualities in a great plain, and if the State exhibits the same qualities the reason may be geographical. The nature of the State is subdued to what it lives in.

On the old map there were three towns, Yankton, Vermilion, and Sioux Falls. When, in the experimental eighties, I came, there must have been several score—or hundred. Now there must be twice—or ten times—as many. The railroads came and made them. The railroads did not have to be coaxed to South Dakota; there was something to come for: Wheat. Everywhere Wheat. Number one hard. While they were building the station, and before the trains began to run, the settlers would bring it in and pile it up. It grew, and still grows, as if indigenous to the soil. Number one hard. There was, and is, no other Wheat like ours.

Still, though the railroads were eager to come, I believe a benevolent government at Washington did present some of the roads with every other section of the good rich land, though by chance, I think, this all occurred in the northern half of the Territory. With the man who wanted to acquire a farm and home, the dear thing, our government, was less open-handed. "Root, hog, or die, for you, old man!" it said to him. And he truly had to, or he did; built his house of sod, twisted wild hay for his fuel, greeted the uprising sun from the field, and plowed two furrows after this luminary had set; and his wife had a harder time than he. But if he didn't die, and became the "following-named settler"—I quote from the notice he had to put in the local paper, and pay for—when the gentle powers finally gave him a patent to his land—if he didn't die, I say, and if the local money-lender (equipped with extra rows of teeth) didn't get him, he has now, I am assured, an immense barn, a big house, a telephone, a phonograph, a radio set, a motor-car. I hope he has; and I hope, too, he has the same wife.

And of these original settlers who came into South Dakota from thirty to fifty years ago, there are still many thousands, grown a bit sedater, it is true, and less inclined to make merry of nights with barber poles and other movable objects. This may be understood when you remember that we Originals on our advent were usually in age somewhere between eighteen and twenty-four; with a few graybeards verging on thirty. We were young, but we didn't know it. It was before Youth was looked upon as a career in itself. There were a few middle-aged men with families; and if one of the families chanced to include a growing-up daughter, he was the most deferred-to man in town, and was immediately elected Justice of the Peace. As for the girl, marriageable age was desirable, but not necessary; age sufficient for the purpose of courtship would do—say fourteen. The really marriageable girl had to keep a card index of her young men. The sexes are now more evenly balanced, though still with the emphasis on the male, and it might pay any young woman in the East who is beginning to feel the least bit anxious to drop in casually. Of course our best men are already married; but that is the case everywhere.

In the old days prairie fires illuminated the night, coming winking over the tops of the little hills, zigzagging down their sides and rushing literally on the wings of the wind with the ranker grasses of the lower land. The old days were, too, the heroic age of the tumble weed. I am tempted to boast of their speed. They suggest another fast-moving object, the county court-house of the early days. In a county each town aspired to be the county seat, and most of them were, sooner or later. I lived in a town, new-planted by the railroad authorities; two miles away on the open prairie stood the county capital, two buildings, a farm-house and a small structure containing a safe for the records. A bright legal mind in our town showed us how we could incorporate the town, with a shoestring gerrymander to include this county building, and thus become the county seat. We warmed to the thought, and took up a collection to pay the fees at Bismarck, the capital of the Territory. Alas! "That very night the Romans landed on our coast," coming in the guise of practical men and mule teams from the rival town, and took away the county building on wheels. We never saw it again. The bright legal mind refused to return the collection.

Taking into consideration the proportion of our people still living who came here to virgin soil, I sometimes think that South Dakota is the youngest State in the Union, though of course in this respect it must stand beside its northern twin. The other Western States it seems to me, with the possible exception of Oklahoma, were settled more gradually. The Territory of Dakota was settled with a bang. Since practically everybody is either an Original, or but once removed, how can the State have developed much individuality? The fact is, it hasn't. Our people are still "from" some place. Even though you were born and brought up here, if your father and mother were from Indiana, and they talked Indiana, and got letters and newspapers from Indiana, and visited Indiana years when the crops were good, you find yourself a good deal of a Hoosier. South Dakota was settled chiefly by people from Minnesota—from Minnesota and Iowa and Wisconsin. But even these States, especially Minnesota, were so young that their people were "from." Thus, though people directly from New England, New York, or Pennsylvania, for example, were not numerous, these regions were well represented among our settlers either by real natives who had tarried awhile in the newer and nearer States or by the second generation. Even the Scandinavians, who seem to liquefy at such a low temperature in the melting-pot, usually reached our prairies from some neighboring State.

These Scandinavians of whom we have so many—though our northern neighbor is much ahead of us in this respect—have made a good record in the State. At least, they readily become Americanized, which may be a desirable thing if you are going to stay in America. They take kindly to our politics and our cooking, which in another generation or two will probably have a baleful effect on the honesty and clearness of their blue eyes. A long way after the Scandinavians in number come the Germans, and I know of nothing that can be said against the way in which they have comported themselves. Our percentage of foreign-born population is somewhat smaller than that of the average of the neighboring States. In the matter of Indians, the statistical tables give South Dakota third place, Oklahoma standing first and Arizona second. One wonders where they keep themselves. Still, there are reservations, and there it is fair to assume they stay, except for neighborhood excursions. In a newspaper printed close to one of these reservations there appeared recently an account of how Frank Bear Running, Charles Kills First, and John Brown Wolf came to town and stole a—there, gentle reader—I've caught you! You've guessed that they stole a Ford car. You're wrong! They had a Ford car. They came to town in it. What they did, while Jim Eddy, a ranchman, was getting a noonday snack at the hotel, was to steal the engine out of his new Ford car, transfer it to their own car, and "light out across the country like greased lightning," as the local paper expressed it. "Sheriff Bender," the paper adds, "started in hot pursuit in his Pierce-Arrow." But can a Pierce-Arrow overtake a Ford where buffalo wallows and prairie-dog towns abound? I think not.

It will be seen from this that our Indians are also becoming Americanized—if an Indian may do so. These Indians, I think, are mainly natives of this State, or the immediate region. Their fathers and grandfathers must have seen the exploration parties of Captain Sully, Lieutenant Warren, and Governor Medary marked on the old map as occurring in the fifties. Think of the talk these hurried and rattling military passings must have made around the Indian campfires.

Too, perhaps, a little examination of arrow points, and plans for trips down the Missouri to trading posts where peltries might be exchanged for that emblem of civilization, the powder-and-ball gun. The savage has a most contemptible habit of taking a hint. Especially when, after having been shot at by a flock of Christians, he finds another flock anxious to sell him arms with which to shoot back. Showing, it must be confessed, a sporting spirit on the part of the Christians.

Still, none shall deny us the beginnings of State personality, even if that personality consists of having next to none. Our northern twin is given to political experiments. Our southern neighbor has brought forth Mr. Bryan, contains Omaha, shares a boundary with Kansas. And why need we dwell on the varied distinctiveness of our two eastern and two western sisters? Now what is there about South Dakota to put one's finger on, to point to with pride?

Once we had a Senator at Washington named Pettigrew, R. F. Pettigrew, the only man of distinction we ever had at Washington in any capacity. But we did not keep him there. He tells why in his latest book. No doubt there is another side to the story, but that doesn't matter. I wish every voter in the State could read the book. There are three or four Senators from other States who are troublesome, sometimes wrongheaded, often cantankerous, who are not understood by their constituents, and who represent the universe rather than their State. Still their States keep them in the Senate. If South Dakota had done the same with Pettigrew it would have been a good thing for South

Dakota, the Senate, and the country. Who ever hears of South Dakota's Senators today?

I have been mentally struggling to think of something to say that will reveal the Soul of Our People, but I shall have to give it up. Barring the mining in one corner, where the Black Hills beckon to their parent Rockies, we are an agricultural folk, caring more for sufficient rain and warmth in June than for Mr. Einstein's ingenious theory, Mr. Hardy's most recent book of poems, the movement for freedom in India, or even the probable state of our own souls. The price of wheat in Chicago comes home to our business and bosoms. "How a good yoke of bullocks at Stamford fair?" How, indeed! And freight rates too high. And what is that feller we sent to Washington doing about it all? Yes, we are an agricultural folk, and pluck the bright dollar (silver—weighing a pound, more or less) from the reluctant earth. We have no large cities, or prospect of any. Perhaps there is nothing to make them.

Our only navigable river has ceased to be so. I wish the Missouri could be dredged out and the delightful old steamboats restored. But perhaps the water would have to be strained first—I am no engineer. Besides, I may be prejudiced about the Western river steamboat; I love the various noises it makes. To me a steamboat always comes round the bend with "a nigger squat on her safety-valve, and her furnace crammed, rosin and pine."

This lack of large cities may be only what should be expected in an agricultural State, not admitted to the Union till 1889, but the absence of any towns of distinction may be less easy to explain. Stop a man on the street in New York or San Francisco and ask him to name a town in South Dakota. "Why—er—yes," says your man. "Yes—Sioux City!" "But Sioux City is in Iowa." "Why, to be sure—yes—good day!" If your man is elderly he may answer your question with Yankton, because time was when it was the capital of Dakotah Territory, and the only town. If he is middle-aged or younger he may say, "When I was a boy I read a bully story about Deadwood Dick—Deadwood, of course—it's in South Dakota—or is it Wyoming?" Pierre boasts (boasts is a figure of speech) of being the smallest State capital in the Union, always excepting Carson City. Our largest town, Sioux Falls, had only a few over 25,000 people in 1920. There were but eight towns of above five thousand population—but two above ten thousand. Still the population of the State was over 636,500. We are country dwellers; we live on our prairies.

As a people we are liberal financially toward education. Of course we don't know what education is; but what State does? We seem to have our fair share of the regulatory spirit, perhaps derived from our New England blood, or perhaps not. We took up with Prohibition before the country did. My recollections of observed effects of strong drink in the early days seem scanty. I do recall an immense Scandinavian who would come to town driving a yoke of oxen. On occasion he indulged too freely, and then invariably sought the grocery store, bought a package of soda crackers, begged a soap box, and repaired to where his patient oxen stood in the street. Standing the box in front of them he would sit down on it and proceed to feed the crackers to the oxen, a single biscuit at a time, alternating between the two animals. It was a scene of tranquillity and loving-kindness calculated to touch the heart of the most callous. On another occasion a visiting clergyman, mistaking, presumably, the potency of the cup before him, ventured too far, and later, making his way across town in the dark of a moonless June night, fell into a new cellar. Unable to deliver himself therefrom, he became so singularly vocal that the reverberations have come down with me through the years, haunting my ears when other sounds are momentarily hushed.

What if Christ came to South Dakota? Absurd; such things only happen far off in time and space. But if He did come it is hoped that He would get a quarter-section of our superior land and, through diversified farming, acquire the point of view of our leading people. Any funny notions put into the heads of our hired men with regard to hours or wages—quite unthinkable! If a miracle were really required—impossible things, of course—but if there *must* be one, say a good soaking rain, without clouds, in the latter part of May. Great for the Wheat. Naturally, no turning of portions of this rain water into any other liquid. The authorities—and so forth.

So runs the world away; but even after all these years I sometimes wonder if it was best that the old Territory was divided into two States and given names which, when their handles are considered, are not impressive. In those old days Congress was slow, and State conventions before there was any State were common. These were always held by but half of the Territory. Some of us, contrary-minded children of the Opposition, thought the Territory should become one State, and called by its own truly beautiful name of Dakota; and we talked of how it would be the second in size in the Union, surpassed only by Texas, a grand, imperial State, striking terror into the other States. We accused the two-staters of being a hungry generation, anxious to make more offices. They called us impractical, visionaries, unmindful of the need in the Senate of four more members of the True Party; finally they threw us out. But after upward of forty years outside the hall on the sidewalk I still say I think we were right.

And yet—if they hadn't! Dakota might have been a turbulent, a strong, a virile State, a leader, a maker of movements, a State to shatter precedents, a State of destiny. But is it not well that one, just one, of These United States should keep, should be, the spirit of the great plains—unending, unchanging, calm? South Dakota . . . the prairie. . . .

OREGON

A SLIGHTED BEAUTY

By CHARLES H. CHAPMAN

WHEN it first occurred to Oregon some years ago to put up her charms for sale she found the market monopolized by a more sumptuous beauty in the south. Competition was risky and the advertising it seemed to demand was expensive. One may possess beauty enough for an adored wife and mother without quite coming up to the mark of a reigning belle. The Creator slighted Oregon when He bestowed Mt. Hood, Crater Lake, and Neahkahnie upon her by scattering those picturesque assets too widely. It is a long journey from each to the next one and the intervening stretches fall regrettably short of heavenliness. When the tourist at last reaches the marvel toward which he has been straining through monotonous sagebrush or the still more monotonous Willamette Valley and compares it with the Grand Canyon or Rainier Park or the Yellowstone he can seldom suppress a sigh. It is not a sigh of disappointment precisely but rather one of melancholy that anything so lovely should, by a hair's breadth, miss being of the loveliest.

The Emerald State put more than common dependence upon the sale of her beauty because it was about all she had received from nature that seemed to promise quick returns without much work. A little coal, a little gold, a little quicksilver had been strewn here and there in her wide territory, but not enough to make a spread over. The forests could not be shipped to market as they grew. Wheat, apples, prunes, and live stock hardly yielded more wealth in the long run than human hands and brains sunk in them.

When it came to sea-going commerce the Creator had slighted her again. He had given her but one harbor and that not His best sample. Ships can sail up the Columbia to Portland if not too big, after they once surmount the obstacles at the river's mouth, but if they are too big they must sail away to some other port; if they are wrecked crossing the bar that finishes them so far as trade is concerned. Portland, therefore, is obliged to seek the consolations of philosophy when she contemplates the vessels in her harbor.

It takes as much philosophy, perhaps more, to bear the slight the railroads have put upon the city and State. They sheer off to the north and south perversely aiming at the deep waters of the Sound and the Golden Gate, as if conspiring to keep Oregon forever blushing unseen in her continuous woods and deserts, a wallflower at the commercial dance where richly married sisters of the north and south disport themselves.

The immigrants of the days before the railroads played the same trick upon her. They strayed away from the Oregon Trail to California seeking gold and left only the weary and second rate to drift down the Columbia into the Willamette Valley. It would be inaccurate to say that the State was born tired, for the earliest of the immigrants, the primeval Jason Lees and the later Applegates, had vim enough for any enterprise. It was Oregon's hard luck to have that tired feeling thrust upon her by the cracker infusion of the years to follow. But the State never has been positively overwhelmed by a flood of immigrants either good or bad. The population has grown slowly like her business. Lured by deep water and railroads Portland's business kings are apt to have more of a stake in Seattle than at home. Lured by the climate of paradise they hope to die in California.

Oregon's climate is not bad enough to make anybody curse it nor good enough to make anybody love it. The winter rains just barely fail of being execrable. The summers would be divine if it were not for the smoky haze which hangs over the landscape and hides nature's miracles. What thanks does Oregon owe the Lord for giving her Mount Hood when He blots it out with a veil of smoke in summer and a veil of mist in winter? The smoke is the unkindest cut of all, for after obscuring everything all summer long it clears away in the fall when the tourist season is over and leaves the scenery in crystalline glory with nobody to pay for looking at it. Mt. Hood is a veiled idol ten months in the year but Portland adores it for its potential vendibility and dreams passionately of a day to come when tourists will flock to see it as they do to the Jungfrau. Doubtless they will when the mists have cleared away. Meanwhile they swing off to the Yellowstone, the Grand Canyon, the Yosemite, and leave Oregon to theorize with empty pockets over their neglect.

She has framed an hypothesis to account for it. There is a conspiracy between man and nature to slight her. Nobody can stay long in the State without catching on to the prevalent sense of slight and the resentment against it. The resentment is only half articulate. It is a good deal like those suppressed reactions in the brain of an unappreciated youth who has stayed too long in his home town which work out finally in an inferiority complex. The poor fellow comes to believe that there is neither fame nor fortune in doing what he was born to do and tries to win out by imitating gifts alien to his nature.

If Oregon would work out her native qualities in her life she might make herself a world's delight and wonder. Blooming as she does on a mossy bank in the shelter of the mountains under the shade of the evergreen forests, she might be the sweetest violet ever seen, but she pines to be a sunflower. She has every chance and allurement to sow and harvest a unique civilization. Her geographical situation means exactly that, and so do her mental and material resources. If she chooses to imitate the cheap and tawdry on the outside it is not for want of fine possibilities at home nor of men who understand how to make the most of them. Oregon has always had men, from the first of the pioneers, who comprehended her vocation to original beauty and greatness but the call of the sham has put them out of business before they got very far.

The first thing the primeval pioneers of the Jason Lee stamp did when they reached the Willamette Valley after their trek across the continent was to found schools. Every settlers' camp had one—the Methodists at Salem, the Congregationalists at Forest Grove, the Presbyterians at Albany, the Baptists at McMinnville, the Wesleyan Methodists at Corvallis, the Quakers at Newberg, the Campbellites at Monmouth, strung along the Willamette River for a hundred miles or so. The schools went by all sorts of names, academies, institutes, colleges. They had no money, no buildings, no football teams, no booster presidents—nothing but consecrated teachers, ambitious students, and the divine fire.

In those days Harvey W. Scott, a wild and woolly young man, footed it down from the Sound to Forest Grove with his blankets on his back and entered the college there. He turned out, as it happened, to be Oregon's one big man. Whether his Alma Mater made him so or not, at any rate the good creature did not spoil him. During the forty years and more that Scott edited the *Oregonian* newspaper at Portland he put his college into his editorials. He wrote crisp, bold, positive English. He whaled away at every religious superstition in sight even when it cost his paper money, and between elections at least he railed at the sacred Republican tariff, although the *Oregonian* was a Republican organ. In the afternoon, when his editorial was written for the day, he read Ovid for recreation. He could recite from memory page after page of "Paradise Lost." He modeled his style on the English Bible and his political philosophy on Burke. Cant and humbug he hated and said so in print. Free thought and free speech he preached and practiced. Now Scott is dead and the *Oregonian* has flatted down to the pitch of the New York *Times*. There is less free intelligence in Portland than there was thirty years ago when he was in his prime. The little college where he got his fine education does not produce any more like him, but it has an enviable football record.

The Campbellite academy at Monmouth, small and hungry as it was, sent out a group of men to whom must be attributed an altogether disproportionate share of whatever nobility Oregon's life and politics can show. This mother of men with high brows and big souls has been transfigured into a State normal school which makes over farm girls into schoolma'ams without changing anything about them but their handwriting and the way they do up their hair. When I visited it two or three years ago the president was feeling jubilant over a new building he had just squeezed out of the overtaxed public. I remembered the boys who had sat under great teaching there long ago in a little shed and asked him what was doing along that line. He did not know or did not care. He could talk of nothing but his new building. He died soon afterward and went to heaven, and when Peter examined him at the gate, he found that new building tattooed on his presidential heart. The inferiority complex has got in its work on every last Alma Mater of that Willamette Valley bevy. They are out for cash and buildings with football teams and booster presidents. Their first love is forgotten.

It has never been much the fashion among Portland's millionaires to bequeath money for public purposes. When the city was young its frugal proprietors pinched it up along streets too narrow for anything but camel traffic and the same thrifty spirit has animated their real-estate deals and commercial policy ever since. But with all their vigilant husbandry of pennies few of them have been comforted at death with the assurance that they had saved more than enough to provide for their own families. The shining, or prodigal, exception to their strictly Biblical deathbed policy was Amanda Reed, who bequeathed some three million dollars to found what she supposed would be a technical school but what has turned out, oddly enough, to be a rather ordinary college of arts and letters.

Amanda Reed's bequest was Portland's opportunity to work out something new and big in education. The city lies so far away from current academic idiocies that there was nothing to hinder, except its fear of being original. The first president of Reed College, W. T. Foster, a young man of brains and ideas, saw the possibilities in the situation and set out to realize them. He chose for himself the maxim that "college students are there to study" but the studies he dealt out were of the free, noble sort that youth thrives on. Foster's plan was to connect up the college with the city's intellectual resources, making it a central ganglion for the civic body. With the courage of a very young president he shut his doors in the face of intercollegiate athletics. Well, President Foster got just so far with these big notions of his and then the inferiority complex closed down on him and extinguished him. Portland did not want any grand, original experiments in education. It wanted an obsequious imitation of the commonplace colleges in the East, and that is what it has got out of Amanda Reed's bequest.

W. S. U'Ren is another adventurous soul who has

tried to make Oregon travel the road on which the pioneers started her, the Pacific highway of free thought and original experiment. He saw what a chance she had to become the world's political laboratory in those remote mountain solitudes unpestered by big business and big cities. The pioneers themselves had been practical anarchists. They had no political government, needed none, and perhaps never would have had any but for a wrangle with the British Hudson's Bay Company which infected them with the disease of patriotism and in due course erupted in a written constitution. Up to that time schools and churches had sufficed to keep the settlers straight, but the first act of their new government was, characteristically, to build a jail and then to fill it. With this grand political start Oregon outsped some of her sisters on the downward way. When U'Ren came on the stage in the 1890's politics was flowing in a sticky, malodorous stream bearing along the usual stuff of sewers.

U'Ren was a student, a thinker, and a man of constructive imagination. He knew the dreams the sages have dreamed of a perfect democracy and by what a close shave the pioneers had failed of realizing them. Perhaps it was not too late to recall Oregon from her paddling in the political sewer. An accidental eddy in the current enabled him to launch his "Oregon System." The State legislature had, in literal fact, so clogged itself with its own offal that it could not stir hand nor foot. It had ceased to function. The people were out of all patience with it and sick to death of the bosses. The time seemed ripe for something bold and big and U'Ren rose to the occasion with the Initiative, Referendum, and Recall.

It was Oregon's chance to move in one leap from foul politics to the golden prime of democracy, but the chance was not taken. His system was adopted formally and that was the end of it. It has not been worked to see what there was in it. The novel scheme scared the politicians into fits at first. They expected that the people would use it to buck them off their backs and run the State government for their own benefit, but the people did nothing of the sort. The inferiority complex busted them as deftly as a cowboy does a broncho by warning them how unsafe it was to set out on a political experiment so bold and unprecedented. Of course it was gloriously alluring but think how outside statesmen would talk. Oregon would get a bad name. She would be called the fool of the family. By the time the flurry was over the politicians had patched the Oregon System so neatly into the seat of their old overalls that they could sit on it and graft as comfortably as if U'Ren had never been born.

In spite of the frugality of her founding fathers Portland has one wide and beautiful street downtown. It runs about halfway through the city from south to north and all of a sudden it stops. The Arlington clubhouse has been built squarely across it and bars its course to the logical terminus. "Thus far and no farther" is the edict of the brick walls and the street peters out into shanties. That rich men's clubhouse, standing where it does, is the concrete embodiment of Oregon's inferiority complex which sooner or later has blocked every move toward beauty and greatness. The wonder is that the fine ideal survives in spite of all the times it has been killed. It is an invincible spark of heavenly flame, the significant thing in Oregon's life. No sooner is one idealist flattened out than another jumps up waving the torch. It extenuates many sins, even the Rose Festival.

There is enough in the experience of Portland and the Willamette Valley to work up into an incomparable annual pageant. This could be done without trenching on the territory of romance preëmpted by Pendleton in the Inland Empire and the cow country. The Indians, the missionaries, the pioneers, the mountains, and the Columbia are waiting for their poet and there must be some young genius at Reed College bursting to answer their call if he could get the chance; but he does not get it. The pageant he would build, with all its living beauty, might not pay at the outset and Portland, true to the spirit of the men who laid out her Oriental streets, wants quick returns. So she wastes herself competing in a display of roses with cities to the south where roses bloom like weeds. When the perverse June weather blights the home supply she imports a few carloads. The inferiority complex entices her from what she could do supremely well into a competition where at best she can only be second or third rate. The situation is about the same as if Cinderella had been tempted by the slights of her stepmother to despise her native beauty and had painted her face for the King's ball.

Pendleton's Round Up is in the same boat. This has become a settled yearly event and might have a world-wide charm. For Pendleton lies in the rich bosom of the wheat country, at the door of the cowboys' home, with the Indian tribe which murdered Marcus Whitman still at hand, the sagebrush aromatic on the hills, and the keen air bright with the sunshine that never was anywhere else on land or sea. Pilgrims would come from the world over to smile and weep at the vanished range life she could evoke, its romance, its hardship, its invincible gayety, its sleight of hand and horsemanship, and its fidelity to everyday work. But she does not evoke the vanished life. She calls instead from the vasty deep a commercialized substitute which is supposed to pay better. Half the cowboys are cowgirls, incredible monsters that never rode the range, and the other half are roped out of dime novels. They travel over the country from show to show exhibiting their unreality for a livelihood. Round Ups are now as common as flies and Pendleton has frittered away the opportunity of a thousand years.

Oregon prides herself on her literary eminence almost as much as she fears the Pope. The tradition of letters runs down unbroken from the Protestant missionaries who wrote polemics against the Jesuits for their imagined complicity in killing Marcus Whitman to Mrs. Dye, who offers an agreeable home brew of fiction and history in "The Conquest" and other books. Frank Norris is counted among Oregon's authors because he once worked on an Astoria newspaper and Joaquin Miller because he is said to have held up a man east of the mountains in the placer mines. H. W. Scott's editorials have a good deal of the flavor of genuine literature. His family has published them in two gigantic volumes. I do not know that anybody reads this formidable collection but it is far less a waste of money than most tombstones. Some of the lads who work on the newspapers have written verses of promise as a matter of course, but Oregon's truly great poet was Sam Simpson, who courted the muse in the days when an apple from California sold for two bits in the Willamette Valley and everything else, including poetry, was priced on the same scale. Whether his local fame needs deflation or not the curious may say for themselves after reading his poems, which are on the market under the title of "Songs from the Golden West."

Thus far the inferiority complex has been too much for Oregon's idealists. Some of them it has killed outright with the deadly sickness of hope deferred, some have wearied of the everlasting fight and compromised with the second rate for the sake of peace and a living, some go to San Francisco and New York for a breath of the keen air of freedom, but there are some, too, who will not die and who will not run away from the tournament. A newspaper published in Rome must be Roman or else perish of inanition, but the *Journal,* of Portland, lives and makes money in spite of flashes from the eternal light that sometimes streak like chain-lightning down its columns. Around the *Journal,* for example, is a group of Oregonians to whom politics is something more than graft and life a little better than penny-pinching. Their ideals hark back to the pioneers and the brave old academies strung out along the Willamette. They are pioneering yet, out on the old trail, following the stars. I have seen U'Ren with a mob of supporters cheering him on and I have seen him plodding forward all by himself, but I have never seen him discouraged or afraid.

This loyalty to the ideal has been the saving factor in Oregon's life so far. Who knows how soon it may become the dominant factor? The faith in Oregon's unique vocation to a great destiny is a living faith. It is not dead yet and it will never die. I could name men in Portland and Salem and Pendleton who understand that her geographical situation, her resources and climate, and the prepotent genius of the pioneers have destined the State not to be an imitator of the sham and shoddy in outside civilization, but to create a civilization of her own for outsiders to imitate if they know when they are well off. And there are enough of those men to keep the pioneering ideal alive and to pass it on. By and by the idealists will win out. They will frame another Oregon System and not leave it mummied between the covers of a statute book but work it out in life. Then we shall see something in the Willamette Valley and the wheat and the cow country that it will be worth a trip across the continent to look at.

PENNSYLVANIA

STILL A KEYSTONE

By REGINALD WRIGHT KAUFFMAN

GIVEN a chance of making it—but particularly making it—the Indianian proclaims himself a Hoosier, the San Franciscan announces his California birth. That Southerner whose father came from Naples yells when the band plays "Dixie," and the New Yorker is ostentatious in his ignorance of anything west of Riverside Drive. Why is Pennsylvania diffident?

In a world so mixed as this of 1922, metaphors cannot escape the general *mélange*. We Pennsylvanians —and the politico-economic "we" means, of course, the controlling majority—used to speak of our commonwealth as the Keystone State. It is still that; but we don't say so. We don't say anything about it, and our silence is a symptom of our disease; nevertheless, we hope that ours will become the Keystone State, and therein lies our chance of cure. For we are suffering from over-immunization against the present epidemic of radicalism, and so soon as we are convinced that the plague has run its course, or that at least we are safe, we shall recover from our reaction. We trust that the orchestra of the Union will tune its instruments to ours; but *we* are going to be right, anyway.

"It seems to me," wrote *The Nation's* managing editor, "that you might effectively give Pennsylvania her place as the keystone of the American industrial edifice. Leaving out New York, it cannot be questioned that Pennsylvania is the most important State in the Union. One can well imagine any other withdrawn without affecting our national life. Upon the steel and coal of Pennsylvania has been built our vast economic structure—indeed, Wall Street is but the retail office of the power that comes from Pennsylvania."

The truth, but not the whole truth. He might have added that Lancaster County is agriculturally the richest land of its extent in the world, and that Chester and Berks and Bucks are not far behind. Nowhere is there a valley like our Donegal, scarcely anywhere such food as comes thence: the fat sausages, the gray pork puddings, the mush, the sauerkraut, the scrapple, proud capons and mighty beeves, cream cheese and cottage, meat-jellies, and apple-butter boiled in vast caldrons over veritable conflagrations—we live well and grow fat on them among things good to look upon. Our lowlands are yellow with the grain or green with the tobacco; the Alleghenies, the Tuscaroras, the Blue Ridge—to learn them is to lose your taste for the ruder Rockies; our Susquehanna is as beautiful as the Rhine and more beautiful than the Hudson.

Out of the beauty that is ours and the wealth, we have, indeed, extracted what the journalist just quoted precisely describes as "the very essence of American feudalism, imperialism, materialism." But not all at once. In production, the State has held its own; my thirty-five-year-old school geography adequately describes the Pennsylvania of today. As to mental and moral changes, most that was written of us in the eighties would still apply: our thinking people, and those wise enough to know that they don't think, have not, thank God, gone far in the direction that those who think they think call "forward." But socially we used to be paternalistic, whereas, though we need not, we have become indeed imperial and, consequently, material. We have stepped too far aside to avoid modernism, when, really, it is less annoying to stand quiet, or to go back, until this year of grace shall have become "one with yesterday's sev'n thousand years."

A pugilist that I know put it: "Pennsylvania's lost her pep." The protest against industrialism we have met with more industrialism; and industrialism has sorely wounded our enthusiasm. Now we can manufacture everything save that. Lately, we have produced only Woolworth and the five-and-ten-cent store, which, in turn, gave New York the biggest building in the world. Repeat the name of Keith to our average citizen; you will evoke no mention of Sir William, the first royal governor to espouse the popular cause: what you will evoke is a reference to that enterprising person who brought "refined vaudeville" to the Quaker City.

"Where," inquired a French friend of mine, "is Independence Hall?"

And a native Philadelphian answered: "Downtown, near the Curtis Publishing Company Building."

"For unknown geological reasons," says Lesley, "Pennsylvania is peculiar for exhibiting the Paleozoic system in its maximum development." For clearly discernible historical reasons, Pennsylvania's natural state was long paternalistic. Not only did the 1681 grant of Charles II give William Penn the patriarchal powers conferred by most royal grants; its recipient wisely, for all his immediate erection of popular suffrage, proceeded to administer his powers paternally. One of the greatest of advertising geniuses, he saw that his immigration prospectuses went to a list that, enormous as it was, was carefully "selective." He made his "holy experiment" upon people chosen for its success: in bestowing liberty of conscience, it is well to be sure that the freedmen are a sort whose ideas of liberty will not conflict with one's own. The land that had been given by the King had to be taken from the Indians: the English Quakers only sometimes cheated them; the Scotch-Irish Presbyterians only sometimes massacred them; the French Huguenots left them alone; the Swiss and German Quietists made friends with them. Then all these elements patterned their microcosms after the Proprietor's Manor.

An Englishman's house might be his castle: a Pennsylvanian's land was his kingdom. He held it in fief to an emperor vaguely personified in the Commonwealth, to whom he paid certain taxes and to whose general laws he was amenable; but he was its liege lord. Notwithstanding its religious precepts, the Society of Friends was composed of feudal-minded individuals, and the Friends' neighbors were their political brothers.

When, in the Maryland Border War, unarmed John Wright met the raiders alone, he was protecting that which was John Wright's, and, although his reading of the riot act was performed in his character of royal magistrate, it was his sermon as a Quaker owner that induced the invaders to down arms and help him with his harvest. Lord Hardwick's decision in chancery and Mason and Dixon's subsequent survey did divide the North and South, but they also "confirmed the original claims of Penn" and protected the border dependencies of his dependents. Even the Revolution respected the paternalistic point of view; the annulment of the old charter in 1778 carried a payment of £130,000 in satisfaction of the Penn demands.

Until time within living memory, there was no substantial change in the Pennsylvania attitude. The French and Indian alliance compelled a synthesis between non-resistance and self-protection; the balance swung toward self-protection in the Revolution, and self-protection became patriotism. The State's war records are among its proudest; but even its defense of the Underground Railway was in part a defense by individuals maintaining the sanctity of their own bits of earth. Until twenty-five years ago, we Pennsylvania-Dutch always referred to a large landholder as *König* So-and-So.

And, in the old days, the administration of those little kingdoms was beneficent. First on the farm, then at the mill, and finally in the mine, it was a point of honor and a badge of pride that one's employees should be contented. We had our "Coal Families" that owned the fuel-veins, our iron and steel families that worked the ore-banks and ran the furnaces; one clan possessed a little mountain-range and kept its hold on the lumber until the great rafts had escaped rock and rapids as far south as Peach Bottom or Port Deposit. Homestead is a red blot, but, excepting that and a few minor outbreaks in abolition days, there have been, even to this date, only four bloody internal disturbances: the Whisky Rebellion, the affair of the Molly Maguires, and a couple of sanguinary railway strikes. My Marxian friends to the contrary notwithstanding, the workers were better educated than now—knew just as well what was good for them and yet were satisfied: they had no chains to lose and, consequently, no ambition to gain a world.

Later immigration was slow to affect the old order. The Germans that came to us in the nineteenth century were largely law-abiding Western Catholics; so were the Irish, and so have been most of the Italians that followed these. Our later Hungarians and Poles stand in the same faith, and our Russian and Serb miners, our Greek confectioners and bootblacks and our Syrian merchants are Eastern Orthodox: they obey the catechism of Platon of Moscow.

It was the employers themselves that made the change. Not even a manifestation of economic determinism did it. The feudal holdings of life's necessities were so large a proportion of the whole nation's store that the holders could have maintained their position. They simply didn't want to.

We still boast an entire town making chocolate under family rule: it is a survival. Most of us went corporation-mad. The Pennsylvania Railroad became the best railway in America, and it was too much for us industrially; John Wanamaker happened into the Bon Marché, and our retail system, though bettered in twenty particulars, could never be the same again. We opened our gates to the new movement; the mountains were "lumbered" above until naked; they were mined below until city streets caved in. Many a mine-owner lost his badge; combinations of capital produced combinations of labor. Then we discovered that among other guests whom we had invited was the radical. It was the reaction of our paternalistic inheritance to this discovery that produced our present plight.

The process pursued in our economics had to be pursued in our politics. There has been a deal of nonsense talked about them; representative government is still on trial; our sort has not been the best imaginable, but we considered it plenty good enough for us and long perpetuated it. Mark Sullivan, in the *Atlantic Monthly,* once blamed our Quietists: he said they wouldn't interfere to set up their own ideals. He was wrong. Our Quietists do not interfere for the excellent reason that their ideals have been set up. When their ideals are endangered, they go to the polls.

The Amishman is the standard type of our non-voter, yet he was the silent cause of the abnormally large Republican vote cast in Pennsylvania at the Congressional elections of 1918. After them, an Amishman came to Columbia—which, as Wright's Ferry, escaped from being Washington by one vote in the Continental Congress—to attend the funeral of a brother who had "turned Methodist." Another brother, turned member of the Church of God, sat beside the coffin. During the services, the Amishman plucked this one's sleeve.

"Well," he said, "we done it, ain't?"

"Done what?" asked the backslider of the Church of God.

"Woted," explained the Quietist. "Sink o' this

here Wilson tellin' us a Democrat Conkress had ought to be elected: him sendin' word to us yet, orderin' us how to wote—*we woted!*"

No, we Pennsylvanians were the satisfied subjects of paternalism: Stevens died on a Tuesday in the August of 1868; the Lancaster County Republican primaries for the nomination of a Congressman had been set for that Saturday; no candidates would present themselves while the body of the representative whom the people loved remained above ground; the voters knew that he was dead, yet, when the ballots were counted, it was found that every one had been deposited for Thaddeus Stevens.

The Cameron Dynasty, father and son, ruled us to our taste. Quay was their heir; even his factional rivals like now to think that no other State has produced so great a master of political strategy. Then Penrose came, Harvard *magna cum laude,* holder of the bequeathed power *magna cum laude,* too. But at his death there was the fear of the radical. Heretical *tirailleurs* were advancing toward the electoral field of the coming gubernatorial contest, and, at the primaries, there were the schismatic Vares from Philadelphia. Being conservatives, the paternalists followed a well-worn recipe: they chose as their candidate a man that the onward-lookers believed to be a vessel of Progressivism, but a vessel that the Organization believed to be by no means full of that liquor. Far from being the triumph for reform that it was heralded as being, Pinchot's nomination was due to the 5,000 votes given him by Buck Devlin, the Penrose boss of the Eighth Philadelphia Ward—Penrose's own.

Over-immunization. The Pittsburgher journeying into Canada puts a full flask in his suit-case. If that Act which Miss Laura Volstead so ably drafted for her father depended upon the majority of our Pennsylvania voters, it would not be invalidated: it would be decapitated. We are not for things as they are; certainly not for things as they threaten to be elsewhere; we are so much for things as they were with us that we are a bit rough-handed.

Our conservatism best exhibits itself socially, our over-immunization in education, science, and the arts. The Lincolns of Berks County, who sound their second *l,* were not asked to Reading charity balls just because their kinsman became President; the clan that forbade a marriage with the young Carnegie because he was "in business" would not have changed its mind when he became the man that could not die poor; Market Street is still a dead-line in Philadelphia, and the Dunker farmer knows the Christian name of the least important of his great-great-grandfather's brothers-in-law.

"Mom," asked Joe Ritner's children, after their father's election in 1835, "are we *all* governors now?"

"No," answered the Governor's wife: "only me an' pop."

That concept of the family remains among us, and with it the old concept of chivalry. If you are a woman, Pennsylvania is a good State in which to kill your husband; in substituting barbarous electrocution for dignified hanging, we have not extended our acceptance of woman's rights to her right to death when she has taken up the sword; but if you are a man, you had better do all your murders in New Jersey.

Of course, at least in the countryside and the small towns, we have remained a friendly folk and tolerant. The Quakers are passing, but the Mennonites in their shovel-hats, the Amish—the "Beardy Men"—in the brown homespun that bears hooks-and-eyes instead of buttons, because "buttons is a wanity": they reap by turns, for each helps his neighbor bring the harvest in. Does the girl cashier in the county town embezzle a little money? She was underpaid; we raise her salary, and she makes restitution on the installment plan. We have little drifting labor, and our jails are seldom full.

Nevertheless, we are answering our radicals with more of what they object to. It is denied that Bryn Mawr uses an expurgated Iliad or bans "Othello" because of that dark warrior's love for a white lady; but the University of Pennsylvania's Wharton School of Finance cannot be concealed, and our "business colleges" are a contradiction in terms the most thorough in the world. We have more kinds of religion than any other State, but our most popular preacher's most popular sermon is called "Acres of Diamonds." James M. Beck is in Washington; John G. Johnson is dead, and the world-wide proverb about a Philadelphia lawyer with him. The Da Costas, the Solis-Cohens, De Schweinitz, and Keen did not graduate from our medical schools yesterday; it is a long time since Henri, Sloan, Parrish, and Scofield left our Academy of the Fine Arts. The Philadelphia Orchestra flourishes, but many a Pennsylvania town has 12,000 population and no library. Out of such hands as Wister's the literary tradition has passed into those of Mr. Joseph Hergesheimer.

Is all this a mere lament for "the good old times"? It is. But it must not end in a dirge: it must rise to a fanfare. For Pennsylvania is that State of life unto which it has pleased God to call me, and I love it; in its kindly earth lie the bones of all my people for the past two hundred years and more: my own bones will lie easily nowhere else. Again, then, the truth, but not the whole truth: I have tried to tell what Pennsylvania peculiarly is; what she will be is another matter. Economically there will be little change for long, radical or other. But spirit is more important than economics, and stronger: already there are signs of a return to former days.

Charles M. Schwab wanted to move a house; in the route stood a tree that his mother loved: he had the house lifted over the tree. There is something more than materialism in our capitalists.

In that something-more in everything about us waits our salvation. Even now our farmers have ceased buying gold-mine stock. The black smoke is not symbolic of Pittsburgh; Philadelphia holds promise of deserving again the priceless epithet of "slow." In Scranton, Altoona, Columbia, York, Lancaster, and Bethlehem men and women are getting drunk once more, and drunkenness is one of the commonest, if most misdirected, expressions of divine discontent.

We procure our beer, though we must drink it quietly. Our people don't want to marry either above or beneath them. Welfare-work and the pension-system are softening the Pharaoh-heart of Labor. In our

Episcopalianism the Highs have it; Bishop Darlington is friendly with the Eastern Orthodox; Western Catholicism gains converts; Zionism has returned hundreds of Pennsylvania Jews to their fathers' faith; our Lutherans are beginning to think of what they call their Orders; Methodists have "vested choirs." The day may yet dawn when we shall recover form in the arts, and when the rich man of a small town will again support it rather than exploit it. After all, the Republican Organization is still in power: our next Governor after Pinchot will not even seem to be a Progressive.

Over-autonomic-immunization against certain specific disease-tendencies: S. Solis-Cohen, who belled that cat, has given it a beautiful name—vaso-motor-ataxia. It is significant that he is himself a Pennsylvanian; his disease, as I have said, is Pennsylvania's trouble. But Cohen, in his contribution to the Osler Seventieth Birthday volume, bears hope:

"The writer has felt justified in reassuring patients who—presenting marked autonomic disorders, and aware of tendencies to tuberculosis or carcinoma in their families—have expressed a fear of developing cancer or consumption, by telling them that they are protected; that they are, in all probability, suffering from an 'excess of protection.' Thus far, the assurance of immunity, the prediction of safety, has not proved false in any known instance."

With us Pennsylvanians, the malady is only mental. When our subconsciousness has been convinced of our immunity, we shall resume the paternalistic attitude in everything possible; we shall return to—*normalcy.*

TEXAS

THE BIG SOUTHWESTERN SPECIMEN

By GEORGE CLIFTON EDWARDS

TEXAS, it should be observed by a native anxious to begin on the right note, is great. It is great in size. As it shows on the map it is as large as New York, Pennsylvania, Massachusetts, Illinois, Ohio and Wisconsin, all in one. It is larger than France; larger than Germany; and, in products, more abundant. We produce more cotton than any other State; more oil, both cotton-seed and Standard; more cattle and sweet potatoes; more peanuts and mules; more brass-bound Democrats and Democratic office-holders; more Ku Klux Klansmen, killings, and lynchings. We sent to the Baltimore Convention a group of shock troops that came away shouting that they won the nomination for Woodrow Wilson. Mr. Wilson must have believed this, for he allowed Texas to contribute to our country's welfare the slave-driving Burleson, who used the post office to abolish freedom of the press; T. W. Gregory, who developed a spy system vaster than the Czar's; and Colonel House, who abolished secrecy in diplomacy. But size and raw products are not our only grounds for complacency. We have a remarkable history.

One of our school histories is called "Under Six Flags." The French, under the adventurous La Salle, made the first settlement in 1685, but dissension and starvation wiped this out. During a century and more, the Spanish, from Mexico, slowly established ranches and missions, villages and presidios, far spread but thinly settled. In 1820 the Mexicans broke away from Spain and established a republic, which in due time brought forth a dictator, who did not get along with the English-speaking colonists coming in from the States. After many quarrels and compromises the Americans revolted in 1836 and set up the republic of Texas with a constitution, a president, an army, and a miniature navy. Ten years later the Republic came into the Union; the State seceded and joined the Confederacy; and was brought back into the Union, after a bitter reconstruction experience with Republicans and Negro soldiers. It is true that Texas is now fully within the American industrial machine; but no other State had as vivid and varied experiences getting there.

This history left some marks. It left us with a tendency to act first, and to think later, if ever; and it left us with a scant regard for human life when feelings are stirred. Of the early French there are few material traces. Spanish influence has not been obliterated, however. Thousands of Mexicans have remained, unchanged and unassimilated. Texas law contains many Spanish survivals, particularly concerning land, the family, and the rights of married women. Franciscan missions, combinations of fort and church, the Alamo, San Fernando, Concepcion, and San José, still stand, relics of Spanish architectural grace and of Spanish devotion to the Indians whose souls the friars sought to save.

This vast State is far from uniform, physically. In

the southeast, about Beaumont, are forests, swamps, and rice fields; and in Democratic war days, shipyards. It is low, moist, warm, and busy. About San Angelo, in Tom Green County, it is bare, high and dry and drowsy, except, as it seems to a visitor, for the evidences of the State's fight against tuberculosis. At the State Sanatorium, where the principles Trudeau developed at Saranac are admirably carried out in this more genial climate, a poor "T.B." from Beaumont once expressed it thus: "It's hard that I can live out here where I can't make a living; at Beaumont I can make a living but I can't live." Of course they do raise cattle and sheep in Tom Green; and also, in the rare rainy years, a bountiful crop of false hopes. Water is all that country needs. Where they can irrigate, they manufacture garden truck at will. To the south, in the lower Rio Grande valley, it never freezes, and irrigation produces even more bountifully, with oranges and grape fruit. Half a thousand miles northwest and four thousand feet higher, the Panhandle country knows winters piercingly cold, with northers, the ranchers say, straight from the Pole, broken only by barbed-wire fences. Sometimes it snows in the Panhandle as late as May; but the May snows quickly vanish and in a few days the plains are an endless exquisite green. On the eastern side of the State are dense pine forests. On the western edge, near El Paso, the Guggenheims operate one of their largest smelters, and the United States holds its army crouched for the spring on Mexican oil fields.

But these extremes do not express the spirit of present-day Texas as does the middle: the cities to which the rich "black waxy" land counties and the oil counties are tributary, where the population is dense, the tenant farms numerous, the banks powerful and interlocked. Here are no arid plains, no wind-swept plateaus, no forests, no rice fields, no cowboys. The rich little city of Waco has one twenty-story skyscraper sticking up like a totem pole among the Baptists. Houston (which we call "Hewston") has more skyscrapers; Dallas more and higher; all modern machine-made, as much like the north as may be; crammed with offices, bankers, lawyers, oil men, "realtors"—effective Texas of today. For landscape and Old World atmosphere, history and heroes do not occupy our thoughts much. The substantial characteristics of Texas are suggested not by the flower-glowing prairies under gorgeous skies or the mellow Spanish missions, but by the ubiquitous oil tanks and the electric power lines.

To be sure, the masses of Texans are not business men and do not make much money; they are hard-working people, and just get along; they do not starve, and rarely suffer from cold—except in the winter. Few farmers make anything above a living unless by some rise in land values; farm laborers live as wretchedly as tenant farmers, who are not much better off than serfs. But we are easily taken in by the business men and the newspapers. The larger our city, the larger our capacity for being fooled: cities are the habitat of the corporations and their lawyers, pleasant, facile sophists, with all the ancient and modern skill in making the worse appear the better part. In Dallas, for example, from the time it first became a paying field for franchise-holders, every city government has been dominated by business and the public-service interests. Some administrations have been more eager than others, but all, without exception, have served the interests primarily. When a utility (street railway, electric power, telephone, or gas) wants a measure and the people do not, the people are beaten, sometimes openly, sometimes secretly, but always effectively.

The telephone company has just hired off the bench the chief justice of the Supreme Court of Texas. The man who was lately supposed to exercise, for the people, the highest impartiality in deciding fundamental law questions, is now running hither and yon, before courts, city governments, and commissions, for the telephone monopoly and against the people. The president of the most powerful street railway in Texas, a system owned by absentee capitalists, is a former mayor of Dallas, a lawyer with no knowledge of railways but with a commanding ability to fool the people by his pose as a good citizen of the home town. This man was, with possibly one exception, the most subservient mayor the interests have ever had, and they have had them all. In 1918 the mayor, specially elected by the street-railway company, and the commissioners, allowed the street-railway company to add to its capital account an item of $100,000 expended by the company in "promoting the franchise." Which, being interpreted, meant in electing that mayor and getting for nothing a franchise worth millions. Dallas is paying and will continue to pay dividends on this $100,000, spent not to buy cars or to lay tracks, but to debauch an election. This is one reason for the six-cent fare in Dallas, established during war prices as an emergency and continued now after deflation as graft. Against this domination of the city by the utilities there is scarcely any citizen's protest, and no newspaper protest whatever. The rewarding, after the fact, of men chosen to serve the people who instead served the corporations is regarded as good business. Modern Texas considers it the proper thing for such officials to be on the make, so long as they pay virtue the proper tribute of canting talk and are "good men."

In State politics the situation is the same. Politicians and business men tell us, and we swallow, huge and solemn lies. In 1919 a start was made toward a minimum-wage law for women and minors. It had some teeth. As soon as the employers found this out they had it repealed, which the legislature did on the ground that it was impracticable "without doing serious injury to the female and minor employees"! Our child-labor law, city home-rule law, and workmen's compensation law, viewed from the theoretical purpose of the laws, are about as bona fide as the anti-trust law: which last is as much a joke in its ultimate effectiveness as the Sherman law. Once the Standard Oil Company was fined a million dollars, which we, the consumers, paid; and was driven from the State, but after walking through dry places for a while, it came back with seven, or more, other spirits, and we are now worse off than before. We have an "Open Port Law," so named because it was designed, it was said, to keep "open" the port of Galveston. The day before election our young Baptist Governor would not use it, seeking union votes. He got them, and the day after election, it was put into effect to break the railroad strike at Denison four hundred miles from any port. He estimated rightly our capacity for being fooled.

Nearly all our politicians are lawyers, and in the courts they apply the same sort of skill they use in politics. In Texas, as elsewhere, men are sentenced to the penitentiary, in pretense for crime, in fact for being poor. No one who is able to hire the "best" criminal lawyers need worry about being hanged or about staying in jail. It is a fact that there is a son of a rich Texan in one prison convicted of robbery with firearms. But his accomplice is under death sentence—being poor. That this rich man is actually in prison is such a wonder to us that we never cease talking about it.

With the introduction of modern business spirit, our killings have changed somewhat. Very rarely in Texas do we now have a killing like that in which an early Dallas mayor and a brother lawyer were looking for each other in the court-house. They drew on sight, but the lawyer drew first. The death of Brann, the "Iconoclast," our Waco literary light, was old-fashioned. He had quarreled with the Baptists—and many others—and an acquaintance shot him, mortally, from behind; but Brann braced himself against a telephone pole, turned, and killed his fellow citizen. This is not the modern style of killing. It is not businesslike and involves some risk.

The best preventive against conviction in a Texas murder case is money. The best trial defenses are the "unwritten law" and the "hip-pocket move," both of which are based on solemn fooling. The "unwritten law" is large and liberal as the all-embracing air of rumor. It is, as it works out, that any person who can allege that a man has committed adultery with, or insulted, or "talked about" a female relative (marriage, blood, or step), can kill that man on sight, shooting from front, side, or back, without word or warning. Recently a young man was accused of having had a sexual adventure with a young woman. The father of the young woman and her stepfather, that is, the present husband of her mother, got the young man into a hotel room, by himself, unarmed, and killed him, shooting him nine times. These killers were, for a long time, not indicted; it was doubtful whether they would ever be indicted; and it will be a waste of time to try them in a Ku Klux court, now that they are indicted. After the preliminary hearing on bonds, the Ku Klux lawyer stated that he was greatly surprised that the prosecuting attorney would not agree to a low bond for "these Christian men." Yet no one should get the notion that the men of Texas are Miltonic in the practice of chastity. They are much as other men; but it is the custom of the country to talk as did that Ku Klux lawyer.

The Texas "hip-pocket move" is pleaded against a person who after death by shooting is shown to have had nothing in his hip-pocket. It is quite distinct from the effort to draw a weapon, a movement where the person killed has a gun. Three recent Texas cases typical of the "hip-pocket move" reveal a man killed with a cigar in his mouth; one standing talking at a wall telephone; another, sitting at his desk, with a fountain pen in his hand.

Texas early established a court devoted entirely to

criminal appeals, the industry having grown too large for the Supreme Court to handle. Except for one short period this court has been one of strict construction. It stands on the letter of the law, and in so doing has shown surprising skill. Consider this. There is a rule that the best evidence must be adduced. Circumstantial evidence is not the best if direct evidence is obtainable. Richard Roe's horse is stolen. He gets John Doe arrested, charging him with the theft. Roe testifies that he owned the horse, that his horse was "stolen," using that word, and that Doe was found with the horse. This is not enough. The State is required, when the owner is present and testifies, to prove "want of consent" in terms. Therefore, if the State did not ask: "Mr. Roe, did you consent to Mr. Doe's taking your horse?" and did not get the direct answer "No," the rules of evidence have been violated and the conviction of Doe will be reversed. The line of decisions supporting this absurdity extends from the first volume of Texas Criminal Reports down to Volume 231 of the Southwestern, and is the law today.

The Supreme Court, on the civil side, is capable of equal ingenuity, but is more modern and businesslike. The Dallas city charter provides that "any proposed ordinance" may be submitted to, voted on by, and adopted by the people. The Supreme Court, on the suit of the telephone company, says: "Yes, that is true, and that is good law. But 'any proposed ordinance' does not mean 'any proposed ordinance.' It plainly means: *any proposed ordinance which is, in our judgment, suited to the initiatory method and which is not within the powers of the Board of Com-*

missioners." Now the commissioners can pass practically any sort of ordinance. The initiative, of course, was intended as a means for the people to pass those ordinances which they wanted but which the commissioners would not pass. But the fact that the commissioners can pass an ordinance (though they will not do it) is, in the mind of the Supreme Court of Texas, a sound reason why the people shall not be allowed to pass the ordinance, in spite of the words of the charter authorizing them to pass "any proposed ordinance." Thus Dallas has in its charter a perfectly good-looking initiative and referendum section that has as much vitality as the wooden Indian that used to stand in front of our cigar stores. The Supreme Court indulges here in excellent fooling; but it is good up-to-date law fooling, quite on a level with the child-labor decisions of the United States Supreme Court.

The open-shop movement in Texas is active; and it exhibits the frauds we are gulled by, in purest form. In theory, the open shoppers are animated by devotion to abstract justice and make no distinction between union and non-union men, loving them equally. In practice, the open shop means a scab shop. Its most liberal supporters are those corporations, in particular the utility corporations, that as a matter of principle, fire every employee who joins a union. Yet day after day, in letters, speeches, circulars, and newspapers, the statement is repeated that the open shop is not fighting the unions. Every one of its speakers, and every informed man, knows this is a brazen falsehood, but the open shoppers know our Texas public. They know it is not informed and that it loves the process of being fooled. And fooled or not fooled, after we make up, or have made up for us, what passes for our minds, we act as if there were only one side, and that the stronger. We are intolerant of minority views and rights. There is no peace without victory in Texas. It is a Versailles treaty the defeated expect, in politics, industry, or religion.

Morality—the compulsion upon others of the ideas of the old men of the various religious groups—we talk a great deal about; but we have little interest in scientific, or indeed in any sort of knowledge, from books, unless immediately merchantable. We are not hostile after a matter has become a commonplace of the newspapers and the *Saturday Evening Post,* which we buy by the ton. Before it has been thus diluted and denatured, we will have none of it. It is hard to believe that a large, rich, technically, and mechanically efficient newspaper can fill its editorial page, eight long columns, 365 days a year, without indicating somewhere in it that sometime, some editor has read a book. But the Dallas *News,* our greatest Texas daily, achieves this. About the only book ever named is the Revised Statutes, and the only one ever reflected is "Science and Health," this reflection appearing every Sunday in a column of editorial bathos. Sometimes the hostility to a new idea is quite frank. The editor of another Texas daily printed a characteristically violent attack on the Plumb Plan. Shortly afterward, in his office, he kindly hunted up a little book on the Plumb Plan to give me. "No," he said genially, "I haven't read it and I don't want to. I can lambaste it better if I don't." At the top of this paper's editorial column, the editor prints a classic quotation from the well-known Mr. Bartlett; and he has thereby a great popular reputation as a reading man. Just equally interested in books is the Dallas Scripps paper, our representative of liberal thought; but it is strong for morals. It modestly admits in 12 point black on the front page, editorially, that it is "run on the Golden Rule." And few laugh in its face.

The most prominent and "eloquent" preachers in Texas expound doctrines as primitive as those of the Salem witch hangers. They are as certain as Bryan and Billy Sunday that there is nothing to evolution save a slander on humanity: they call it "monkeyism." They believe in and teach the actual physical resurrection of the body, and the actual physical flame and burning of hell. Toward which well-deserved fate, of course, free thinkers and Unitarians are moving directly. The preachers are vastly patriotic. They still talk about "Hunnishness" and about the "war for democracy," though it must be admitted that they do not claim now that the war ended war. In the cities the preachers are apt to be good business men. The active young Episcopal bishop of Dallas was one of the organizing committee from the Chamber of Commerce, to establish the open shop. The most lurid of our Texas Baptists is generally believed to have set fire to his own church as an advertising stunt. This man is very successful in Texas.

It is a matter of pride to us in Texas, that our early statesmen, preoccupied as they were with the violence and the difficulties of their times, did plan for a good educational system. The public schools and the State

University were bountifully endowed with gifts of land; but these have not been well managed. Our country schools are poor, and the teachers miserably paid. In the cities the schools are far better, and the teachers fairly well paid; but it is made clear to them that they are to stick in the rut, must not be too much interested in learning or books, and shall be strictly conventional if they desire to get on. City school boards repeatedly refuse to "reëlect" [the teachers hold by one-year tenure and are "reported on" regularly] teachers who show any signs of thinking and speaking independently. What is wanted in schools and colleges is the industrious type that will not do or say, or be caught thinking, anything except what is approved by those factory directors, the trustees. Some men have been let out of the University of Texas for matters of opinion purely; but mostly this censorship intimidates in advance. Teachers very frankly admit that they cannot teach what they think or follow to conclusion lines of thought constantly reached in classes. They either decline to speak or they evade issues: their jobs depend on it. The Damoclean sword of "investigation" hangs over all, save the machine-minded and the time servers. A Texas legislator recently charged that the University was teaching Socialism, and cited the catalogue, where in plain black print it was set out that there were classes in and teachers of *Sociology*. Rice Institute, a millionaire-endowed college at Houston, discharged a teacher for his opinions, expressed outside of the college, in reference to justice to the Bolsheviki. Baylor University, a large and rich college, but Baptist, "investigated" and discharged a teacher who wrote a very conventional text-book on Sociology that aroused the Baptist ministerial hatred of science and evolution.

The Southern Methodist University at Dallas was established to take the place of Vanderbilt University, which had fallen from grace and its Methodist swaddling bands. Dr. John A. Rice, one of the teachers, published a book on the Old Testament. There was nothing startling in the book unless one excepts some of his personal testimony on the extremes to which Southern Methodist literal belief can go. But as soon as the echoes of this book (the book itself they would not read) reached the Methodist preachers of the State they went after Dr. Rice's scalp. And there was no lack of frankness. He was fired for cause, and the cause stated. An incident showing the connection between business and intolerance in the schools developed shortly thereafter. In one of the student publications, a writer took a fling at the president, charging him with "playing politics" in the Rice case. The president called a meeting of the students, demanded the passage of a resolution stating that the article was false, and made this argument: "There are three men who have put in their wills big endowments to the university who will withdraw these endowments if the student body does not support the faculty in this matter." Plainly the president regarded his action toward Dr. Rice, if not as politics, at least as good business. The resolution was passed. The three endowments are safe. The president has since been made a bishop.

The intolerance that depresses our schools and intimidates the teachers exists nearly everywhere. The lunch clubs defend all existing means of exploitation, boost public-utility schemes, afford publicity to attacks on unions and strikers, entirely refusing to hear the other side. One club denounced the Plumb Plan at a time when most of the lunchers thought it a new method for fruit raisers. The only speech that I ever heard in Dallas openly advocating violence was at a lunch club. At a Rotary Club luncheon a very rich and prominent corporation lawyer advocated summary shooting for all I.W.W.'s, agitators, and soreheads against the Government generally, the method of identification not being specified or regarded as important.

But there are no I.W.W.'s in Texas. The unions are pure and simple after Gompers's own heart. The labor leaders are conventional, generally ignorant of the labor movement outside of their personal experience in their own craft. Often the leader is subject to purchase or pressure because there is neither idealism nor principle in his equipment. His office means to him merely a steady job to collect at least the full wage scale assured by keeping in line a majority of his local or council. The labor press is venal, paid for in advertising. Dallas is the head of the open-shop movement in Texas; and the Dallas official labor paper carries constantly large well-paying advertisements from the utility interests that are the brain, backbone, and treasury of the open shop. Though this is the frankest sort of bribery, resentment by the simple union men is lacking.

The unions last year, however, under the leadership of the Farm Labor Union, joined a non-partisan political conference, and tried in the Democratic party to emulate North Dakota's success in the Republican. The farmer-labor nominee was not successful in the primary, but more union men than ever before voted for a man they themselves, with the farmers, had selected. There is hope in this showing, even though the platform and the candidate both evaded the Ku Klux issue and the use of troops and rangers against the strikers. What political progressive activity there is in Texas has its origin among the farmers, for the union men are befooled by the daily papers and hoodwinked by the Gompers type of labor leader.

All of our present-day characteristics—our fondness for being fooled, our subjection to big business, our intolerance, our hatred, our preference for violent action, our prejudices against the Negro—have flowered in the Ku Klux Klan. Dallas, the city most thoroughly dominated by the utility interests, is the Klan stronghold. There is no complete record available to "aliens" of its achievements; but no less than sixty mobbing episodes took place in Dallas before the anti-Klan elements began to organize last spring. A Negro, with his back lashed and his forehead branded K. K. K. with acid, was thrust into the Adolphus, the showy, leading hotel of Dallas. Then we learned that before we had waked, at a special election in the preceding summer, the Ku Klux had elected a State Senator. Other mobbings took place, of Negroes and whites, and finally a reputable business man was taken from his home, dragged from the presence of his daughters, one of whom was knocked down by the chivalrous knights, taken to the river bottom and terribly beaten. Not once did police or sheriff find any of the mobbers. The only two men arrested charged with offenses were police officers, and both were promptly acquitted. The Dallas sheriff and the Dallas city police commissioner are leaders in the Klan. At the great Dallas Ku Klux parade the electric company kindly cut off all the downtown lights and let the masked men march in their desired darkness.

The Ku Klux Klan came into Texas with a selling organization that beats the installment furniture collectors in effective personal work. Its paid organizers made money as the snowball grew. They took in the small church people who wanted to vent their virtue on others. The head of the Dallas Klan now is a Christian preacher, an oil speculator, and an Elk. The most wholesale approval of the Ku Klux was expressed in a Dallas speech by the man whom the Methodists have just elected head of the church in North Texas. While he made a little lip protestation of belief in law and order, he promptly added that not one person had been attacked by the Ku Klux who had not got what he deserved. The very officials, police, sheriff, judges, prosecutors, who are charged with responsibility for law enforcement, were solicited and, with few exceptions, taken in. A newspaper man, friendly to, if not a member of, the Klan told me in answer to my question about the men guilty of one flogging. "Why, it's the police. But they can't prove it on them. They ought to have killed the damn Jew." "It's a fine grand-stand play the mayor is making over that Jew, ain't it?" I heard one plain-clothes officer say to another. "It's all a bluff. He's one of them himself." This is the

Dallas feeling about the Ku Klux, the church, and the officials.

The women of the churches were not taken in directly, but effectively annexed in a capacity that the "alien" world thought a joke when it was first announced—namely as "rumor spreaders," who charged opposition candidates and officials with being Catholics, or having Catholic wives, or with being about to be Catholics. True to our Texas practice, the dentist Evans, high man in the State Klan, announced that the "Klan is not a political organization." This buncombe was carried on by Earle B. Mayfield, who was on the Ku Klux ticket last election, but refused to answer any question about it or to discuss it "because it was not an issue." Not until he had won the nomination for the United States Senate did he admit that he had been a member; then he asserted that he had resigned, but he continued to attend the Klan meetings. This combination of officials, fanatics, preachers, and politicians has finally gone into partnership with the great utility corporations. The campaign manager of the Klan in Dallas was the law partner of the ex-mayor of Dallas who is the president of the Dallas street railway company. This union of fanaticism and finance has swept Dallas and the State.

The governor, the house of representatives certainly, and the senate probably, most of the trial judges, sheriffs, and the police—practically all are Klansmen in membership or in spirit. In Dallas the entire county government, prosecuting attorney, sheriff, judges, all the clerical officers, were elected by the Klan. Now they are openly planning to take possession of the city government, get the offices for themselves and furnish the electric interests with an enthusiastically, not a grudgingly, subservient administration. They will probably be successful. The electric interests are powerful and will take much other business along with them in their raid on the city hall. They will, however, probably soft-pedal the mobbing industry in Dallas. In fact this has already been done. There has not been a case of mobbing in Dallas since the fight on the Klan began last May: the leaders have been too intent on offices to let the mobbers act. The more hopeful of us think that as the Klan gets better known and its connection with the utilities is exposed, it will lose some of its power. This is not likely to happen in the smaller towns. There the mob spirit and the church fanaticism will bear bloodier fruit. Catholic priests have been, and will be, taken out and whipped for "pro-Germanism" at this late day. One woman was mobbed, beaten, her hair cut off, and brought back to the little town half naked. There is no measure that can be given of the cruelty this movement has brought to bear on the Negroes. The Ku Klux has, of course, simply exaggerated the feeling that is common in the South and in Texas. Here men will discuss the weather, a lawsuit, a grocery bill, or a building scheme and use their best intellect; let them touch the Negro question and they are no longer dominated by their thinking—they become a mass of feeling and flaming prejudice. And this is truest of those who are themselves almost as poor and wretched as the Negro, economically. And while thousands do not believe in any sort of mob law, do not desire to oppress the

Negro, and realize that religious intolerance is a pure curse, they are not in an effective majority now.

The regulation question in Texas as elsewhere in the United States, addressed to one not properly commendatory of the herd's ways, is "Why don't you go back to where you came from, if you don't like it here?" My answer satisfies me at least. I was born in Dallas, and I am not a workingman or a farmer. The Texas climate is good and the utilities do not yet own it. It is true that we have a difficult social situation, but few other States are in a position to throw stones at us. Little as can be said for Texas justice, it has no Mooney case, nor such anti-thought laws as California. We cannot match Ludlow; nor the Chicago riots and East St. Louis riots; nor the cold infamy of the mine owners of West Virginia; and if we have no Socialist legislators, we have not thrown any out as has New York. Our school intolerance is due to ignorance and not crystallized into Lusk Laws.

As for the other Southern States, they are no better than Texas. We have the worst case of the Ku Klux but Georgia invented it. Texas lynches, mutilates, and burns Negroes; but, except for this, the Ku Klux year, other Southern States rank ahead of us in this pastime—they have more Negroes to lynch. But the mass of Texans, in varying degrees, are suffering and will suffer from the reactionary Democratic party, oppression of the Negro, corporation domination, church fanaticism, and the perfect embodiment of them all, the Ku Klux Klan, just as the whole South suffered from slavery. These things are a denial of civilization, and a lover of civilization cannot be comfortable here.

Why any workingman or farmer, or any person who expects to live by honest toil, should come to Texas, or, if he is footloose, should stay here, is hard to see—except that there are few better places to go. Texas is not attractive to labor or to liberal thinking. It is a good State for exploiters to profit by credulity and fanaticism, by defrauding and oppressing the weak. But, after all, is it not, really, just the big Southwestern specimen of American capitalism?

ARIZONA

THE LAND OF THE JOYOUS ADVENTURE

By MARY AUSTIN

It would be easier to treat of Arizona as Dominion than as one of these United States. Not that there is any question about the swift and whole-hearted allegiance of Arizona, but there are distinctions. Her territory is about equal in map miles to the combined areas of New York, New Jersey, Delaware, Pennsylvania, and Maryland, which means, taking the mountainous nature of the country into account, that there are about as many more miles standing straight in the air, lying at the bottom of deep canyons or doubling in immeasurable folds of crumpled rock. To this dramatic variety of contour is added color and a play of light and atmospheric effect which for pure splendor and subtlety is not elsewhere matched. This superlative intention exhibited in the topography is reflected in the history of Arizona to an extent that makes it obligatory to add -est to every adjective that describes it. Not only is its Grand Canyon the grandest and its cotton staple the longest in the world, but it is the newest State and the seat of the oldest civilization within the territory of what is now the United States. In Arizona one finds the scale of amazing things running from petrified forests to common weeds that produce rubber in what promises to be commercial quantity.

First of all we hear of this country emerging from a

cloud of legend in the report of one Cabeza de Vaca who had come first to Florida with Narvaez, was thence wind-driven in an open boat as far as the coast of Texas, and wandering, in the longest walk ever recorded by a European, heard of—and possibly touched—what is now Arizona, as a land of many-storied cities, true prototype of the modern American skyscraper, using gold as common metal, having door lintels crowned with turquoises. Later its wilderness was certainly traversed by Estevan, a Barbary Moor, slave of that Dorantes to whom were given the five emerald arrows, and by Fray Marcos de Niza, who confirmed the report and enlarged upon it in the manner of all subsequent visitors. Of all the joyous adventures undertaken there since Coronado's to find the Seven Cities of Cibola, no report of failure, hunger, thirst, or torturing savages has dimmed the bright appeal of Arizona's beauty and mystery. There can be no adequate discussion of a country, any more than there can of a woman, that leaves out this inexplicable effect produced by it on the people that consort there. It is an effect that primitive men seem to have responded to as readily as moderns, for a cut across the human history of Arizona reveals almost as many stratifications as the banks of the Grand Canyon. When the Mormons built their first irrigating ditch at Mesa, they saved $20,000 by utilizing the gradients laid down by prehistoric peoples, so ancient that the traditions of the present Indians have no reference to them, and every spade that the archæologist puts into the soil puts back the record of the dust of another cycle.

It is the peculiarity of the human history of Arizona that its strata seem not to show those interpenetrations of the diverse elements which, in other environments, make up the amalgam of State character. Indian tribes in Arizona are as distinguishable from one another and from Indians elsewhere as Frenchmen from Italians. The Spanish-speaking Arizonian is removed in type from the Spanish-speaking New Mexican as the Scotch are from the English. And yet nowhere is the State type more definitely localized. Somehow the land has found a way of imposing its free dramatic quality on the inhabitants, which gives them a likeness to itself more evident than their likenesses to one another.

It is reported that during the late unpleasantness in France an Arizona teamster, delivering ammunition to the firing line under cover of darkness, lost the road and ran into a listening post from which he was frantically warned to turn back and not to speak above a whisper while he was doing it. "Whisper, hell!" said the Arizonian, "I got to turn four mules around!"

Something of this clear concentration on the task in hand and a magnificent unawareness of any reason for not proceeding directly to its accomplishment, is the note of Arizona. It is always coming to the surface of the political and social life of the people in ways inexplicable to communities in which the lack of sharp structural lines in the environment has permitted the local character to run into a somewhat flavorless plasticity. There is a story that when Arizona applied for stateship, President Taft objected to certain items of the proposed constitution. Did that worry Arizona?

Not that you could notice. "Rip 'em out," was the general verdict, "and as soon as the first legislature meets we can put 'em in again." Which was done to the satisfaction of all parties. In much the same spirit of adaptation of immediate issues to an ultimate good, woman suffrage and prohibition were put through far in advance of communities that prided themselves on their sociological sophistication. Both woman suffrage and prohibition contributed to place social control in the hands of the superior racial groups, and neither the rancor of sex antagonism nor the moral fanaticisms which retarded these movements elsewhere played very much part in the Arizona decisions. Something of the same values were expressed in Arizona's election of a labor governor. Nothing could be more mistaken than the conclusion drawn by the political friends of organized labor, that Arizona was thereby committed to its program, or viewed its objective with a selfsame eye. Almost nothing, indeed, can be prophesied of Arizona on the same basis that makes prophecy possible in older communities. The most, and by no means inconsiderable, comfort that can be drawn out of such incidents is the assurance that nothing is going to be retarded in Arizona by the fear of newness.

The one thing that might retard the necessary free experimentation in economic adjustments natural to a unique natural situation, would be the settled determination of the rest of the country to regard them as the fruit of policies and agitations to which they bear only passing resemblances. Like Kim, confronted with the soul-loosening vistas of the Himalayas, Arizona has "flung its soul after its eyes." Its economic horizon is as vast, as vague, as absolutely unterrifying as its landscape. It can afford to experiment in local devices, just as a man going from Flagstaff to Dokoslid can afford to take any promising detour without fear of missing the mountain. This quiet certainty of having all the room they need to turn their mules around in, rather than the persistence of any given party or policy, is the key to the political development of Arizona.

To understand how, without theatricality and with very little intellectual sophistication, such a common consciousness comes about among such dissimilar elements as make up the population of Arizona, we must turn again to the interactions of history and topography. Arizona is protected on the east and south by pure desertness, screening out of successive waves of invasion all but the types in whom the pull of adventure is stronger than most other considerations. The many-colored dragon of the Colorado canyon curving about the north and west, prevents the overflow eastward of the complacent and comparatively commonplace cultures of the Pacific coast. The Indian tribes incorporated within the State are most of them of superior type. With the exception of the diminishing Hopi, none of the Arizona tribes have been communistic to the degree that has made of the Rio Grande tribes an economically satisfied and socially inbred people, incapable of assimilation except by a slow and wasteful process of absorption into the Spanish-speaking population. In Arizona more individualistic cultures have made possible a more citizenly type of coördination, in which the Indians give promise of becoming, as an intelligent Navaho once put it to me, "a pulse in the side of the white race." They have contributed the largest quota of place names, their trails have become automobile roads, their ancient ruins are public monuments, their dances and festivals are occasions of general entertainment. All this must eventually be felt as a formative influence in the art and literature of the State. If the rule holds good here that, in Europe, produced the most outstanding cultures out of a successful intermingling of aboriginal and conquering peoples, we should be justified in expecting more of the Arizona of the future than of any other single State. But for the present the aboriginals live alongside the invading settlements with, except for the brief period of Apache wars, a remote but amiable toleration. The Navaho and Hopi together cut out a section of the northeast about the size of Connecticut. The Haulapai and Havasupai are distributed along the Grand Canyon, the Apaches in the White Mountains, the Pimas in the Gila Valley, the Papagoes and other remnants along the most senseless bit of boundary in American history.

The political stupidity which deflected the southern boundary of Arizona from its original intention of proceeding directly from Nogales to the Gulf, thus giving us a deep-sea outlet, no doubt altered the whole course of political and economic development in the Southwest and probably in Mexico also. Its chief result has been to make of southern Arizona, which was naturally laid out to produce an agrarian and mercantile culture comparable with that of ancient Egypt or the valley of the Euphrates, a land-locked, commercially introverted community.

The interactions between Arizona and Mexico,

checked by this illogical political interference with a natural, trade-provoking situation, have nevertheless been a considerable item in the commercial prosperity of the southern towns. During the Mexican revolution gold shipments to Tucson were not uncommon and much of the Mexican Government's banking was carried on through the local banks. Settlement from Mexico never flourished within the territory of Arizona as it did in New Mexico. In the Rio Grande country, pioneer colonization carried two distinct strains; scions of old Spanish aristocracy and peasant colonists who intermarried first with native Mexicans and later with local New Mexican tribes. The result was an almost feudal social organization which persists in the economic and political life of New Mexico to this day. But in Arizona settlement was much more a matter of individual adventure than of political enterprise. There are many more squatter's rights than royal grants among the early land titles. The Jesuits and Franciscans during the first hundred years of Spanish occupation both tried their hands at establishing missions among the Indians, which were somewhat feebly enforced by colonization. The remnant of Mexican population drawn to Arizona in their wake, functions chiefly as a medium for ameliorating the social environment for reserves of labor drawn across the present border. Mexican labor properly handled is likely to prove a steadily appreciating factor in the development of southern Arizona. A Sonoran Yaqui will do twice as much work as a white laborer and show a steadier sense of responsibility toward his job.

The bulk of this Spanish-speaking population is

centered around the Gila River and its tributaries. At Tucson the lovely mission of San Xavier del Bac preserves the best of Spain's contribution to the Southwest, a style of architecture, so right in its relation to the conditions of church and home building that it has become part of the Southwest's contribution to America, and a tradition of an intimate and releasing art of life and decoration.

Impinging on the Spanish-speaking culture, often in direct conflict with it, came successive waves of adventurous overflow from the United States. As early as 1803, when the Louisiana purchase had made what was then known as Nueva Mexico contiguous territory, American trappers began to explore the lower spurs of the Rocky Mountains. Incidents bearing the names of Kit Carson, Lieutenant Beale, Zebulon Pike, Frémont, the Pattees, Captain Cooke, leave a rich detritus of romance; filibustering episodes, Apache raids and counter raids, lost mines and lucky strikes. Stuff of this nature, drawn out of the history of their own community, is excellent filling for the imaginations of the younger generation. Actually the new romantic period of Arizona, which lasted from about the beginning of the nineteenth century until the separation of the Territory of Arizona from New Mexico in 1863, has left fewer visible traces on the life of the State than the period of the old romance, which began with the exploration of Fray Marcos and Estevan the Moor in 1539, and lasted until the death of Maximilian. Mexican interest and influence dwindled rapidly during the years between the founding of the Mexican Republic and the treaty of Guadalupe. American settlement had already begun when annexation took place. Development since the separation of the Territory of Arizona from that of New Mexico has been so rapid that, to all appearances, the pioneering period has been completely submerged by it.

Over all the social and commercial life in the larger communities of Arizona has been spread that shining surface competency made possible by rapid transit, the wide use of electrical appliances, popular magazines and the possibilities of mail-order shopping. The uninquiring stranger might spend months in the cities of Arizona without discovering anything that distinguished them from other American cities except a faint Spanish flavor kept alive chiefly for the delectation of the tourist. I have addressed a teachers' institute in Tucson without finding it any less competent or any freer from conventional teaching limitations, than similar groups in Kansas or Pennsylvania. I have lectured to Arizona women's clubs on precisely the same subjects that make club programs elsewhere, and with almost identical reactions. Arizona women are a trifle less familiar with the "patter" of culture east of the Mississippi; they are also a little more accessible to new points of view. But this is a distinction that can be made in other Western States in direct ratio to the distance from New York.

The things that are peculiarly Arizona's are expressed in the quality of the attack on the environment, rather than in the surface forms of culture. To many people Buckey O'Neill and his Rough Riders are the quintessence of this Homeric Arizona strain, but even to get the full flavor of that, one must know such nuances as that the redoubtable Buckey himself fainted at his first sight of a legal execution, and that the massed church choirs and a chorus of normal-school girls saw him off from the station to the Spanish War singing "God be with you till we meet again."

Perhaps this native attack on the environment is best described in material less Homeric, and easily assembled out of the annals of trade in almost any small Arizona city. The freight rate for Tucson, for instance, included at one time charges to some point on the Pacific coast and back, as in the days of Frank Norris's "Octopus," used to be the case with all points in California. But the Arizona merchant wasted no time in raising an Iliad of woe over his situation. He shipped his goods in bond through to Guaymas, or some point in Mexico which has a water rate: shipped back to Nogales and hauled them the remaining seventy miles in wagons.

All around Tucson and Phoenix and Prescott you will find the evidences of true American normalcy, wide streets, beautiful homes, orange orchards, cotton fields, crop rotation, automobiles and Rotary clubs, but, underlying them, strategies and toils of the dimension just quoted, rooted in the rich stock of pioneering life of no more than a generation or two ago.

If you examine any list of names of those pioneers you will find English, Scotch, and Virginia-Irish names —a great many Southerners drifted in that direction after 1864—and in any collection of pioneer likenesses you will find one type of physiognomy predominating, tall-bodied, broad-browed, wide between the eyes, and in spite of the Viking mustachios and long curls which gentlemen of that period generally favored, a look of almost childlike mildness. You will find a good many faces of that type looking out at you from any group of University of Arizona students, with the far-fixed gaze of generations who have "stretched their vision" over the great spaces of the arid West. They were hard livers, those Arizona forbears, slow talkers, quick doers, chivalrous toward women, and within their concept of justice and honesty, incorruptibly just and honest. But it will be another generation or two before the stock comes to flower.

This Arizona which I have described, with its agreeable and promising mixture of modern American "pep," pioneering fiber, and Spanish-Mexican flavor, is concentrated almost wholly in the river valleys south of the Rim, the cutting edge of the Mogollon Mesa, running slantwise of the State between the Hualapai and Fort Apache Indian reservations. Northward the character of the land changes to vast stretches of sagebrush and bunch-grass country, sparsely dotted with cedar and piñon, cut with great gorges and outcrops of brown and ocher and vermilion rocks. The Rainbow Bridge is in this country, the Painted Desert, the Hopi pueblos, and the most interesting of the cliff-dwelling remains. It is also a cattle country within which is nourished, almost as much apart from the rest of Arizona life as if they did not occupy adjacent and overlapping territories, one of the three C's—cotton, copper, and cattle—which keep up the economic life of the State.

Cotton is raised in the valley of the Gila and in irrigated lands under the Roosevelt Dam; cattle are raised chiefly north of the Rim; and copper, together with silver and lead, is produced out of widely distributed mountain regions. Between these three industries there is only the thinnest integument of commercial interchange. Any one of the three could fall out altogether without in any way affecting the entity that is Arizona. In times like the present when every one of these industries has experienced a slump, the personnel items shift and are replaced as the land calls its own out of the most unlikely quarters, calling "Come and find me!"

The relation of the great mining industries of Arizona to the features that have just been described requires a certain amount of explanation. Productively their output must be credited to the wealth of the State, but actually they are mere isolated spots of infection, of industrial enterprise or corruption—as your point of view inclines you to regard them—taking their life from New York. Whole towns spring up overnight or are depopulated by mandate. Clashes between employer and employed take place in their streets, motivated by issues at stake in the capitals of the world. Only occasionally Arizona takes a hand in the proceedings. When it does everybody knows it, as in the case of the Bisbee deportations. Also everybody else is more worried by it than the native Arizonians. In spite of the effort of organized labor to make of what happened at Bisbee an item of capitalist strategy, it remains in fact a characteristically Arizonian incident. There was at Bisbee at that time real apprehension of Mexican raids. There were also at Bisbee certain representatives of a not much-loved labor organization making the juxtaposition of the tinder pile to the Mexican match. Promptly, efficiently, and wholly illegally the native Arizonians removed the tinder to a less threatening neighborhood, and nothing in their experience surprised them more than the fuss that organized labor and the liberal element generally made about it. In the press the incident was made to appear as a result of hysteria engendered, according to the political bias of the organ, either by the I.W.W. or by the mining interests in an effort to discredit organized labor. But so far as the social consciousness of Arizona at large was concerned, the truth of either, or both, or neither of these allegations did not enter in the determining degree. The deportees were handled much more in the spirit which, in the old days, made it obligatory on the other gentlemen present to throw the drunken cowboy out of the dance, without inquiring too closely who paid for his liquor, than, as it was generally treated by the press, as an incident of the welter of our civilization in the bog of economic stupidity. Politically it harked back to the period in which the *jefes* and *governadoras* of remote communities were allowed to dispense justice and equity in all cases except the most overt to their satisfied tribesmen, as might be easily deduced from the nature of its reactions in the State at large. The Governor, a Republican in an overwhelmingly Democratic State, lost no votes by his public utterances as to the extra-legality aspects of the affair; and the most public of trials, with actions in State and Federal courts, with no avoidance of the actual facts, brought no convictions, in accordance with a prevailing public sentiment. This also is part of the adventure.

There does not appear any immediate reason for thinking that Arizona will outgrow her right to the Joyous Adventure. The irrigated valleys are due to become opulent. But a rod beyond the furthest ditch the desert waits with immeasurable beauty and mystery. New mountains not yet worn down to the soothed contours of maturity lift the vision and color the aspirations of men as they stain the air with splintered light. Beyond the rim of Mogollon, irreducible spaces of open wood and wind-sculptured rock and ancient ruins intrigue the imagination.

There is an effect of beauty upon the spirit of man that escapes measure and definition. So much of Arizona is by its natural constitution conditioned to be always beautiful, and to serve only by its beauty, that we cannot suppose that it will fail ultimately to produce some equivalent uniqueness among its inhabitants.

CONNECTICUT

A NATION IN MINIATURE

By DON C. SEITZ

CONNECTICUT has been humorously described as "ninety-five miles long and seventy-five miles thick," these being roughly the State's geographical dimensions. Contiguous to Long Island Sound for the entire length, its bare ledges and deep valleys are credited with contributing their top soil to the making of Long Island itself, the detritus having been swept to sea in the days of the glacier, taking away much fertility and leaving mainly the picturesque behind. But picturesque the State is to an extent undreamed by the traveler who shoots through on the railroad touching mostly factory towns and glimpses only occasional views of water and nothing of the hills. The interior is singularly wild. There are long reaches of forest, great areas of idle land, vales that rival those of Cashmere, less its mountains, and that of Yumuri without its palms. Three noble rivers find their way through it to the sea, the Housatonic, the Connecticut, and the Thames. Of these the Connecticut travels farthest, its springs almost touching the Canadas and glorifying four States with its pride. As the country rises from sea level to the Berkshires on the west, or follows the rivers in the east, it develops great ridges, some of which are backed by hills, the chief of which, Bear Mountain of Litchfield County, reaches the respectable altitude of 2,355 feet. Eminences of from 500 to 1,200 feet are plentiful and high uplands border wide valleys that spread out refreshingly to the eye.

The artists discovered the charm of Connecticut years before the automobile gave people in general a still neglected chance to see and know this miniature wonderland. More than a quarter of a century ago John H. Twachtman, Childe Hassam, Harry Fitch Taylor, A. F. Jaccaci, Leonard Ochtman, and Elmer L. MacRae located Cos Cob, and George Wharton Edwards later visualized Greenwich. The art colonies at Saybrook and Old Lyme have become famous. Other groups inhabit Westport, Norfolk, and Silver Mine.

In the rough country made by the broken terrain are stored quaint villages, untouched by the rush of the day, lakes unpolluted, and here and there fat farm lands enriching their owners with an exotic plant—tobacco. Once the "Connecticut filler" was a plebeian. Under improved breeding it has become an aristocrat, as a "wrapper" for the finer-flavored brands of Cuba. In warm summer days to ride among the plantations is to scent the dreamy narcotic and to know why Sir Walter Raleigh loved the weed at first sight. Beyond tobacco the farms contribute little. Connecticut raises only enough mutton to meet its needs for a single day, enough beef for eight days, and enough potatoes for fourteen. The rest of the supply must be imported and to procure this, cunning artisans in brass, silver, and fabrics toil in many towns. Some industries the State has made its own. The copper of Anaconda and Cerro de Pasco becomes clocks, rods, and sheetings of brass in Ansonia, Waterbury, and New Haven, while the hats of Danbury, Bethel, and Norwalk cover many heads. Stamford and New Britain put hinges, locks, and knobs on our doors. Manchester specializes in silk, Glastonbury in soap, and Willimantic in thread. In Bridgeport the typewriter, the corset, and the cartridge rule. In Meriden the silver spoon and its counterfeit began their lives. Far-away New London and Stonington recall through stable fortunes the whale fishery and the seal hunting of the Antarctic, with not a few shekels wrested from the sea by venturesome privateers in 1812. In sleepy Middletown, now noted for Wesleyan University, money gathered by merchant mariners still earns its increment and—shall it be said? —echoes the scandal of the wooden nutmeg and the basswood ham!

The "factory towns" can be put by as blots on the landscape, though not all are to be condemned for their abasement to utility. One of them, Stamford, is a model of what a complete city can be without smothering its soul in size. Its 35,000 people enjoy a fine theater, clubs, schools, library, commodious, handsome churches, and best of fire departments, and indeed all the elegancies as well as the comforts of life. How better it would be if the United States could possess 5,000 Stamfords, rather than the congested centers of New York, Chicago, Philadelphia, and their lesser kind into which our people are packing!

Despite the Puritan grimness of its birth-throe Connecticut became the father of the circus in its modern magnificence. If P. T. Barnum is not truly one of the immortals it is because there is no justice in the process of selection. Bridgeport built itself around him and his fame, and though the genial exhibitor long since passed away he left in its parks and public works a monument to his memory. And this is not all. The Greatest Show on Earth still winters there. The local boys take kindly to acrobats and are indifferent to elephants.

Hartford is a gay combination of Life Insurance and Death, for here the former had a pioneer foundation that has brought in great accumulations of cash, while Samuel Colt's "revolver" has grown into "Browning guns" and many forms of deadly repeaters that wipe out a regiment at a discharge. A dip into history reveals that the warehouse of one Major Selleck, of Stamford, sheltered a share of Captain Kidd's much-hunted booty, while a contumacious person named Clark acted as agent for the whilom pirate in defiance of authority and to the great wrath of the Earl of Bellomont, King William's Colonial Governor.

But the State can be truly described as a nation in miniature. It has made itself. It could be argued that Connecticut, not Necessity, was the mother of Invention. Eli Whitney produced the cotton gin and Elias Howe the sewing machine, the two greatest advances in civilization after steam and before electricity. It has been claimed that the Yankee did not invent so much from innate ingenuity as laziness. He wanted a machine to do the work and save muscle.

Behind all this varied industry and energy stand Education and Congregationalism in high companionship, adding to the sum of wisdom and salvation. Although Elihu Yale—

Born in America, in Europe bred,
In Africa traveled, in Asia wed—

hanged his servant in India for misusing a favorite horse, his dollars laid the foundation for one of the greatest of universities, whose charter is firmly embedded in the constitution of the State. Article 8 provides that "the Charter of Yale College as modified by agreement with the corporation thereof, in pursuance of an Act of the General Assembly, passed May 1792, is hereby confirmed."

There is much in this constitution that is notable besides giving shelter to Yale. Its first two sections contain all that need be said of the Rights of a People in establishing a government, viz.:

1. That all men when they form a social compact, are equal in rights; and that no man or set of men are entitled to exclusive public emoluments or privileges from the community.

2. That all political power is inherent in the people, and all free governments are founded on their authority, and instituted for their benefit; and that they have at all times an undeniable and indefeasible right to alter their form of government in such manner as they may think expedient.

Alas, that this clear and potent view can no longer seem to prevail among us! It is no more in force in Connecticut than elsewhere in these United States. The sturdy independence of the Charter-makers that began when Joseph Wadsworth concealed the first one in the famous oak, is not echoed in the practices of their descendants. They can still resent mandates from without as they withstood the orders of Massachusetts Bay in Colonial days, as witness the drag on suffrage and prohibition, about which they took their time. In the case of suffrage the amendment reached Hartford while the legislature was not in session. The ladies were eager to have Governor Marcus H. Holcomb call a special session to secure its acceptance and so give them the vote at once. The Governor could see no exigency and declined to act, but as the legislature in Connecticut can summon itself when need be, he yielded to the prospect that it would do so and convened its members. The Governor, true to the traditions, thought that prohibition and suffrage were questions that belonged by right to the State alone to determine. But for most local uses, sections one and two are writ in water! It was in Connecticut that a man was recently sent to jail for six months for saying that Lenin was "the most brainiest man on earth."

The political processes by which the American people have been separated from their liberties have ground over Connecticut as the glaciers did long ago, leaving a sterile "freedom" behind. In the beginning Church ruled State. The much-vaunted "Blue Laws" were not so blue as many that prevail on the statute books today. They were merely enforced. When the church ceased to have political power parties contended with some diverseness until Insurance came to the fore and its magnates in Hartford took over the legislature, as later the same sort did in New York. When all their needs in lawmaking were satisfied, the control was handed over to the "Consolidated," that being the local name for the Interstate Railway combination, better known as the New York, New Haven and Hartford Railroad, reversing the New York order, where the law factory was first owned by the Central interests.

This lasted until the dethronement of Charles S. Mellen as the railroad head. For a few years the legislature has been free of corporations, but like a prisoner released after long confinement does not know what to do and sits blinking at the light.

The cities are not permitted to dominate the towns. Though sixty-one of the latter have but one legislator, the remainder send to the capital two each, and the large centers of population receive no consideration for numbers. Two is their allotment. This is a grievance with the big communities, but the little will not yield them more. The total membership of the Lower House is 262. Representatives receive $300 a session and meet biennially. The 1921-22 body contains thirteen miserable Democrats and one Independent. The others are Republican. But one Democrat sits in the Senate.

The Master of the Legislature is J. Henry Roraback, the Republican "leader" of the State, and its National Committeeman. He comes from the pleasant land of Canaan up in the hills, is president of a big water-power company, which is taking 35,000 horsepower from a new development on the Housatonic, and is secure in his saddle. For some years he was assailed by the rivalry of John T. King, a carpet-bagger from Brooklyn who rode into control of Bridgeport on a garbage contract. He followed Roosevelt and came down, not to earth, but alighted neatly in Wall Street, where he is reputed to serve in some way the great House of J. P. Morgan & Company. The antithesis of political leadership with Roraback is the Democratic National Committeeman, Homer S. Cummings, of the silver voice and velvet paw. But he, it must now be told, is an exotic—born in Chicago. Each gentleman is careful to see that no real harm comes to the other.

Although the Republican margin of votes is normally small, Connecticut has had but two Democratic Governors in forty years, Thomas M. Waller and Simeon E. Baldwin, both of whom owed their success to discontent in the opposition. Each did much for the State, Governor Baldwin taking the roads out of politics in such a way as to keep them out up to date, the State Highway Superintendent, Charles J. Bennett, whom he appointed, being a sound engineer with a policy that has developed permanent pavements laid on trunk lines, where his predecessor spent millions on useless sections of temporary construction scattered to please localities and doing no one good.

The State has been chary in the past about enacting general legislation. It is less than ten years since it passed a banking act. The general railroad act was wiped out when Mellen moved in. Petty judges are appointed by the legislature, members not infrequently naming themselves for the honor. The constitution's plea that there should be no monopoly of office-holding is often grossly disregarded. Though the faithful be plenty, there are many cases of double place-keeping that pass unrebuked. Clifford E. Wilson, Mayor of Bridgeport for many years, enjoyed three terms as Lieutenant Governor, while holding his city job, and another genius in office-getting contrived to be State senator, State treasurer, and county judge in one overlapping period of bliss. Local officials are constantly picking up State or county jobs under this kindly system of respecting their several terms.

The electorate, it may be sadly said, is corrupt. I myself, in the course of several political adventures, have been three times offered the "control" at the polls of the richest community under town government in the United States. The offer was made in good faith by a man quite competent to carry it out. The poor towns are just as bad as the rich in this respect. Election Day is a biennial harvest. The Republicans are the usual purchasers. The practice began in a desire to save the country and become permanent as part of the process of saving themselves. One factor in the corruption of Connecticut local politics is the system of minority representation. A town Board of Selectmen consists of three members. Four candidates run. The highest three win. An aggressive nominee for the minority is readily beaten by a deal with the majority which can head him in the poll. So good men who might truly represent rarely win. The third man is usually a dummy or a conformer. The same method applies to the choice of assessors and justices of the peace. Well meant, it leads to party treachery and individual chicane through which the minority often has worse than no representation.

Under a system of privilege-selling the citizens of the State have been deprived of much that was their own. For example, nearly all of the long waterfront with its rocks and beaches, bathing facilities and the liberty to dig shell-fish in the sand has passed into private ownership to the great hardship of the people at large. Maine, Massachusetts, and Rhode Island, with jealous eye, have guarded "fisherman's rights" and so have preserved access to the sea. The proudest estate at Bar Harbor, Nahant, and Narragansett must provide a pathway to the shore. In Connecticut "No Trespass" signs mock the people. From Byram shore to Stonington the story is about the same. Greenwich has preserved to itself a waterfront fifteen feet wide, and Sound Beach, imposing as is its name, is little more than a few grains of sand for the public. Here and there a town has salvaged some of its former possessions. Stamford, though it lost possession of the glorious shores of Shippan Point, has established a park on old meadows and given it a sandy shore, and Westport makes the proceeds of a town-owned bathing beach pay a good slice of its expenses. The State also suffers scenically from the invasion of the rich. The segregated shore front, where the "villa" prevails, is further monopolized by the planting of trees and shrubbery, so as to cut off the view. Even on the uplands, where the wealthy have come to live, the roads are girded with walls of stone or hedges of privet, so that one can no longer look across the land.

Industry, too, has dealt hardly with nature. The rivers and bays are polluted. The shad that once crowded the Connecticut come in scant schools, where once they were legion, and the salmon come not at all. Menhaden exterminators have driven bluefish, striped bass, and weakfish from the Sound and the minor species suffer from the sewage in the harbors and the poison in the streams. In remote shore spots lobsters still hide amid the reefs and command metropolitan prices when caught. A few men live by an occupation that once supported many.

Beyond this the franchises of railways, water, and light are mainly in outside hands. It was considered "slick" to unload them as was so generously done during the Mellen régime. The result was not so satisfying. So great a burden was laid upon the New Haven road, in which many had their hoard, as to crush its earning power, while the costs of travel, of light, of water, and of power have gone up. These the public pay. Their increment in the main goes elsewhere. The State's system of justice does not work for the general advantage, but since the railroad quit naming the judges the bench has greatly improved. The jury system continues bad. Jury lists are compiled by the town selectmen, who reward all too often men of poor caliber with a chance to earn the fee. The Town of Greenwich was a conspicuous sinner in this respect, so much so that Chief Justice George W. Wheeler, found it necessary not so long ago to warn the selectmen that he would punish them if better material were not forthcoming.

Grand jurors are elected by the towns, but do not sit as a County body to consider complaints and hand down indictments. Their functions are limited to transmitting information of law infractions to minor jurists and the powers given are so limited as to be practically nil. The ordinary run of criminals pass through the hands of a town prosecutor; important cases, through those of the State's Attorney, who serves the county. The decision of guilt rests in their hands. This leads sometimes to extraordinary miscarriages that need not be listed here. Coroners are appointed by the judges of the Superior Court upon the recommendation of the State's Attorney. Persons reporting the finding of a body dead from violence are rewarded with a tip of fifty cents. An appeal from a local to the county court begins the case *de novo*. The State's Attorney decides whether or not he will go on, regardless of the local official. So the accused has always what is pleasingly called "a chance." This power sometimes becomes visible in local politics.

Taxation is, on the whole, light. There is an elaborate personal-tax provision, but it is not enforced by penalty, so it is generally disregarded. Four dollars per $1,000 is levied annually on bonds held in the State. There is no remedy for non-compliance until death, when the State steps in and collects five times the amount and retroacts it for five years. So it gets something. Under its charter the New York, New Haven and Hartford Railroad is expected to turn all its earnings above ten per cent over to the State. In its most prosperous days the prudent management always contrived so that nothing accrued to the commonwealth, but it found that it was much easier to deal with a surplus than a deficiency. One thing the Mellen régime did besides electrifying the line to New Haven deserves remembering. It planted both sides of the track from Mount Vernon on for many miles with ramblers of the Dorothy Perkins variety. These have flourished in sand and cinders, in all the hard soil along a railroad cut, so that in the month of June the path of the commuter is strewn with roses, even if there are none for the stockholders. It is a moot question whether the obligation to pay the State all returns above ten per cent does not constitute an obligation that would annul the wrecking of the road's earning power by loading it with worthless properties, like the unlawful dissipation of assets by a creditor, making the lines eligible for seizure by the State as in violation of contract. No lawyer or citizen has ever taken steps to test the point, while of course the State government itself is supine as usual in corporate matters. The Attorney General is seldom selected for aggressiveness.

The communities are curiously self-centered. The many excellent newspapers circulate closely at home. There is no journal with a State-wide distribution. New York to the west and Boston to the east smother them. This does not mean that they are not profitable. Usually they are—some of them very much so, like the pair in Hartford, which probably earn more per capita of population than any other sheets in America. They simply do not reach out and there is no covering editorial influence. In the paternal days of the railroad management the train service was so arranged as to keep the New York and Boston papers back until the news grew cold as a form of protecting the local press and keeping it amiable. This ceased during the Spanish War, when the city papers bought train service, which later became regular, not the least to the disadvantage of the home journalism, so far as profits go. It has prospered since as never before. A misfortune it is that some of the cities are dominated by journals grouped together by the National Manufacturers' Association; not that this does their owners much good. It is simply against the interests of the community if there is any merit in the theory of a free and untrammeled press.

The cities have become strongly foreign. The country is still strongly native. The melting process is slow, because the large immigration to industrial centers broods together by nationalities. Italians are the strongest force industrially, the Irish politically. The Democratic mayors of New Haven, Waterbury, Hartford, Meriden, and Middletown are of Celtic descent; New Britain's ruler is Italian. In some of the rude reaches of the north, middle, and east bordering Rhode Island, where the scenery is best, dwell grades of people whose minds and habits make the observer regret the extermination of the Mohegans and Pequots. It seems to be the mood of nature when on show to breed the poorest samples of mankind. These back countrymen are not influenced by newcomers of wealth or by the nearness of cities. When a traveler expressed astonishment at one living but an hour away from New York who had not "been thar" for eighteen years, he replied: "Why should I go—I've plenty to do here." And he had!

The State is New England in epitome. It has character, often too latent in these latter days. That this will soon reassert itself through the coming of women into political life is my profound belief. Just as Barbara Frietchie "took up the flag the men hauled down" the new owners of the franchise will surely elevate its political morals, abashing the careless and corrupt males and lifting up the parties above sordid office-getting and the selling of popular rights. These women of Connecticut who have picked up the gage are not "flappers" or notoriety seekers. They are the sort a real man likes for a mother.

Incidentally it may be added that Connecticut has mothered much. The now overcrowded Dartmouth College began as Dr. Eleazer Whitlock's Indian School in Lebanon, with Joseph Brant, the "cruel Mohawk," as one of the first pupils. She mothered Ohio, whose "fire-lands" given to pay the State for British raids during the Revolution became the Western Reserve of Connecticut, giving it and us the Shermans, the Tafts, and other worthy names. She mothered the assault on Ticonderoga during the early hours of the Revolution, when Ethan Allen with Connecticut troops took the stronghold in "the name of the Great Jehovah and the Continental Congress." Her soldiers under Israel Putnam and his like followed the English flag to Quebec and the Havannah. She built a navy of her own to aid the Continentals as bravely by sea as her men had done by land, and the graves of her dead lie thickly in the fields of France.

A land of steady habits, not all good, but her own!

ARKANSAS

A NATIVE PROLETARIATE

By C. L. EDSON

"The one State in the Union that I still have a seething curiosity to visit," wrote H. L. Mencken recently, "is Arkansas. I have never met a man from that State, and I hear that it is a peculiar commonwealth." If the relentless hunter of the Americano should ever reach this last Carcassonne of his critical desire he would at last have had one wish-fulfillment that was up to expectations. For Arkansas is our most distinguished State. It is the one member of our glorious Union that has actually accomplished all that it set out to accomplish, has lived up to its highest ideals, and stands today the only commonwealth of its kind on earth.

What then are the ideals of this State? The motto in Latin on her State seal says: "The People Rule." They do. But to what end? Arkansas has its own popular motto and it is this: "I've never seen nothin', I don't know nothin', I hain't got nothin', and I don't want nothin'." These fundamental aims the people of Arkansas have achieved in every particular. Therefore the Arkansawyers are happy, the only happy and successful people in America. But it was luck that did it. Happy is the State that has no history—and Arkansas has none. It was not founded by a pious Æneas, nor fought over by Hannibals and Scipios. It just grew up out of seepage. While the ports of Louisiana, Florida, Carolina, and even New Amsterdam were being struggled for by Frenchman, Spaniard, Dutchman, and Britisher, old Arkansas, having no port and lying on the road to nowhere, was free to grow up without a history. The Mississippi River, highway of the old adventurers, lies broadside the whole length of the State but there is no landing place. Mississippi has Vicksburg, Louisiana has New Orleans, Tennessee has Memphis, and Missouri has St. Louis. But where is the old port of Arkansas; where its ancient capital of Creole days? A belt of mud a hundred miles wide in places prevented Arkansas from having a port and denied to her a metropolis, a civilization, and a history.

A people who were willing to foot it a hundred miles through the muck to get nowhere founded Arkansas and achieved their aim. Mighty planters, greedy merchants, daring pirates, with beautiful hot-blooded women; these came not to Arkansas nor founded there an aristocracy of strength and cunning. But the kind of folk that pirates terrorize, and merchants cheat, and planters impress into peonage were the wandering sheep that grazed their way into Arkansas to establish there a morons' paradise. No strong men arose to oppress them because the pirate-merchant-planter breed was not in them. They could not raise up strong-arm Cæsars among themselves because there were no Cæsar chromosomes in their blood. They were an infiltrate, and in seeping into Arkansas through a mud filter the Cæsars had been strained out.

The Arkansawyers are of the type of the old

Hoosiers, Crackers, Pikers, and the Big Smoky mountaineers. The Hoosiers themselves were descendants of the bond-servants of Colonial days and being of low degree sought their own kind while the great migration going "out West" moved along the Ohio. They settled in the malaria swamps of Indiana and Illinois, but that was on the highway to empire and civilization drove them out. They colonized again in Pike County, Missouri, and made the name "Piker" notorious throughout the West as denoting a fellow of feeble wit and feebler initiative. Other migrations of the bond-servant stock found their way into Arkansas, and as no strong tribe followed them into this retreat they were never driven out again. "Crackers," descendants of the Georgia convict colony, also found refuge in Arkansas. The mountain people, too, came gradually onward, proliferating in their beloved highlands till they crossed the Mississippi and peopled the Ozarks. But these people are not mentally dull nor physically inefficient. They are simply a highland race that loves solitude and scorns comfort, literature, and luxury.

These three strains, the mountain people, the Crackers, and the Piker numskulls, have united to make the Arkansas nation; for they are a nation, as distinct from the other peoples in America as is a Swede from a Dane. Whenever Arkansawyers appear in Kansas, California, South Carolina, or Texas the natives hold up their hands in horror, fearing that their Spartan State will be erased by the obliterating helot swarm. The high wages in the agricultural Northwest during the World War drew a few Arkansawyers to Nebraska, whither they took their dogs and women, their customs and ideals—and labored for the Swedish and Teutonic farmers. The sturdy Nebraskans (from North Europe) were shocked by the general worthlessness of the Arkansawyers and were heard to declare: "If they keep on letting that kind of people into this country, America has gone to hell." The Arkansawyers are a race compounded as we have seen of three strains of American roughneck blood with no trace of gentility, no Cavalier. The captains and the kings have departed, have been bred out from their stock entirely. No stream can rise higher than its source, and Arkansas has proved it.

There is one great quality that is not an attribute of the superior classes, and that is wit. The Arkansawyers have it. It reaches its highest notch in such blithe fellows as Will Rogers and Tom P. Morgan. To be an immortal wit is no mean distinction. But wit is so common in Arkansas that it does not distinguish a man—not while he is in Arkansas. It is the tradition of the land. No nation so young as Arkansas has produced as great a mass of comic legend and genuine native humor. But its people are not a literate people and you seek in vain to find their glory on the printed page. Perhaps one can best approach this pathless subject by facing about and going back to Davy Crockett. Crockett was a Tennesseean by birth who roved through Arkansas and made his mark in Texas. He spent some years in Congress. Crockett was severely in the Arkansas tradition. He boasted that he was so rough that he could take a porcupine under one arm, a wildcat under the other and climb a thorn tree without getting a scratch. He was a dead shot with the rifle and a rough-and-tumble virtuoso of the bowie-knife. He loved the wild, hard life of the pioneer woodsman, saw the fun and poetry in it, and was equally at ease when clowning from the stump before his backwoods "constituents" and when speaking at an Ambassador's dinner in Washington. London has discovered the American backwoods through the writings of James Fenimore Cooper, and the literary spotlight swung this way and provoked the inquisitive visits of Dickens and Thackeray. The stage was set for the emergence of an American Leatherstocking, and Davy Crockett stepped out and "took his bows."

There spoke the spirit of Arkansas. "Wild and woolly and full of fleas, I've never been curried below the knees." Imagine a Massachusetts statesman or a Carolina gentleman making such a claim. But such coarse boasts are the glory of the Davy Crocketts. The smart Londoners were "charmed," as they are charmed by a woolly rhinoceros, and Davy Crockett was all the rage. He was genuine, he was American hickory with the bark on; and he was so witty that his every word was caught and saved and became a treasury of Americana, recalled for a generation and not wholly forgotten now. Typical was his best-remembered boast from the lecture platform that he was recognized as such a faultless marksman by all the denizens of the woods that a coon in the tallest tree, seeing Crockett priming his rifle, would cry: "Don't shoot; I'll come down."

Such humor is the common intercourse in Arkansas, but when it penetrates to the polite world it is believed to be fabulous. Will Rogers, the jewel of the New York Follies, was born in Arkansas and has carried on the Arkansas tradition. Cracking jokes about princes, prime ministers, and metropolitan foibles while he does miracles with his cowboy lasso and loudly chews his "chawin' gum" he is but the reincarnation of Davy Crockett, who could skin a panther with his bowie-knife while making quips to set the gilded capitals of Europe laughing. These feats build no triumphal arches nor give new work for the map-makers, but they are no easy accomplishments. The men that do these tricks have achieved heights of mental agility that few attain. And the race that can produce such men is as salty as the race that flowers in Napoleons and Foches. Arkansas is that race. One such wit might be an accident. But Arkansas repeats. She does it again and again.

Uncouth audacity is the tradition of Arkansas. The trick of the Arkansawyer is to capitalize his boorishness. It solves his problem in a flash. Why did no other race think of this solution? What medicine for the New Englander fighting his "inferiority" until it drives him crazy? The Arkansawyer says: "Look, I am a buffoon. With one hand I drive my mule, with the other I toss off epigrams." He therefore has no desire to ape gentility; he knows he is as good as anyone. Even as the Southern Negro long believed that the white race was made for him—to amuse him, shelter and feed him, and protect him from his enemies, so the Arkansans believe that the duller race of Rome and Paris and all the glittering world of white shirts, table linen, chefs, opera, tiaras, and taxicabs were made for them—made as a background and a setting for their inspired buffoonery. There is no Freudian grouch in the soul of Arkansas. This is the unique distinction that makes the tribe worth while. They have not, in all their philosophy, any complaint against anything. They are the only white tribe among us that habitually fiddles and sings.

But why has the Arkansawyer never pushed this claim? He doesn't know it. What then does he glory in? He's a joiner of high-sounding, meaningless societies. He prides himself in the fact that "Albert Pike, America's most illustrious Mason, reached the zenith of his career while a resident of Arkansas," and that "the poet laureate of Masonry, Fay Hempstead, is a native Arkansan," and that "the only man ever invited to speak before the New York Lodge of Elks, not a member of the lodge, was an Arkansan." These claims were put forth in the *Congressional Record* last year to show what Arkansas has accomplished in eighty-six years of statehood. The non-member that appeared before the New York Elks was probably Will Rogers. His appearance before the Elks seems to the Arkansans a greater distinction than that his wit has made him a favorite with the smartest audiences of a world metropolis. Another claim that the Arkansas Congressman makes is that Arkansas was the "first State to pass the bone-dry law." But this is typical Arkansas ignorance. Maine and Kansas voted dry a generation ago, while State-wide prohibition came to Arkansas during the World War. But the Arkansawyer's scorn of history and letters and of all things outside of

Arkansas has long been the trait that distinguished him in the eyes of other peoples.

So here is a civilized tribe—civilized in the sense of the "Five Civilized Nations" of the Iroquois—that has no literary tradition. Few can read in Arkansas, and those who can, do not. Their own legends, jokes, and coonskin fables suffice them. They hark back to no classics. They have as little use for Greek culture as a Nevada dry farmer for the canals on Mars. An Arkansas printer named Fields recently removed to Orangeburg, S. C., and there started a paper, the *Daily Field!* At the beginning of each editorial stood the caption in black letters: "Fields Says:" And what Fields said was distinguished, but one perceived he did not write the stuff himself. He told me that he simply couldn't write general editorials. But in an old house he had found a book full of the sayings of Bacon, Swift, Johnson, Addison, Thackeray, and Lamb. These he ran in his editorial columns as original matter. The Arkansawyer supposes everyone to be as unlettered as he is. This "editor" had never heard of Addison and Thackeray and he supposed that his Carolina readers were equally ignorant. Yet Thackeray had actually walked on the soil of South Carolina, and that State has inherited the English literary tradition *in toto*. Who but an Arkansawyer would dare hope to palm off on South Carolina the old British classics as new and original writing?

I know a merchant in Leslie, Arkansas, named George Smith, who made a wager with the first typewriter salesman he ever saw that he could writer faster with a goose-quill pen than any man could write with "that 'ar machine." The test was made and of course the typewriter far outdistanced the merchant's quill. With wonder and frank admiration the merchant bought the typewriter. The Arkansawyer, like the backwoods Missourian, will believe nothing that is told him. It must be demonstrated before his eyes; it is the "show me" trait of the self-reliant man who has had no contact with the recorded experience of the ages. And that is why an Arkansawyer in South Carolina was willing to risk printing the classics as his own compositions. That sanguine fellow would not have felt safe in offering to the Carolinians as his own work such masterpieces as "The Speech of Senator Jones on Changing the Name of Arkansas," "Way Down in Arkansas," "Slow Train Through Arkansas," or the quaint farewell song, "When I Left Arkansas." And yet he would have been much safer in printing these, for although these native classics are known to everyone in Arkansas they do not unfortunately belong to the literature of the world and few men outside of Arkansas have heard them.

When the imitative voices of Virginia and Carolina were rhyming with considerable skill in the meter of Pope and Dryden and changing with the changing mode to the Byronic lyric the people of Arkansas were thriving in utter ignorance of all this—and with the contempt for literature which ignorance always bears—but they were producing a "literature" of their own that stemmed from the wild highlands of old Britain and flowered in Arkansas with a spicy flavor that is native to those hardy, artless people and rooted in the soil that they are rooted in. Little of it has ever been reduced to manuscript and less to type. But it is living and virile, and it sustains the Arkansawyer so that he has no need for contact with the world of written history, literature, or ideas. So I repeat that, culturally, Arkansas is a nation to itself. It stands confidently on its own feet and drinks life to its fill—to the fill of its own little vessel.

The unwritten lore of Arkansas is self-reliant, witty, and grotesque. Its utter vulgarity may be explained by the lack of any strain of gentility in the Arkansas race. The "Speech of Senator Jones," known to every adult in the State, and treasured by him as the New Englander treasures the "Ride of Paul Revere," begins, "Mr. Speakeh, God damn you, Sah, I've been trying for half an hour to get your eye," and proceeds—amid the most unutterable coarseness, phrased in rounded periods, the eloquence of the hogwallow—to argue heatedly against the bill to change the name of Arkansas to Arkansaw. Who was Senator Jones, and where did he make this classic address? (The pronunciation of Arkansas was indeed changed to differentiate its sound from that of Kansas.) Who composed the endless ballads, fables, and droll tales that constitute the Arkansas legend? We do not know. There is no scholarship to expound them.

The Arkansawyers have a legend, a ceremony, and a ballad for every occasion, from the planting of a turnip to the cutting of a bee tree. When I was buying shoes preparatory to shaking the dust of Arkansas from my feet, the merchant laid business aside for the moment and sang me that twenty-verse ballad: "When

I Left Arkansas." It is full of pathos as well as rollicking fun, and concludes with this line:

> And I got drunk as a boiled owl when I left Arkansas.

Every old Southern State has produced scholars, except Arkansas, according to Mencken's dictum, and no man of first-class intellect was born in Arkansas, lived there, or even passed through that State. That is why he has a curiosity to go and look upon that peculiar human kennel. And why shouldn't he? For it is high time that some critical mind turned inquiringly to these people and added to the American archives their short and simple, but not uninteresting story. Washington Irving crossed the State of Arkansas, but merely to enjoy the beauties of its natural scenery. Arkansas has mountains of quartz that glitter in the sunlight with every color of the rainbow. It has marble of all kinds and colorings, the outcrop of a single marble bed being visible a hundred miles along the White River. There is no part of Arkansas, save where man pollutes it, that is not beautiful, no spot that is not a veritable mine of wealth. Its soil is rich and varied, its forest covering is of the choicest woods, cypress, white oak, red oak, hickory, and pine, and its mineral wealth is unbelievably diverse and vast. Arkansas is the only State that produces diamonds, and its output of pearls is greater than that of all the others. Truly this is a region where "every prospect pleases." To enjoy this natural splendor, Irving, who had mule-backed over the mountains and deserts of Spain to visit the Alhambra, came in the company of Audubon, who was classifying the birds. It is time for some one to come and view those rarer specimens, the people.

A region as rich as Arkansas would long ago have been exploited by the soldiers of fortune and the planter-entrepreneurs had it not been segregated from the routes of the world. The captains and founders of first families having passed by on the other side, the buck privates inherited Arkansas. Blood will tell, and it told. The struggle of history saw other States rising to the rank of general officers, but first sergeant is as high as Arkansas ever got. But as every soldier knows, good sergeants are the backbone of every successful army. And Arkansas has moved steadily ahead in population, wealth, and industry. Whence came this population of nearly two millions? There is no immigration. Arkansas has fewer unmarried men than any other State. It got its population as it got everything else it has—manufactured it at home. In Arkansas men build their own houses, cobble their own shoes. It is what makes these people bold. In the highland half of the State there is probably not a man over forty who has not once or twice gone into the woods and hewed out a home, that is, purchased a tract of wild timber or received it as a gift from the Government, and with his own hands cleared the ground, split the rails (or "busted 'em open makin' rails" as they call it, the word "split," although used by Lincoln, being unknown in rural Arkansas), hewed the logs for his house or muled them to a sawmill, carved wooden hinges, made the doors, and riven the shingles by hand with a frow. In a word, Arkansas is a land of raw materials and raw people. The people take hold of the materials and fashion themselves such wealth as they desire. And their desire is the only limit to their wealth. They own it all in fee simple; there are no masters to oppress them and they occupy without molestation a land unbelievably rich and a climate most favorable. But they desire little. Had they been greedy for wealth like the New England Yankees or the Virginia Cavaliers they would have piled up fortunes of the first magnitude. But they were not harassed by the febrile urge to pile up treasure for posterity. No ambition consumes them. Their wants are limited to their needs and normal human needs are not much after all. Hence their merry motto: "I ain't got nothin', and I don't want nothin'." In the great war of man against nature, science against ignorance, Arkansas remained a neutral.

Were it not that Arkansas is incorporated in the United System of Go-getters and therefore under the shell-fire of the Pep Secretaries and the propaganda of Better Porkers for Popaloosa County, Arkansas would have remained like the Balkans, a land where men have had forty centuries of farming without a step of progress, that farming being the same as Rome's and Rome's the same as Adam's. But Federal bulletins and State agricultural college bulletins and Ford's tractor bulletins are everywhere, and some of the farming done in Arkansas is scientific. Besides the opulence of timber, soil and water, minerals and precious stones Arkansas was blessed with upland rice. The planters in that State grow fabulous fields of it, ten bushels more to the acre than any other State, according to their claim. It is grown on flat prairie land underlaid with a water-tight clay. They dike it and flood it with pumped water, which because of the hard pan stays there like water in a saucer. When the rice ripens, the water evaporates and the farmers roll in with great harvesters—the machinery of the wheat country—and bind up wealth so fast as to startle the world. The farmers in that region pay the highest income taxes of any like area in this country. The old rice empire of the Carolina lowlands where the rice had to be harvested by hand on boggy ground was ruined by such competition. The rich (rice-sustained) culture of Charleston never had anything but contempt for Arkansas. She was a sister Southern State but not the kind of sister in whose company one likes to be seen. She was a low wench, a throw-back to the groundlings —and they kept her under the back stairs when the other girls were entertaining in the ballroom. And now that wench has married rich while other branches of the family have fallen on low fortunes.

How rich is Arkansas? About the same as boastful Kansas or the once mighty South Carolina. In population also she ranks with these. But Kansas is almost totally literate and was peopled by militant New England idealists. South Carolina was the cradle of aristocracy and literature on these shores and once contained the richest landed society in America. These were the rice planters of the coastland. Arkansas, the land that has no history, the land of illiterates, Arkansas, the moron sister, see, she walks saucily abreast of them now. The richest landed society is in Arkansas today! These are the facts; what can your philosophy do with them? Is it brains or luck that makes America?

I venture the guess that if the Kansans had inherited

this Eden instead of the wind-whipped, arid soil of Kansas, they would have piled up more wealth, for they have that Yankee beaver blood that eats toil with a ravenous mouth; but they would have built no art, no architecture, no grand literature, no poetry. They have not done it in Kansas; they could not do it anywhere. If the old Carolinian captains had seized on Arkansas they would have used this wealth to build a sweet and virile culture and a literature to invite and captivate the world. But the proletariate got there, and Arkansas is a blind spot on the map of States. But though these people have never used their rich estate, they have not betrayed their blood heritage. They have gone as high as proletarians can go. Art, music, poetry as you who read this essay know them are far beyond the comprehension of the proletarian mind of Arkansas. The muses play on lofty notes that you and I hear well, but they are above the highest mouse squeak on the Arkansas fiddle; they are not sounds at all to him, he hears them not. And he will tell you that they do not exist. So here is a happy commonwealth of inferior men, inferior not in physique, morale, audacity nor humor—indeed, they can laugh at themselves, supposedly the test of the superior man—yet inferior to the best branches of the British descendants because they maintain no link with the past, have no aim for the future, have low standards of comfort and cleanliness, and are mentally incapable of art and life in the grand manner.

Arkansas claims to have produced one protrait painter and one attorney general of the United States, but neither of them is memorable. It has originated more than forty varieties of superior apples. The soil is so marvelously adapted to apples that their sports are treasured and propagated thereafter by the outside world. But the soil can work no such magic on the people. In a hundred years the State has not thrown off one human sport to entice the world with the flavor of genius.

Nearly every State has produced great journalism. Not Arkansas. The leading daily of the State circulates in every community where there are persons who can read. It was founded in 1819 and is said to be the oldest paper west of the Mississippi. It prints only one column of strictly Arkansas matter. The rest of it is Associated Press and *cliché* shipped by mail from a New York press syndicate, matter prepared for cajoling the metropolitan polyglot booboisie and is as Greek when laid before the Arkansas rustic. The one column for which the people take the paper is called "All Over Arkansas," a score of clippings from the native press with comment. Since all Arkansawyers are humorists these clippings are boisterously funny. The comment in the same Arkansas vein by Fred Heiskell, who inherited the paper from his father, also a humorist in his day, is equally so.

> Little Rock is in Arkansas
> And the damndest place I ever saw.

This song was composed in the gold-rush days; men were used to seeing some pretty rough camps, but Arkansas's capital city was so much ruder than most border camps that the traveler was shocked. It isn't much better today. It is there that the State-wide paper, The *Arkansas Gazette,* is published, printing from mats the grotesque pictures sent from New York. The arts so languish in that commonwealth that no man can etch a plate to reproduce a local picture. It is necessary to send the photograph to Memphis, Tennessee. The country printers nail a piece of leather on a block type high and carve pictures similar to linoleum cuts, and the "city" papers use pictures of Harlem and City Hall Park furnished by a New York syndicate. Arkansas has no cities, Little Rock being but a large village. Kansas has no cities either, but it has several famous newspapers and any New York reader can name more than one Kansas editor. Kansas was founded by pamphleteers. Arkansas was founded by wittier but illiterate men and has never developed a journalism.

At the opening of the World War, Arkansas was for Germany to a man. The people were still in the mood their fathers were when they threw the British out of New Orleans. They had to make a complete about-face when they were drafted. There is no foreign population in Arkansas to speak of. Yet the Union Station in Little Rock has a great "immigrant section" occupying three-fourths of the station, and it is filled with ragged, ill-smelling, greasy men and women with sacks, bundles, and bedding, with dogs and innumerable, miserable young. This mass of nondescript humanity sleeps huddled on the station floor as best it can and remains herded there until the trains they are awaiting are announced and Red Caps lead them in bewilderment to their cars. These "immigrants" are the native Arkansawyers! In Hot Springs, Arkansas, the Government maintains one of the world's great resorts, and visitors from all the civilized sections come there in rolling Pullmans. En route they behold around them the mangy herd of Arkansawyers and they shrink away shocked and questioning: "In the name of God, what manner of men are these?" In this inadequate essay I have tried to suggest the answer. Here is the dictatorship of the proletariate in America. These scrub-stock people have been free to work out their own destiny under ideal conditions. They have had no intelligent class among them to prey upon their dullness. Capitalism has not laid heavy hand on them, for they have been always in touch with free land, free water, and all raw materials free. And where labor is free and land is free there can be no capitalism. The lumber companies and the railroads in the past have tried to exploit these simple folk, but you can't lay hands on a land-scratching people roving through forests of free land. Like a greased pig, they elude you. Money has been kept down by barter—corn and pork being used as an exchange medium when there was no cash. For tax-money the people could always trap a few coons and sell their hides. Some of the more obliging officials as late as five years ago would accept coon skins in lieu of taxes due, and cash the furs in the best market. This is in the highlands of the State. The lowlands have their cotton and rice to sell.

No, Arkansas cannot say that any class, régime or social system has held the people down. It has been and is simply a nation of proletarians with nothing in them except what has come out of them. And the result is a State that judged by the standards of the other forty-seven is zero in the world of ideas and cultural achievement, and a people so vulgar, ill-smelling, and outlandish as to shock the people of the other commonwealths when they behold them.

COLORADO

TWO GENERATIONS

By EASLEY S. JONES

THE snap of the whip over the six-horse stage where it bowled between red cliffs, laughter of bar-rooms louder than the ring of poker chips, the volley of dynamite opening the gold wealth of the hills: these voices of the frontier are gone, and in their place have come the purr of taxis, the chatter of tourists, the rattle of teacups in the summer hotels. In fifty years the rip-roaring life of gold, adventure, cowboys, pistols, ran to its climax and subsided; the mines, yielding their richest ores, were abandoned on a thousand hills, the forests were hewn down, the prairies fenced with barbed wire. The restless, kindly, spendthrift pioneer has given place to a still genial, but a calculating, penny-saving race; Colorado has become a taker-in of summer boarders, another Switzerland, flaunting the sign Rooms for Rent under the blue shadow of every mountain.

While it lasted no State had ever a more spectacular youth. The sense of conquest, the marching of caravans into unexplored forests, the exhilaration of active life in the clear mountain air, the prospect of wealth to be made overnight, the springing-up of mushroom settlements gave a zest that has not since been rivaled, and the glitter of firearms served to keep nerves tingling. Liquor was strong; a lusty music animated the dance halls; it was a commonplace to shoot the clock and pay the fiddler with a pinch of gold dust. The world was not only young, but on the eve of fortune. Beggars might be lords before another sunset. In the rudest camp of pine-board saloons, canvas hotels, and sod houses every penniless rogue assumed the manner of a millionaire, spoke a language of gross exaggeration, and indulged in flamboyant humor, even at his own expense. The names the early adventurers gave their mines reflect the expansive spirit of the day, mouth-filling or defiant names: Golconda, Mantinomah, Onondaga, Brazilian, Ace of Diamonds, Newsboy King, Invincible, Silver Serpent, Revenge. For a score of years, shifting its center from camp to camp with each new rumor of discovery, the turbulent life of the frontier reeled upon its headlong course. It seemed impossible to believe that the enthusiasm roused by gold could ever have an end. But it did.

As the mines failed or became worked out the names of the lodes gave evidence of the change: Last Chance, Hard Times, Grubstake, Esperanza, Hungry Dog, Up Grade, Blue Monday. The decline of the price of silver in 1893 was a heavy blow. And in another twenty years the increase in the cost of living, which is to say, the decrease in the value of gold, reduced the metal industry to one-fourth its activity in palmy days. Newspapers periodically announce, "Mining in Colorado is about to enter upon an era of great prosperity"; but no one is deceived. Shaft-houses and mills now sprawl upon the steep slopes, picturesque in semiruin, with sunken roofs, sheet-iron swaying to the winds, logs upended and overgrown with clematis, ore-dumps covered with berry bushes where scamper fugitive chipmunks. The great camps, Cripple Creek, Leadville, Blackhawk, Silverton, Ouray, Creede, have become ordinary languid villages piled about with red and yellow worthless heaps of mineral, waiting for a revival that never comes. In the two decades following 1900 the annual production of gold, silver, zinc, lead, copper declined from fifty to twenty million dollars, and the value of agricultural products rose from seventeen to 181 millions. The irrigated areas produced grain, alfalfa, and sugar beets; "dry farming" on the highlands above the ditches, at first timid, experimental, attained unexpected success. Smelters were established in Denver, steel works in Pueblo, sugar factories in the prairie towns; the mountain torrents were harnessed for electric power. The era of high spirits passed; the devil-may-care swagger had served its turn; the hair-trigger guns so long worn and used in the open day were put on the shelf. The influx of new migration gave the population more and more the character of the States eastward along the fortieth parallel: Nebraska, Iowa, Illinois. The Wild West was overrun by the tame Middle West, tempered with its practical wisdom and forethought, its shrewdness, its concern for proprieties and amenities.

Another destiny overtook Colorado when tourists began to flock to the State in armies outnumbering those which followed the discovery of gold. In 1922, against a native population of one million, the tourists numbered three-quarters of a million, and the wealth left by them was something like forty-five million dollars. Since the war the number of visitors has doubled every two years. If the increase should continue at the same rate, in 1925 the tourist army will be larger than was the American military force in France, an army to be housed, fed, entertained, and sent away satisfied. Every year in June the deluge begins. From Texas, Oklahoma, Kansas they come, from the central States sweltering in heat, on trains, in automobiles, school teachers, clerks weary of the counter, business men sick of ledgers, and not the ultra-rich, but the middle class grown prosperous since the war. They come with endless questions, and not a few misconceptions. They expect to discover Indians, cowboys, prairie schooners; they find instead electric interurban trains, and Chautauqua lectures by Dr. Steiner and Lorado Taft. They are sure that Pike's Peak is the highest summit in the State, and are surprised to discover at least two dozen peaks higher. They whirl through Estes Park in taxis, taste the mineral water at Manitou with a wry face, and buy gorgeous post cards of "Sunset behind the Spanish Peaks." They write eloquent letters home, how they scaled Sierra Blanca (on horseback), how they slid down snowbanks in August. The men wade in cold streams with rod and line, where the trout are long since grown wise or scared to death. The women throw aside their georgette waists for flannel shirts, and appear transformed, but still charming, in khaki trousers and shoes full of little bright nails. The children ride burros, throw stones until their small arms ache, or shout madly where down both sides of the street race irrigation ditches full of shining water. The tourists go frankly in for pleasure; they uproot wild flowers; they prefer movies to books; they are indolent enough to want to climb hills by automobile; yet for all this they have a certain eager sparkle of curiosity; the mountains have not ceased to be for them a splendid novelty.

The ironical fate is that of the natives, sons of the free, strong race that Mark Twain wrote about—and Bret Harte and Eugene Field and Walt Whitman and Horace Greeley—tied to the treadmill of shop and boarding house, fated to become the keepers of a nation's playground. For in comparison with Bret Harte's men, breakers of the wilderness, founders of cities, the present generation appears to shrink in stature. One perceives a change even in the names of mountains, streams, and towns. These the pioneers created from the first material at hand, careless, homely names: Wildhorse Creek, Dead Man Gulch, Lost Lake, Quartz Hill, Riflesight Notch, Rattlesnake Butte, Three Cottonwoods, Rabbit Ear Peaks. The later generation of small business men, the race that had read Tennyson and Harold Bell Wright, sought purring, soothing, or bookish names, like Idylwilde, Brookvale, Ferndale, Glenwood, Rosemont, Montrose; or some bit of cleverness to scrawl upon a cabin door, like Seldom Inn or the Jazz Whisper. Many of the pioneer names they made over. They turned Skunk Canyon into Bluebell, Red Bull Draw into Antelope Glen. A prize was offered for a name for an upland park, and the best that came forth was Panorama. The greatest modern triumph was Mount Sanitas, triumph because people could really be persuaded to repeat the word, and the mountain thus libeled is standing yet. One has only to let the mind sweep along in time, from the earliest Spanish names that blazoned the snowy peaks with memorials of Christ and the saints: Sangre de Cristo, San Miguel, San Juan; from the Indian names of as stern dignity as that of the hills themselves: Navaho, Arickaree, Ogallala; from the pioneer names which, lacking dignity, had still the smack of an outdoor energetic life: Powderhorn, Dripping Rock, Lone Pine; to the culmination in Ingleside, Sanitas, to get an impression of a late generation feeble in invention, yawning beside the fire, jaded by comforts the frontier never knew, reading the ten best sellers, tired and tiresome. The pioneer, if we are to believe a hundred legends, was a prince in hospitality, and scorned to take a penny. His sons show an increasing desire to take all they can get. Some comparisons lead one to believe, not that the race has degenerated, but that it has at least passed from an adventurous, generous, impulsive life to a shrewdly reasoned, narrow one. The mind of the frontiersman occupied itself with uncounted herds of cattle ranging over ten square miles of pasture, with the need for bridging a roaring forest stream, his only domestic care being to provide the four staples—whisky, coffee, bacon, bread. The modern mind is occupied with minute complexities and hesitancies: whether the salad shall have caper sauce or only mayonnaise, whether to play bridge whist or see Salome in the movies, and (this particularly) what the neighbors think about it all. In the face of natural beauty that towers half up the sky, it is still possible for human nature to be servile. In streets pleasant with flowering hollyhocks under the beetling mountains gossips meet and snigger, repeat contemptible trivialities, virulent pin-pricks of rumor, concealed weapon of enslaved minds. Blue through the orchard-tops, eagle-haunted summits shimmer in the slant of sun, or darken with forests and the purple shadows of clouds, home of mystery and adventure, a challenge to the imagination forever. In front of a barber shop a man buries his head in the Denver *Post,* the most ill-mannered and vindictive yellow newspaper that money can buy. The tragedy of Colorado is that her race cannot measure up to the scene which it inherits. The stage is set for heroic action, or a theme of beauty, but the actors are raising the room rent or winding the phonograph. The race is dwarfed by the epic mountain theater where its life is cast.

Or do we deceive ourselves in making sharp the contrast between two generations—one romantic, dare-devil, open-hearted, the other humdrum, nicely moral, calculating? Is the difference only subjective, our mistaken feeling that the race has changed? Or is it part subjective and part actual? Was the pioneer truly a "prince of hospitality"? Was he not, as much as any now, a conniving rascal, except that we have chosen to forget the petty element and remember only the glorious feature of his rascality? Was his era a true youth of the race, or only the rawness (often mistaken for youth) of an old race greedy for gold? Was his largeness of spirit born only of speculation, waste, wealth easily got? Do boarding-house keepers lack strong will, generous impulse, the free, large mind we attribute to the earlier day? If we push the inquiry only a little, we find qualities of the pioneer which are active at the present time. Even the wildness of the frontier reappears in curious ways. For let the news fly of tungsten or oil shales discovered, or free lands opened in remote corners of the State, and the old fever returns, the phenomena of the frontier repeat themselves on a smaller scale; the same frenzy is astir as when George Jackson discovered gold in Idaho Springs. Exactly as in 1859 one may hear men say: "Here's where we make a strike. Let's drop all, take bag and baggage, and go." Susceptivity to the idea that fortunes *may* be made overnight, that all things are possible with the aid of some great luck that waits just round the corner—this is one heritage that the frontier left to its sons of a more sluggish generation. The outdoor tradition, too, maintains itself in the midst of an indoor age. Camping, anywhere, is a natural impulse; but in Colorado it is a mania, a compelling influence in the blood, perpetuating in men the ways of their fathers who tramped the granite peaks and slept under the blazing stars. The expansiveness of the gold-mining era, its frankness, its democracy, its humor are met today in unlikely places, even in the summer hotels. The Western landlord does not bow the knee before the tourist; he baits him, or meets him as an equal. The mountaineer does not covertly smile when the Eastern schoolmistress asks questions: he laughs aloud. "What is that feather you have in your hat?" "That, madam, is a woodchuck feather." "A woodchuck? Why, I didn't know woodchucks had feathers." "Ah, yes, madam, *at certain seasons.* In winter their plumage is pure white; in spring, green; in autumn, red and brown. This feather, as you can plainly see, was picked in the autumn." Thus the tourist is received, not as a lord to be fawned upon, but as a lineal descendant of the greenhorn, the tenderfoot of the earlier day. This raillery is the humor of the frontier, and if the sons of the frontier choose to keep it, it will prove to be their most precious inheritance, and an armor against which all that critics may say against them will be futile.

These and other sturdy qualities of the frontier remain. Actually there has been a gain in comfort, manners, intellect. It is not reasonable to compliment one generation at the expense of another. Both share certain virtues. Both have in common many faults. The raw, wealth-greedy pioneer could not mine ores less rich than forty dollars a ton; more than half his gold he wasted in the process of extraction. He slaughtered part of the forests and set fire to the rest. He impoverished the soil. He could only exploit nature, rob her, and he sometimes robbed his fellow men. His record is a continuous story of colossal waste. And the son of the raw pioneer is still an exploiter, except that he has no bonanza or forest, easily accessible, rich, to waste. It takes hard work and thought to exploit ten-dollar ore, without labor wars. He therefore sinks into small business, establishes a factory in which the employees are always threatening to strike, or exploits the most available resource, the tourist. The generation that shall merit compliment, at the expense of both pioneer and present age, is one that shall conserve and build—that shall learn to extract the gold from ten-dollar poor ore, or even five-dollar ore (without labor wars into the bargain), that shall make forests grow, one foot of clear timber for every foot cut down, that shall return chemical values to the soil and conserve the moisture of the arid lands, that shall conserve childhood and manhood, that shall establish tolerable factories, and make the conditions of industry and bread-getting human.

Colorado as an industrial battlefield has furnished the nation at intervals during thirty years with spectacles of violence amounting almost to civil war. The most bitter conflict was the coal strike of 1914, directed against the Rockefeller interests, marked by brutality on the part of both operators and miners. The culmination was Ludlow, a settlement of wretched tents and hovels on the bare prairie where more than twenty miners and women and children lost their lives. Ludlow is the contribution of Colorado to the list of scenes of industrial terror, the black list that includes Homestead, and Herrin, and grows longer year by year. One feels the tragedy of such warfare less keenly when any permanent good results, and the lessons of the strike of 1914 were not lost. The operators undertook to improve the conditions of living at the camps, and succeeded beyond anyone's expectation. More important still, the public conscience was, at last, profoundly stirred. The most amazing feature of economic struggles is the haste with which public opinion jumps to a conclusion on the first false rumor, and the reluctant slowness with which it arrives, when the facts are sifted, at a just decision. The question public opinion immediately asked concerning Ludlow was, who fired the first shot? Popular judgment was based largely on this question; yet it was a cheap and superficial inquiry. The underlying issue was not who fired the first shot, or even who accumulated guns and bullets. The issue was, what grievances and tyrannies had accumulated, over a period of years, that could make men want to break the law. Few citizens have patience to seek the truth thus far; it is easier to dismiss Ludlow with a wave of the hand, and some remark about maintaining law and order. Other coal camps, under other corporations, still squat upon the bare plain; large families of Mexicans, Italians, Americans, are crowded into two-room shacks. The land, streets, houses, churches, schools, police, and even the administration of justice, are controlled by the mine operators, and many of these camps have squatted flat upon the flat plain twenty years without anyone's attempting to plant a tree or a blade of grass. No citizen interests himself enough to know whether the coal diggers have a tree and a home or not. It is cheaper to let grievances run to some bloody conclusion, and content oneself with a virtuous remark about the necessity of obeying law.

Other ugly social phenomena occur in Colorado, as elsewhere, and the wonder is not so much that they occur as that they are so little regarded or remedied. Abuses of political power pass usually without much protest. Mineral and timber lands, sources of water power, are unscrupulously gobbled up; the beet-sugar corporations haggle to escape taxes. Freedom of speech is so far from being realized that a labor organizer, scheduled to give in Denver the same speech he had delivered in Eastern cities, was seized by police and dumped across the border upon a neighbor State. A millionaire makes a present of a building to some college and nominates himself for the United States Senate. Educational institutions have been a football of politics since the founding of the State in 1876. In those earliest days when institutions were passed out as plums by the legislature, Cañon City, so the story goes, was offered a choice; she might have either the penitentiary or the university. And looking on society as it was then constituted, Cañon City chose the institution which was already a thriving concern, and whose future was not threatened with uncertainty. She elected to take the penitentiary, and the State university fell into the lap of Boulder. The penitentiary has today only one-third as many inmates as the university has students. One may smile, indeed; but it is perhaps too early to laugh. Cañon City's day may come, if the citizen lets public issues drift. For his attitude appears on first observation to be this: Let the politicians be as vicious as they please; business is good, our scenery matchless, the climate perfect. The physical conditions of life are so pleasant that he is deceived into the belief that the world is going well, when so far as the social aspect is concerned it may be going badly, and going fast. From his mountain vantage ship subsidies and tariffs seem small disputes of lowland minds. The hills lull the senses with a false impression of security.

But this view of her citizenship is only half the truth. Colorado adopted the eight-hour day, equal suffrage, prohibition, and had ceased to talk about them before they became national issues. For every name of ill odor, like that of Guggenheim, there is some brilliant name, like that of Judge Ben B. Lindsey, whose juvenile court was one of the first and best of its kind, or that of Miss Emily Griffith, whose Opportunity School in Denver is a model for a new idea in education. Neither the Republican nor the Democratic Party has been able to maintain control of the State, the vote shifting from one to the other according to the issue. What appears to be indifference to abuses is in large part only tolerance, the tolerance of gold-mining days when stakes were great and men did not occupy their thought with small affairs. The Western mind still overrides not only trifles, but hardships, the downright slaps and blows of fate. Things which loom large on the horizon in New England, like a misspelled word, or a breach of formal etiquette, or exclusion from a social set, or even losing a job, give short pause in the rush of Western progress. Here where distances are vast, where between bristling mountain ranges the eye sweeps over valleys deep and wide, into which a Delaware or Rhode Island could be dropped and never missed, the frontier habit of thinking in big terms persists in some measure despite the trivial occupations of a modern day; the imagination, surrounded by scenes of beauty, flatters itself with the delusion that human nature is largely good also, and that what is not good can be dismissed with a clutter of other useless things not worth one sober thought.

The climate encourages this large and easy way of taking life. The greatest distinguishing feature of the State is a subtle atmospheric stimulus, hardly capable of description, further than to say that its immediate effect, experienced by everyone, is a feeling of buoyancy. The clear, dry air prolongs one's cheerfulest moods, releases energy. Its extreme effect is even a kind of nervousness. The phlegmatic, plodding human creature often found in Mississippi Valley regions of sticky days and muggy nights hardly exists in the mountain States; the usual temperament of the high altitudes is sanguine, buoyant, excitable. The teamster shouts a greeting to every stranger in the road; in commercial clubs business men extend the hand before they think of introductions; in a few weeks one calls a new-made friend by his first name. In every physical aspect the country is one of light and color. Nowhere is one confronted by any moldy symbol of decay. Reaping machines remain in the field for weeks without danger of rust; an unroofed wooden house endures without rot the weather of two decades. The cliff-dwellings stand much as they did centuries before the white man turned his thought toward America, not ruins in any usual sense of the word; the charred sticks on their hearthstones look like embers of fires extinguished yesterday. Even the graveyards assume a cheerful appearance, always small, with glistening sharp corners of new stone, no lichen, no tarnishment of decay, no moldering wall, no biting of the tooth of years. The happy-go-lucky weather reminds one of nothing but youth. Day after day the unclouded sky invites to the out-of-doors. When storms venture to show themselves, often as not the clouds settle upon the higher cliffs, bluster, menace, reconsider, and in one hour dissolve back into clear ether. The harsher winds deflect upward and go ruffling far overhead, with subdued complaining in the branches of distant pines. So gently the seasons merge into one another that their